elementary
baking

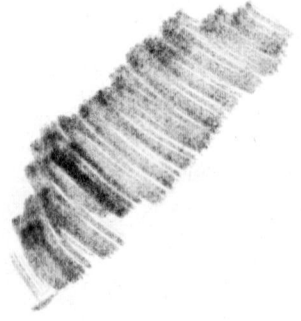

WILLIAM J. SULTAN

Chairman, Food Trades Department
Food and Maritime Trades High School
New York, New York

elementary baking

McGRAW-HILL BOOK COMPANY
New York   St. Louis   San Francisco
London   Sydney   Toronto
Mexico   Panama

TX
763
.S89
1969

elementary baking

Copyright © 1969 by McGraw-Hill, Inc.
All Rights Reserved.
Printed in the United States of America.
No part of this publication may be reproduced,
stored in a retrieval system, or transmitted, in any form
or by any means, electronic, mechanical, photocopying,
recording, or otherwise,
without the prior written permission of the publisher.

Library of Congress Catalog Card Number: 68-29917

62408

1 2 3 4 5 6 7 8 9 – M A M M – 1 0 9

PREFACE

Baking and dessert making are artistic phases of cooking. It is creative to start with basic raw materials and make them into attractive, appealing dishes. Baking can therefore be challenging, educational, and enjoyable. Even when convenience foods are used—prepared cake mixes, self-rising flours, and similar preparations—the same basic skills and judgments are required for completion of the product. Primarily, the achievement and the satisfaction derived from it are measured by the end result—the baked product.

This book is directed toward the student, the homemaker, and the teacher. It may be used independently in a self-teaching situation, or in a more formal teacher-student situation. The basic objective is learning through positive achievement. It is hoped that the student with a teacher's guidance and instruction will also apply the fundamentals of the basic "tool" subjects—reading, writing, arithmetic and science.

The units of work are arranged so that the learner proceeds on a graduated basis from the simple to the complex. Wherever possible, the reader—the student or homemaker—is asked to recall experiences that should establish a more realistic approach to the subject and increase motivation.

Instructional procedures and directions are given in detail for maximum clarity and understanding. In this way the less articulate student may be reached while the interest of the more gifted student is created and maintained. To repeat—the primary objective is to ensure some positive achievement for all students. Special emphasis is placed upon the importance of reading, understanding what is read, making practical judgments, and applying the fundamentals of learning to specialized food preparation.

Functional illustrations showing "how to do it," most often in a step-by-step format, serve as direct visual aids. In relating the reading material to the visual guides, the student should strengthen the associations to be made. In addition, the teacher is urged to supplement this material with techniques and materials which will increase learning.

A series of test questions and special assignments for each unit of work are contained in a separate Student Workbook to be used by the student or homemaker in association with the text. The workbook may be used as a self-testing device or in a classroom situation.

PREFACE

The unit test and research assignments show how other subjects and skills, particularly in a team-teaching program, may be used in conjunction with the learning experiences of this text. It is hoped that the practical work experiences may serve as a motivating force to contribute to the total education of the student.

In special programs of education—such as short, intensive programs to meet special group needs—the text may also serve as a basic tool for teaching and learning the fundamentals of language communication, as well as for its own practical training objectives.

TO THE STUDENT

Cooks and homemakers should know the basic foods they use, understand how they may be used to best advantage, and be familiar with the tools and equipment commonly used in food preparation. In baking, a special area of food preparation, certain basic food materials are used in most recipes. Baking also requires the use of special tools and equipment. In order to prepare good baked products and desserts, you should know these basic raw materials and their purposes, and the tools and equipment required.

Some personal responsibilities should be mentioned. Two kinds of cleanliness are important in food preparation—personal cleanliness, of course, and clean work habits. Clean work habits can be developed with the help of a teacher, if you have one, and by following instructions carefully while you are at work. Once these habits are developed, they become automatic.

Safety practices are also important. You must be careful to prevent injury to yourself and to those who work with you or near you.

Following the instructions you receive on cleanliness and safety will help you to learn successfully and to create better products.

BASIC EQUIPMENT

These are the basic tools, appliances, and other equipment you will need for baking. You will find other equipment listed in the glossary and illustrated in the text. As you read about this equipment and use it in baking and dessert making, you will get to know the items by name.

MEASURING TOOLS

teaspoons	measuring cups	balance scale (*optional*)
tablespoons	quart measure	home table scale (*optional*)

MIXING TOOLS

mixing bowl	mixing spoons	rubber bowl scraper	pastry blender
small mixing machine	grater	sauce pans	wire whip
(*if available*)	egg beater	sifter	

BAKING AND SHAPING TOOLS

rolling pins	pie pans	butter knives	workboard	layer cake pans
cookie cutters	pastry wheel	forks	or cutting board	(assorted)
biscuit cutters	(*optional*)	spatula	wash brush	muffin pans
pastry bag	French knife	table brush	grease brush	tube pans
pastry tubes	(*optional*)	loaf cake pans	baking sheet pans	apple corer

MAJOR EQUIPMENT

cooking stove with an oven chamber
refrigerator with freezer section
sink with drainboard
worktable
storage cabinets
storage cans or jars
deep fat fryer or
    frying kettle with basket (*optional*)

MEASUREMENTS

EQUIVALENTS

3 teaspoons (tsp.) = 1 tablespoon (tbsp.)
4 tablespoons = ¼ cup (c.)
5 tablespoons + 1 teaspoon = ⅓ cup
8 ounces (oz.) liquid = 1 cup
2 cups = 1 pint (pt.)
2 pints = 1 quart (qt.)
1 quart liquid (water, milk, etc.) = 2 pounds (lb.)
4 quarts = 1 gallon (gal.)
16 ounces = 1 pound

INGREDIENT MEASUREMENTS

Apples, fresh	1 pound = 3 cups sliced; approximately 3 apples
Baking powder	1 ounce = 2½ tablespoons
Baking soda	1 ounce = 2 tablespoons
Bananas	1 pound = 2½ cups sliced; about 3 medium bananas
Berries (strawberries, blueberries)	1 quart = about 3½ cups, picked over and cleaned
Butter or margarine	¼-pound bar = ½ cup; 1-pound bar = 2 cups
Cake crumbs	1 cup = 3 ounces
Cheese (hard type), grated	1 cup = 4 ounces
Chocolate, grated	4 tablespoons = 1 ounce
Cinnamon, ground	1 ounce = 4½ tablespoons
Cocoa, sifted	1 pound = 4¼ cups
Corn starch	1 tablespoon = ½ ounce; 7 ounces = 1 cup
Cream of tartar	1 ounce = 3 tablespoons
Eggs, fresh	4 to 5 eggs = 1 cup; 2 cups of eggs = 1 pound
Egg whites	8 to 10 = 1 cup
Egg yolks	12 to 14 = 1 cup
Flour, all-purpose (sifted)	4 cups = 1 pound
Flour, cake (sifted)	4½ to 4¾ cups = 1 pound
Flour, whole wheat	3½ cups = 1 pound

Honey	1 cup = 12 ounces
Molasses	1 cup = 12 ounces
Lemon juice	2 tablespoons = 1 ounce
Lemon rind	4 tablespoons = 1 ounce
Milk, liquid	1 cup = 8 ounces
Milk, powdered	1 cup = 4 ounces
(1 cup of powdered milk mixed with 4 cups of water = 1 quart of milk)	
Oil, vegetable	1 cup = 8 ounces
Orange rind	1 medium orange = 2 tablespoons grated rind
Orange juice	1 medium orange = ⅓ cup juice
Raisins	1-pound box = 3 cups, approximately
Salt	2 tablespoons = 1 ounce
Shelled nuts (pecans, walnuts, almonds)	1 cup = 4 ounces
Shortening	2½ cups = 1 pound
Spices (allspice, cloves, mace, nutmeg)	4 tablespoons = 1 ounce
Sugar, brown	3 cups = 1 pound
Sugar, confectioners'	3½ cups = 1 pound
Sugar, granulated	2¼ cups = 1 pound
Vanilla	2 tablespoons = 1 ounce
Water	8 ounces = 1 cup
Yeast, compressed fresh	1 small cake = ½ ounce
Yeast, dried	1 package dissolved = ½ ounce of compressed yeast

COMMON CAN SIZES

Number 1 (#1) can (tall) = 16 ounces
Number 303 = 16 ounces
Number 2 = 1 pound, 4 ounces
Number 2½ = 1 pound, 12 ounces
Number 3 = 2 pounds, 1 ounce
Number 5 = 3 pounds, 8 ounces
Number 10 = 6 pounds, 10 ounces

COMPARISON OF CAN SIZES

1 #10 can = 7 #1 tall cans
1 #10 can = 5 #2 cans
1 #10 can = 4 #2½ cans
1 #10 can = 3 #3 cans
1 #10 can = 2 #5 cans

GLOSSARY

NOTE These are the *cooking* or *baking* definitions of the terms.

Absorb, or absorption   To *absorb* is to take in and hold; *absorption* refers to the ability of flour or other dry ingredients to take in and hold liquids.

Bake   To cook by dry heat in an oven or closed chamber that has been preheated.

Bag out   To press out a prepared batter through a pastry bag and tube or a cookie press, producing a particular shape or design.

Beat, or whip   To mix air into a batter with a mixing machine at high speed or a hand whip used rapidly.   This mixing method is used for egg batters (as for sponge cake), whipping cream, whipping egg whites, or whipping a gelatin-based solution.

Blend   To fold or mix two or more ingredients together, fairly gently, until smooth.

Caramelize   To burn or brown sugar.   Caramelizing takes place at approximately 320 degrees or higher.

Cream   To mix or rub shortening with sugar or flour until blended.   This incorporates air and makes the batter soft and light.

Crystallization   The reforming of sugar syrups into sugar crystals.

Cut in   To distribute fat into dry ingredients in small particles by using a chopping motion.   A pastry blender or two table knives may be used for cutting in.

Decoration   The art of making designs on cakes and pastries.

Develop dough   To make a dough (generally a yeast-raised dough) smooth by additional mixing after the ingredients are blended.

Dissolve   To mix dry ingredients into a liquid by stirring.   Stirring sugar into water, for example, will *dissolve* the sugar.

Dust   To spray or spread flour (or another similar dry ingredient) on a table or over a dough or product.   The purpose of flour *dusted* onto a table is to prevent sticking of dough worked on the table.

Fermentation   The process of raising a dough (making it rise) through the action of yeast.

Flaky   Made up of many very thin layers.   Such layers of dough are made by mixing fat and flour together to form small lumps.   This is done in the preparation of pie crust dough.

Fold   To mix one substance into another very gently, usually by an overhand motion with a mixing spoon or beater.   Generally, flour or beaten egg whites are *folded* into a batter.

GLOSSARY

Fry   To cook in hot fat (380 to 385 degrees).

Gelatinize   To make into a jelly-like substance, often by the addition of gelatin.

Gluten   A tough, rubbery substance that is formed when flour is mixed with water. Gluten serves as the structure for bread, rolls, and other products made from yeast-raised doughs.

Gradually   In stages; step by step; little by little. For example, if you add liquid, then flour, then other ingredients, you are forming a batter *gradually*. Or if you add a liquid to a batter a little at a time, you are adding it *gradually*.

Grain   The cell structure (texture) of a baked product.

Grease   To apply fat or oil to the bottom and sides (Inside) of a baking pan with a brush or pad. This keeps the product being baked from sticking.

Humidity   The water content of the air.

Ice   To apply a sugar preparation (a frosting or icing) to a baked product.

Knead   To make a dough smoother by additional mixing with the hands. This is usually done on a worktable or workboard after the dough is removed from the mixing bowl.

Leavening   A substance which causes a product to rise during baking. Baking powder, baking soda, and yeast are examples. To *leaven* is the same as to *raise*.

Measure   To determine an amount of an ingredient.

Mix   To blend two or more ingredients into one mass.

Moist   Containing some liquid, or *moisture;* not dry. Many baked products should be a little moist, so that they will stay fresher longer.

Mold, or mould   To form or shape, as in the *molding* of a loaf of bread or a roll.

Rise   To increase in volume and become light and spongy. To *raise* a dough (usually a yeast dough), or units made from it, is to allow it to *rise*.

Roll   To flatten a dough with a rolling pin.

Scaling   Weighing ingredients with a scale (generally in ounces and pounds).

Scrape   To remove clinging batter (or other substance) from the sides and bottom of a mixing bowl or other container.

Sift   To pass a dry ingredient or a mixture of dry ingredients through a sieve or sifter. This serves to remove lumps and foreign matter and to aerate the mixture or ingredient.

Stipple   To make small holes with a fork or the point of a knife, as in the top crust of a pie before the pie is baked.

Stir   To mix with a circular (or "round-and-round") motion, as in dissolving ingredients.

Texture   The character of the grain (smooth—soft and silky, or coarse—rough and crumbly).

Tough   Too firm in texture; too hard to chew; sometimes, rubbery. *Toughness* in baked goods is a condition generally caused by overmixing after the flour has been added to the batter.

Volume   The size of a product, especially in relation to its weight. A product that is large for its weight is considered to have good *volume*.

Wash   To brush a liquid, such as eggs or milk, over the top of a product before the product is baked. Also, to brush the top of a product with syrup after the product is baked and removed from the oven.

Wet peak   When a whipped mixture (eggs or egg whites and sugar, cream, icing) has reached a certain point of stiffness, it will form soft mounds that fold over on top. These are *wet peaks*.

BASIC INGREDIENTS

The following is a brief introduction to the basic ingredients used in baking. It is presented in outline form for easy reference. You are advised to find out more about these ingredients by referring to other books and manuals on cooking and baking.

SUGAR AND OTHER SWEETENERS

Types:

granulated sugar	powdered or	honey	corn syrup	other syrups
brown sugar	confectioners' sugar	molasses	maple syrup	

Sugars and sweeteners provide taste (sweetness), flavor, tenderness, and crust color, and they improve the keeping quality of the baked product (that is, keep it fresh longer). Sugars also serve as the base for various icings and toppings for cakes and pastries. In yeast-raised doughs, part of the sugar used provides a yeast food to promote fermentation.

SALT

Types:

Fine table salt and coarse salt are the basic salts.

Salt provides flavor in baked products. It also helps emphasize other flavors. For example, sugar tastes sweeter when used with salt. Coarse salt is used as a topping for specialty products such as salt stick rolls and pretzels. In yeast-raised doughs, salt controls the rate of fermentation by controlling the action of the yeast.

SHORTENING AND OTHER FATS

Types:

all-purpose shortening (this can be used for baking and frying)   **vegetable oil (varieties)**   **lard**
emulsified or high-ratio shortening (used for special cakes)   **margarine**   **butter**

Shortenings provide richness, tenderness, flavor, volume, flakiness, and good texture. They also help keep the product fresh.

EGGS

Types:

fresh (shell) eggs	frozen whole eggs	dried or powdered eggs
fresh egg whites	frozen egg whites	dried egg white
fresh egg yolks	frozen egg yolks	dried egg yolk

Basically, eggs provide flavor and color in the baked product. They

BASIC INGREDIENTS

also provide liquid to moisten and dissolve dry ingredients in the batter. The protein in eggs help build the structure of the baked product, and the yolk of the egg adds richness. Because eggs expand in the presence of heat, they also help leaven the product and create more volume.

MILK AND OTHER LIQUIDS

Types:

whole milk	**whole milk powder**	**buttermilk**	**fruit juices**
skim milk	**skim milk powder**	**water**	

The most important purpose of liquids is to dissolve dry ingredients and make possible a uniform blending of all materials. Liquids also provide moistness, of course, and thereby improve keeping quality. In baking, part of the liquid in a product is evaporated in the form of steam, and this steam helps to raise or leaven many products. Liquids, particularly fruit juices, may also provide flavor in baked products.

FLOUR AND STARCHY THICKENING MATERIALS

Types:

bread flour (strong or high gluten content)
pastry flour	**whole wheat flour**	**corn starch**
cake flour	**rye flour**	**rice flour**
cocoa and chocolate	**gelatin**	**tapioca flour**

Flour and starches (including cocoa and chocolate) provide body for the product. The proteins form the structure to support other ingredients. Flour used in yeast-raised doughs forms the gluten structure which contains the gas and allows the dough to rise. Flours and starches are used for dusting work areas to prevent dough from sticking while it is being rolled or worked. Cocoa and chocolate provide a special grain (interior) and crust color and taste. Starches and other thickening agents increase the ability of mixtures to absorb liquid.

LEAVENINGS

Types:

Baking powder and baking soda are chemical leavening agents.
Yeast is an organic (living) leavening agent.

Leavening agents make batters or doughs rise and spread before and/or during baking. Yeast is used to leaven (cause to rise) special doughs for bread, rolls, sweet rolls, buns, rich coffee cakes, doughnuts, and numerous other products that are made from yeast-raised doughs.

FLAVORINGS AND SPICES

Types:

Natural spices and flavors are present in various fruits, berries, and plants—such as cinnamon, nutmeg, and many others. Fruit rinds and juices provide the basic source of fruit flavorings. Cocoa is a natural source of the special cocoa or chocolate flavor. There are also imitation or synthetic flavors and spices. These are in the form of powders or liquids such as vanillin, artificial fruit flavors, artificial cinnamon, and others.

> Spices and flavorings provide special flavor, odor, and color. They improve the natural flavor of other ingredients and improve the taste of the end product.

CONTENTS

	BASIC EQUIPMENT	ix
	MEASUREMENTS	x
	GLOSSARY	xii
	BASIC INGREDIENTS	xv
Part One	**QUICK BREADS**	1
Unit 1	VARIETY BISCUITS	2
Unit 2	VARIETY MUFFINS	13
Unit 3	VARIETY LOAF-TYPE QUICK BREADS	21
Unit 4	POPOVERS	27
Part Two	**SWEET YEAST-RAISED DOUGH PRODUCTS**	33
Introduction	HOW YEAST CONDITIONS A DOUGH	34
Unit 5	BASIC SWEET YEAST DOUGH	37
Unit 6	VARIETY SOFT ROLLS AND BUNS	41
Part Three	**FRIED PRODUCTS (DOUGHNUTS AND CRULLERS)**	79
Unit 7	VARIETY YEAST-RAISED DOUGHNUTS	80
Unit 8	VARIETY CAKE-TYPE AND COMBINATION DOUGHNUTS	92
Part Four	**VARIETY PIES**	99
Unit 9	PIE CRUST AND FRUIT FILLINGS FOR PIES	100
Unit 10	SOFT-FILLED PIES AND TURNOVERS	118
Part Five	**LAYER CAKES AND CUPCAKES**	137
Introduction	CAKE MIXING AND CAKE RECIPES	138
Unit 11	THE CREAMING METHOD OF MIXING CAKES	139
Unit 12	THE BLENDING METHOD OF MIXING CAKES	147
Unit 13	THE WHIPPING METHOD OF MIXING CAKES	153
Unit 14	VARIETY FROSTINGS	162
Unit 15	FINISHING AND DECORATING CUPCAKES	168
Unit 16	DECORATING LAYER CAKES	178
Part Six	**PUFF PASTRY PRODUCTS; ECLAIRS AND CREAM PUFFS**	185
Unit 17	PUFF PASTRY DOUGH	186
Unit 18	PUFF PASTRY VARIETIES	192
Unit 19	CREAM PUFFS AND ECLAIRS	205
Part Seven	**VARIETY COOKIES**	213
Introduction	RULES FOR COOKIES	214

xix

Unit 20	DOUGH-TYPE OR CUTOUT COOKIES	**217**
Unit 21	BAGGED-OUT OR SPOONED COOKIE VARIETIES	**223**
Unit 22	ICEBOX COOKIE VARIETIES	**232**
Part Eight	**DECORATING CAKES AND PASTRIES**	**241**
Introduction	PREPARING AND PRACTICING	**242**
Unit 23	DECORATING PETITS FOURS AND FRENCH PASTRIES	**244**
Unit 24	DECORATING BIRTHDAY CAKES AND SPECIAL-OCCASION CAKES	**248**
	INDEX	**260**

PART ONE ■□□□□□□□

quick breads

UNIT 1

**VARIETY
BISCUITS**

AIM   To learn how to make a variety of biscuits.

THINGS YOU SHOULD KNOW   Biscuits that are tender, flaky, and tasty are the pride of the homemaker and cook. Biscuits often take the place of bread in meal planning and meal service, but they also have many other uses. For example, old-fashioned strawberry shortcake has a tender biscuit base to support the strawberries and the whipped cream. Chicken a la king and similar dishes may be served on a baked biscuit base. Small-size biscuits are often used as dumplings. Many of you have seen, perhaps eaten, pizza biscuits. Chicken and beef pot pies are often covered with a biscuit dough rather than a pie crust dough.

When you consider how biscuits can be used in many dishes and as a substitute for bread, you realize the value of being able to make good biscuits and other types of quick breads. Making good biscuits is like making a good cake or a good pudding: you must read the recipe carefully, be sure you understand it, and follow directions exactly.

Variety in biscuits has to do with the way the dough is mixed. A smooth-topped, tender biscuit is made from a dough that is well

UNIT 1: VARIETY BISCUITS

mixed after flour has been added to a batter. A flaky-type biscuit is made from a dough that is mixed very lightly after the liquid (milk) is added to the flour and shortening. Another light, soft biscuit is made from a dough raised, or leavened, by baking powder and yeast; this is called a combination biscuit. Each type of biscuit will be treated separately in this section, but practically the same recipe will be used for each. The difference will be in the way the dough is mixed for each variety. Be sure to *read carefully, understand what you read, and then follow the instructions exactly.*

TYPE 1: SMOOTH-TOP BISCUITS

Yield: *15 to 18 biscuits*

THINGS TO PREPARE Light the oven and set the temperature at 425 degrees. Check the recipe for materials.

measuring spoons	pastry blender	worktable and workboard
measuring cups	baking pan	table brush and wash brush
mixing bowl and spoon	rolling pin	French knife
flour sieve	biscuit cutter	

SMOOTH-TOP BISCUITS

INGREDIENTS (*measure carefully*)		HOW TO MIX
salt	1 teaspoon	Place the salt, sugar, and shortening in the mixing bowl. Mix them together to a smooth, soft paste.
sugar	¼ cup	
shortening	¼ cup	
milk	1 cup	Add the milk and stir it in lightly.

(*Sift the flour before measuring.*)

all-purpose flour	3 cups	Sift the flour and baking powder together into the mixing bowl. Mix in well until a smooth dough is formed. The dough will pull away from the sides of the mixing bowl and be of medium thickness.
baking powder	2½ tablespoons	

CHECK POINTS

1. The workboard, or part of the worktable, should be dusted with flour before the dough is placed on the board or table.
2. Check the oven to see if it is ready at 425°.
3. The baking pan and the small work tools should be handy.

PART ONE: QUICK BREADS

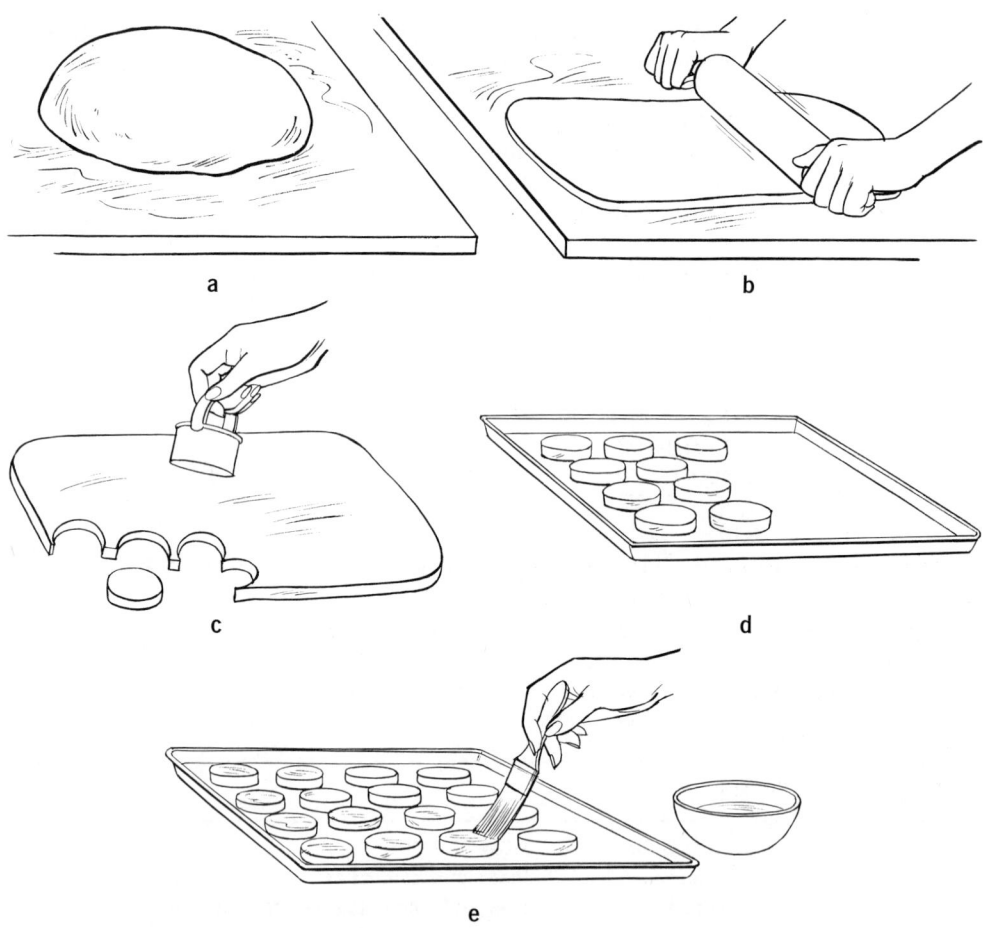

Fig. 1-1 **Rolling and cutting biscuits.**
   a   Place the mixed dough on a flour-dusted work space.
   b   Roll the dough to about ½-inch thickness.
   c   Cut the biscuits out of the dough with a biscuit cutter.
   d   Place the biscuits on the baking pan in straight rows. Space them about ½ inch apart.
   e   Brush the tops of the biscuits with egg wash, melted butter or margarine, or milk.

MAKING AND BAKING THE BISCUITS

Refer to Fig. 1-1 as you work.

1 Remove the dough from the mixing bowl and place it on the floured part of the worktable or workboard. Fold the dough gently to form

UNIT 1: VARIETY BISCUITS

it into a square or rectangular shape with a smooth top. Dust the top of the dough lightly with flour and let the dough rest 5 to 10 minutes before rolling it out.

2 Before rolling the dough, check the bottom of the dough to see if there is still enough dusting flour. If the dough has absorbed the dusting flour, lift the dough gently and dust more flour on the workboard or table. Dust the top of the dough again lightly and dust the rolling pin.

3 Flatten the dough gently with the palms of the hands and then roll the dough gently with the rolling pin. It is best to roll from the center to the sides, lifting the rolling pin when it reaches the edge of the dough. (If you let the rolling pin roll over the edge of the dough, the ends will become too thin.) If the dough sticks to the table, raise it by rolling it up on the rolling pin and then dust the table with more flour.

The dough should be about ½ inch thick when it has been rolled out. Feel the dough with your fingertips to be sure the thickness is equal over the entire dough. If the dough is too thin in spots, you can push the dough together with your hands and then roll it gently. *Be sure that the dough is of even thickness* before cutting out the biscuits, so that the biscuits will be equal in size.

4 Cut the dough with the biscuit cutter. Dip the cutter in flour if the biscuits tend to stick to it. The yield depends on the size of the cutter. For example, a cutter that is 2 inches in diameter (across) will give you fewer biscuits than a cutter 1½ inches in diameter. Cut the biscuits as close together as you can without spoiling their shape, to avoid having much extra scrap dough.

5 Place the biscuits on a baking pan that has been lightly brushed with shortening. Place them about ½ inch apart in straight rows.

6 Gather the pieces of extra scrap dough together and knead them gently into a square. Allow the dough to rest for a few minutes and then roll it out to the same thickness again. Cut out biscuits as before and place them on the pan. Do this until all the dough is used up. Many cooks cut the scrap dough into small squares with a French knife after they have cut out the first biscuits with the round cutter. In this way they avoid having to knead and roll the scrap dough over and over again—this extra kneading and rolling makes the biscuits tough. Be careful when using the French knife to cut the dough into squares.

7 If there is any extra flour on the tops of the cut biscuits, brush it off. Then wash or pat the tops of the biscuits with egg wash. (To make the wash, mix one egg with two tablespoons of water.) The egg wash will give the baked biscuits a shiny brown color. To get a dull brown color—the homemade effect—the tops of the unbaked biscuits may be brushed with melted butter, margarine, or shortening.

8 Check the oven temperature to be sure it is 425° and bake the biscuits about 12 to 15 minutes. (Smaller biscuits need less time to bake than larger ones.) Lift the biscuits gently with a fork or knife to see if the bottom crust is browned lightly. Sometimes it will be necessary to turn the pan around or move the pan from one shelf to another if the oven bakes unevenly. You should get to know how your oven bakes and how you should move the pans to get an even bake and even crust color.

TYPE 2: FLAKY-TYPE BISCUITS

Yield: *15 to 18 biscuits*

THINGS TO PREPARE Prepare the same things as for smooth-top biscuits.

FLAKY-TYPE BISCUITS

NOTE The same ingredients are used as for smooth-top biscuits, but the materials are mixed differently. *Read carefully* and then follow instructions.

INGREDIENTS (*measure carefully*)		HOW TO MIX
all-purpose flour (sifted)	3 cups	Sift all the materials together into the mixing bowl. This sifting will blend them together.
baking powder	2½ tablespoons	
salt	1 teaspoon	
sugar	¼ cup	
shortening	¼ cup	Cut the shortening into the sifted mixture with a pastry blender or two butter knives. (Fig. 1-2.) Cut until small pieces, about the size of grains of rice, are formed.
milk	1 cup	Add the milk and fold the mixture over lightly with the mixing spoon until a sticky dough is formed.

CHECK POINTS These are the same as those for smooth-top biscuits.

MAKING AND BAKING THE BISCUITS

Refer back to Fig. 1-1 as you work.

1 Use extra dusting flour on the worktable or board to keep the dough from sticking. This dough is not smooth and developed.

2 Fold the dough over gently and form it into a square or rectangular shape. Let the dough rest for about 5 minutes and then roll it out as you did for smooth-top biscuits. Use extra dusting flour to pre-

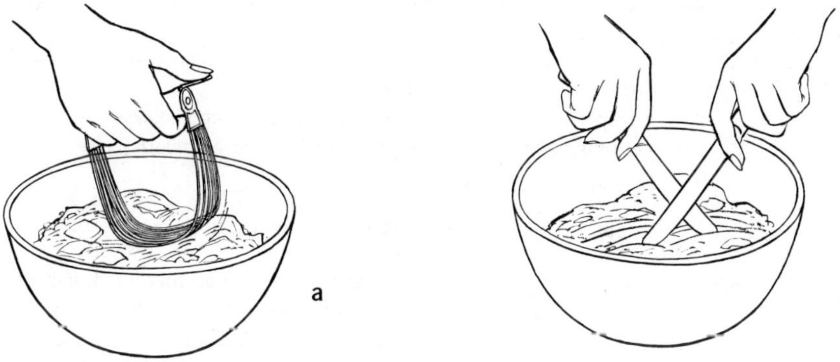

UNIT 1: VARIETY BISCUITS 7

Fig. 1-2 **Cutting in shortening.**
    a With pastry blender.
    b With two knives.

vent sticking. (Be sure to check frequently to see if you have enough flour to keep the dough from sticking to the table.)

3 Follow the same steps you did when making smooth-top biscuits. Space the cut-out biscuits about 1 inch apart on the pan. These biscuits spread more in baking.

**TYPE 3:
COMBINATION
BISCUITS**   Yield: *18 to 20 biscuits*

    Combination biscuits are raised (leavened) by the action of baking powder and yeast. The combined action of both makes the baked biscuits lighter and softer and gives them a lighter grain and texture. Extra care and attention must be given to these instructions. *Read carefully* and follow the directions exactly.

THINGS TO PREPARE Prepare the same things as for smooth-top biscuits. In addition, prepare the yeast. Dry yeast should be soaked for 10 minutes in warm milk before it is used.

COMBINATION BISCUITS

INGREDIENTS (*measure carefully*)		HOW TO MIX
yeast (fresh or dry)	1 package	Dissolve the yeast in the warm milk. Let dry yeast stand about 10 minutes. Fresh yeast may be used as soon as it is dissolved.
milk (warm)	½ cup	

COMBINATION BISCUITS (*Continued*)

INGREDIENTS (*measure carefully*)		HOW TO MIX
sugar	¼ cup	Place the sugar, salt, and shortening in the mixing bowl and mix to a smooth paste.
salt	1½ teaspoons	
shortening	¼ cup	
milk	½ cup	Add the milk and stir it in.
all-purpose flour (sifted)	3 cups	Sift the flour and baking powder into the mixing bowl and stir in slightly. Add the yeast solution. Mix until the dough is smooth and pulls away from the sides of the mixing bowl.
baking powder	2 teaspoons	

CHECK POINTS These are the same as those for smooth-top biscuits.

MAKING AND BAKING THE BISCUITS

Refer to Fig. 1-1 (page 4) as you work.

1 Leave the dough in the mixing bowl, but be sure to cover the dough with a cloth to keep a crust from forming. Crust, if formed, will remain in the dough, producing streaks and toughness in the biscuits.

2 Place the dough in a warm place (near the oven) and allow the dough to rise until it is twice the size it was when first mixed. The dough will feel soft and gassy when touched gently with the finger tips.

3 Place the risen dough gently on a floured workboard or table. Flatten it gently with the palms of your hands and roll it out about ½ inch thick. Be sure to use enough dusting flour to prevent sticking. Check this frequently, and check for even thickness. Cut out the biscuits and place them on a lightly greased pan. Space the biscuits about 1 inch apart on the pan.

4 Place the biscuits in a warm place and allow them to rise until they have almost doubled in size and feel soft when you touch them gently. Brush the tops of the risen biscuits *very gently* with egg wash, melted butter, or margarine.

5 Check the oven temperature to be sure it is 425°. Place the biscuits in the oven gently. Do not move the biscuits as they bake until they have risen and started to show a light brown crust color. Then you may move the pan in the oven if the oven does not bake evenly. Lift a biscuit with a fork or knife to check the bottom crust color. Smaller or thinner biscuits take less time to bake than larger or thicker biscuits.

UNIT 1: VARIETY BISCUITS

HOW TO MAKE BISCUIT VARIETIES

You may use any of the three types of biscuit-dough recipes to make a complete variety of biscuits, in addition to the plain biscuits you have already made. Before you make any variety, read carefully the instructions given for it.

RAISIN BISCUITS

Soak ½ cup of raisins in cool water for about 15 minutes. When raisins are soaked, they absorb some of the moisture, and this keeps the raisins soft and tender during and after baking. The soaked raisins should be sprinkled over the top of the dough just before you finish mixing it. A few more mixing turns, and then the kneading and folding on the worktable, will work the raisins into the dough. Too much mixing will cause the soft raisins to smear and discolor the dough. (You may use regular raisins or bleached raisins, and the amount may be increased to 1 full cup.)

CHEESE BISCUITS

Add 1 tablespoon of grated Parmesan cheese or 2 tablespoons of grated American cheese to the sifted flour and proceed as usual. Baking pans for cheese biscuits should be greased lightly with melted shortening to prevent sticking.

CINNAMON-RAISIN BISCUITS

Any of the biscuit types may be used for cinnamon-raisin biscuits.

MAKING AND BAKING CINNAMON-RAISIN BISCUITS

Refer to Fig. 1-3 (pages 10–11) as you work.

1 Roll out the dough into a rectangular shape about 6 inches wide and ¼ inch thick. Use enough dusting flour to keep the dough from sticking to the table or the rolling pin. Brush the extra flour from the top of the dough after you have finished rolling the dough to the proper size and shape.

2 Brush the top of the dough evenly with melted butter, margarine, or shortening. Vegetable oil may also be used. Sprinkle the top of the dough with some raisins (soaked) and then with cinnamon sugar (½ cup of granulated sugar mixed well with 1 teaspoon of cinnamon). Roll the rolling pin gently over the raisins and cinnamon sugar. This will cause the raisin-cinnamon mixture to stick to the dough.

3 Starting at the edge of the dough furthest away from you, fold the dough over the top about ½ inch and press the folded part down gently with the fingers. (At this point it looks like a hem.) With your fingers, roll the dough up into a tight roll about 1½ inches round.

PART ONE: QUICK BREADS

Fig. 1-3 **Cinnamon-raisin biscuits.**

   a Roll the biscuit dough to a rectangular shape.

   b Brush the surface of the dough with oil or melted fat.

   c Sprinkle raisins over the surface of the dough.

   d Sprinkle the dough with cinnamon sugar.

   e Roll the dough up into a tight roll.

   f Mark off the thickness of the biscuits on the roll (space the marks regularly to make the biscuits of equal size) and then cut the dough with a French knife or other knife.

   g Place the cut biscuits on the prepared pan. Space them about 1 inch apart.

   h The biscuits may be placed in a prepared muffin tin for baking; this gives muffin-shaped biscuits.

   4 Using a knife, cut the roll of dough into 1-inch slices (like jelly roll slices). You will see that the cinnamon sugar and raisins form a spiral effect inside the biscuit dough.

   5 Place the cut biscuits on a lightly greased baking pan about 1 inch apart. Flatten them slightly with your fingers. Brush the tops with egg wash or melted butter, margarine, or other shortening. The cut biscuits may also be put in a greased muffin pan with the spiral or

UNIT 1: VARIETY BISCUITS

HOW TO MAKE BISCUIT VARIETIES

You may use any of the three types of biscuit-dough recipes to make a complete variety of biscuits, in addition to the plain biscuits you have already made. Before you make any variety, read carefully the instructions given for it.

RAISIN BISCUITS

Soak ½ cup of raisins in cool water for about 15 minutes. When raisins are soaked, they absorb some of the moisture, and this keeps the raisins soft and tender during and after baking. The soaked raisins should be sprinkled over the top of the dough just before you finish mixing it. A few more mixing turns, and then the kneading and folding on the worktable, will work the raisins into the dough. Too much mixing will cause the soft raisins to smear and discolor the dough. (You may use regular raisins or bleached raisins, and the amount may be increased to 1 full cup.)

CHEESE BISCUITS

Add 1 tablespoon of grated Parmesan cheese or 2 tablespoons of grated American cheese to the sifted flour and proceed as usual. Baking pans for cheese biscuits should be greased lightly with melted shortening to prevent sticking.

CINNAMON-RAISIN BISCUITS

Any of the biscuit types may be used for cinnamon-raisin biscuits.

MAKING AND BAKING CINNAMON-RAISIN BISCUITS

Refer to Fig. 1-3 (pages 10–11) as you work.
1 Roll out the dough into a rectangular shape about 6 inches wide and ¼ inch thick. Use enough dusting flour to keep the dough from sticking to the table or the rolling pin. Brush the extra flour from the top of the dough after you have finished rolling the dough to the proper size and shape.

2 Brush the top of the dough evenly with melted butter, margarine, or shortening. Vegetable oil may also be used. Sprinkle the top of the dough with some raisins (soaked) and then with cinnamon sugar (½ cup of granulated sugar mixed well with 1 teaspoon of cinnamon). Roll the rolling pin gently over the raisins and cinnamon sugar. This will cause the raisin-cinnamon mixture to stick to the dough.

3 Starting at the edge of the dough furthest away from you, fold the dough over the top about ½ inch and press the folded part down gently with the fingers. (At this point it looks like a hem.) With your fingers, roll the dough up into a tight roll about 1½ inches round.

PART ONE: QUICK BREADS

Fig. 1-3 **Cinnamon-raisin biscuits.**

    a Roll the biscuit dough to a rectangular shape.

    b Brush the surface of the dough with oil or melted fat.

    c Sprinkle raisins over the surface of the dough.

    d Sprinkle the dough with cinnamon sugar.

    e Roll the dough up into a tight roll.

    f Mark off the thickness of the biscuits on the roll (space the marks regularly to make the biscuits of equal size) and then cut the dough with a French knife or other knife.

    g Place the cut biscuits on the prepared pan. Space them about 1 inch apart.

    h The biscuits may be placed in a prepared muffin tin for baking; this gives muffin-shaped biscuits.

4. Using a knife, cut the roll of dough into 1-inch slices (like jelly roll slices). You will see that the cinnamon sugar and raisins form a spiral effect inside the biscuit dough.

5. Place the cut biscuits on a lightly greased baking pan about 1 inch apart. Flatten them slightly with your fingers. Brush the tops with egg wash or melted butter, margarine, or other shortening. The cut biscuits may also be put in a greased muffin pan with the spiral or

UNIT 1: VARIETY BISCUITS   11

Fig. 1-3 **Cinnamon-raisin biscuits (continued).**

cut side showing. This will produce a baked biscuit with a muffin-like appearance.

6 Bake the biscuits as you did the others, at 425°.

NOTE: SPECIAL FLOURS AND PREPARED MIXES USED FOR BISCUITS *Self-rising flours* are specially prepared flours which contain salt and leavening agents (baking powder, baking soda, and other chemicals). When using self-rising flour, *follow the instructions on the label of the package or container. Do not* use baking powder or salt in the biscuit dough. (Whenever self-rising flour is used in *any* recipe, do not add salt or leavening.)

Prepared mixes are mixes which contain all the dry ingredients; you are directed to stir in the necessary liquids. For example, a prepared biscuit mix may simply ask you to add water and stir to make a dough. The mix contains salt, leavening, and perhaps sugar and milk powder. In richer mixes, such as those for cakes, you may be directed to add eggs and milk or water to the dry mix. Some mixes contain dried eggs or egg powder as well as other ingredients and you have to add only water. *When using prepared mixes, it is important to follow instructions on the container or label carefully in order to get satisfactory results.*

NOTE: FOR RICHER BISCUITS Some cooks and homemakers like to add one or two eggs to biscuit doughs. This is an excellent suggestion. Eggs do produce more volume, improved taste, and better texture in biscuits. However, you must also remember that eggs add to the cost of preparing biscuits. Since eggs contain moisture, it will be necessary to add about ¼ cup of flour for each egg added to the recipe. There will be no need to add any more baking powder, since the egg will raise or leaven the added flour.

VOCABULARY

dissolve	knead	mix	roll
dusting flour	leavening	prepared mixes	wash
flaky	measure	rise	yeast

Refer to *Glossary* for explanations if you need to. Some commonly used words are not in the *Glossary;* for these, a dictionary will be helpful.

UNIT 2

**VARIETY
MUFFINS**

AIM   To learn how to make a variety of muffins.

THINGS YOU SHOULD KNOW   Look at a picture of a basket full of assorted muffins, or picture it in your mind. The muffins are warm, smell delicious, and look beautiful. If you could make and serve such muffins at different meals, you would rightly be proud of your baking ability. Would you be surprised to learn that—like fresh biscuits—tasty muffins can be made easily with the same amount of effort and attention? In fact, when you have carefully read this entire unit you will see that you can make a variety of muffins quickly and well.

Some special notes about making muffins should be called to your attention so that you will have a better understanding of the mixing procedure and some other important points. Read carefully:

1   When sugar and shortening are *creamed* (see baking terms in *Glossary*), they become soft and absorb air; this forms air cells in the batter. The more air absorbed and air cells formed, the lighter the batter will be. After the eggs are added, the yolks of the eggs also help to cream the batter lighter. The yolk has a special fat which

13

PART ONE: QUICK BREADS

coats the walls of air cells and enables the cells to become larger without breaking during creaming. It also helps the batter to hold the liquid (in this case, milk) without separating or curdling.

2 Ingredients that are at room temperature (70° to 75°) cream faster. If the shortening is kept in the refrigerator, take it out ahead of time if you plan to use it to make muffins or some other baked product for which the batter has to be creamed.

3 You will note that the recipe instructs you to mix the milk and flour alternately (in separate stages). This prevents a curdled effect. It also makes it easier to mix the flour in smoothly, and keeps lumps of flour from forming in the batter.

4 The leavening used in the muffin recipes (baking powder, baking soda, or both) causes the batter to rise in the oven. It is important that you *measure it carefully and correctly.* If you measure too much leavening, the muffins will rise in the oven and then fall back. The batter may even run over the top of the muffin tin and into the oven where it burns. The muffins will have an uneven grain (large holes) and a bitter taste. If you leave the leavening out or do not use enough, the muffins will be small, heavy, and soggy.

5 All flours, except rye flour, have proteins that form a gluten structure when mixed with water or some other liquid containing water. Bread flour and all-purpose flour have more of these gluten-forming proteins than does pastry flour or cake flour. However, even the proteins in cake flour will form gluten. This gluten formation will become tough with overmixing and will cause the product to be tough when baked. For this reason you are cautioned not to overmix.

6 If you use self-rising flour for any of the recipes, do not add any salt or leavening to the recipe. If you use a prepared muffin mix, follow the recipe on the label but follow our procedure for placing the batter in the muffin tins and baking.

7 A note of caution is necessary regarding the greasing of muffin tins. Be sure that the tins are clean and that they are greased with soft or melted shortening. One small spot in the tin that may not be greased will cause the muffin to stick at that spot after baking. When you try to take the muffin out of the tin, the part that is stuck will not come free and the muffin will tear or break. Check the muffin tins carefully for ungreased spots.

8 As you read the different recipes, you will note that in each one other ingredients, like molasses or fresh berries, are added to the basic muffin recipe. This makes possible variety in muffins. *Read carefully, understand what you read, and then follow the instructions exactly.*

UNIT 2: VARIETY MUFFINS

PLAIN MUFFINS

Yield: *15 to 18 muffins*

THINGS TO PREPARE   Light the oven and set the temperature at 385°. (Observe safety practices when lighting the oven.) Check the recipe for materials.

mixing bowl and spoon	measuring spoons	grease brush	rubber bowl scraper
worktable and workboard	measuring cups	muffin tins	
#16 ice cream scoop	flour sifter	soft shortening	

PLAIN MUFFINS

INGREDIENTS (*measure carefully*)		HOW TO MIX
sugar	¾ cup	Place the ingredients in the mixing bowl and mix to a smooth paste. Scrape the sides of the bowl with the rubber scraper and mix the batter until soft and smooth.
salt	1 teaspoon	
shortening	½ cup	
corn or maple syrup	1 tablespoon	
eggs	2	Break the eggs into a separate cup and check them for freshness. Add one egg at a time to the mixing bowl batter and cream the egg in well after each addition.
milk	¾ cup	Add half the milk, the vanilla, and half the flour and stir them in gently.
vanilla	1 tablespoon	
(*Sift the flour before measuring.*)		
cake flour	2½ cups	Add the rest of the milk and flour (sifted with the baking powder) and mix the batter until smooth. Be sure there are no lumps.
baking powder	1½ tablespoons	

CHECK POINTS

   1 Be sure the worktable and work area have enough room.

   2 Check the muffin tins for proper greasing.

   3 Check the oven temperature to see if it is ready at 385°.

   4 Have the ice cream scoop and other small work tools handy.

MAKING AND BAKING THE MUFFINS

   Refer to Fig. 2-1 (page 16) as you work.

   1 Place the greased muffin tins close to the mixing bowl containing the batter. Now fill the mixing spoon with batter and place it over the muffin tin. With a teaspoon, push enough batter from the mixing spoon into each tin so that the tins are all *half full*. (With practice

16   PART ONE: QUICK BREADS

Fig. 2-1 Making and baking muffins.

- **a** Place the ingredients in the mixing bowl and stir in a round motion to cream the batter.
- **b** Sift the flour with a short back-and-forth motion.
- **c** Fold the raisins into the batter gently.
- **d** Drop the batter into the muffin tin with a scoop or a spoon. Fill each space half full.
- **e** This is a sketch of the baked muffin.

you will learn to pick up just the right amount of batter with the mixing spoon.) The #16 ice cream scoop, if used, should be filled with the same amount each time, and the batter dropped from it

UNIT 2: VARIETY MUFFINS

into the tins. *It is important that all tins are filled half full* so that the muffins are all the same size after baking. If some tins contain less batter than others, the batter in those tins will bake faster, and those muffins will be dried out and have a dark crust before the larger ones are baked. It is good practice to tap the muffin tin lightly on the table to settle the batter and to check the even amounts.

2 Place the muffins in the oven and bake until golden brown. The best test for doneness is to touch a baking muffin gently in the center after the muffins have risen and have a golden-brown crust color. If the muffin springs back to the touch, it is done. Also, the toothpick or straw test may be made. If a toothpick or straw pushed down into the muffin comes out clean, the muffin is baked. If your oven bakes unevenly, move the tins around *after they have risen and have a light brown crust color.* If the bottom shelf of the oven bakes faster than the other shelves, shift the tins after the muffins have risen so that all the muffins bake evenly. *Be sure to use oven pads when moving or removing hot pans.*

3 After taking the muffins from the oven, allow them to cool slightly; then remove the muffins from the tins. Removing the muffins while they are still warm prevents the possibility of their sticking. Also, the muffins may become moist if left in the pans.

**MUFFIN VARIETIES
THAT CAN BE MADE
FROM THE
PLAIN MUFFIN BATTER**

RAISIN MUFFINS

These are made by adding to the batter ½ cup of raisins that have been soaked for 10 to 15 minutes and then drained. Fold the raisins into the plain muffin batter gently. Avoid overmixing, for this will make the batter tough. Bake these as you did the plain muffins.

BLUEBERRY OR HUCKLEBERRY MUFFINS

These are made by adding ½ to ¾ cup of washed, fresh blueberries or huckleberries to the batter after it is mixed. Fold the berries in gently with the mixing spoon in an overhand motion. Try not to break the skin of the berries; this will discolor the batter.

DATE-NUT MUFFINS

These are made by folding in ¼ cup of chopped nutmeats (walnuts) and ¼ cup of chopped, pitted dates. Fold these in gently after the batter has been completely mixed.

PART ONE: QUICK BREADS

ORANGE MUFFINS
These are made by using only ¼ cup of milk in the recipe and adding ½ cup of orange juice and 1 tablespoon of orange rind to the batter. Mix as usual.

CORN MUFFINS OR SOUTHERN CORN BREAD

Yield: *15 to 18 muffins or 1 panful of corn bread*

THINGS TO PREPARE   Prepare the same things as for plain muffins, and 1 pan 8 by 12 inches.

CORN MUFFINS OR SOUTHERN CORN BREAD

INGREDIENTS (*measure carefully*)		HOW TO MIX
sugar	½ cup	Place the ingredients in the mixing bowl and mix to a smooth paste. Scrape the sides of the bowl and mix the batter until soft and smooth.
salt	1 teaspoon	
shortening	½ cup	
corn syrup	1½ tablespoons	
eggs	2	Break the eggs into a separate cup and check for freshness. Add one egg at a time to the mixing bowl. Cream each egg in well until the batter is soft and light.
milk	¾ cup	Add the milk and stir the mixture lightly. Sift the flour, corn meal, and baking powder together. Add them to the batter and mix until all the flour is absorbed.
cake flour	2½ cups	
corn meal (yellow)	¾ cup	
baking powder	1½ tablespoons	
milk	¼ cup	Add the rest of the milk and mix until the batter is smooth.

CHECK POINTS
These are the same as those for plain muffins.

MAKING AND BAKING THE MUFFINS OR CORN BREAD

Refer to Figs. 2-1 and 2-2 as you work.
For corn muffins, spoon the batter into muffin tins and bake, as you did for plain muffins. (Fig. 2-1.)

For Southern corn bread, clean and grease one pan 8 × 12 inches which is about 1½ inches high. (A larger pan may be used; this will result in a thinner corn bread. A loaf cake pan may be used but should be filled only about 1 inch high before baking. More batter placed in the pan will make thicker Southern corn bread, but it takes longer to bake thicker bread.) Southern corn bread in an 8 × 12 pan will take about 20 to 25 minutes to bake at 385°.

Do not move the pan in the oven until the corn bread has risen and shows a light brown crust color. Test for proper bake by touch-

UNIT 2: VARIETY MUFFINS

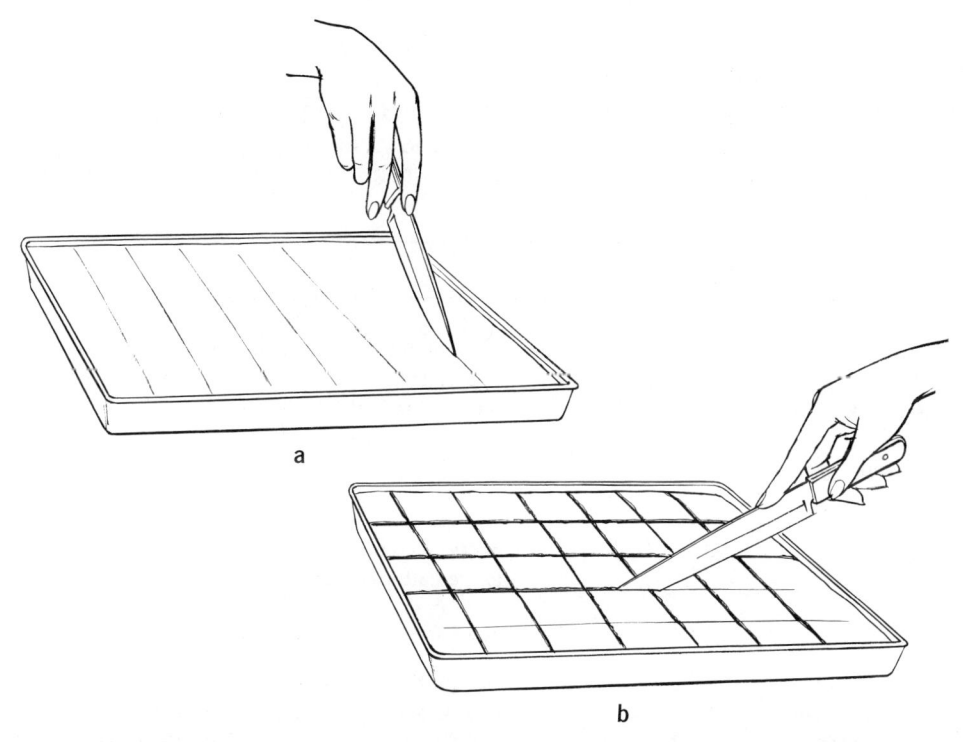

Fig. 2-2a Mark the baked Southern corn bread into 2-inch by 2-inch squares.
   b Then cut the sections, following your marks.

ing the center gently. If it springs back to the touch, the corn bread is done. (A straw or toothpick may also be used to test for doneness.) Remove the pan from the oven carefully and allow the corn bread to cool until it is just warm. The corn bread may be cut into portions while in the pan. Try to cut the portions evenly and equally. Mark off the sections first; then cut the portions. (Fig. 2-2.)

WHOLE WHEAT MUFFINS Yield: *15 to 18 muffins*

SPECIAL THINGS YOU SHOULD KNOW ABOUT WHEAT MUFFINS

1 The molasses used in the recipe gives added sweetness, a darker color, and a special taste and flavor. Darker molasses will make the muffins darker and the taste of molasses stronger.

2 The cinnamon also adds to the taste and produces a darker color. Measure the cinnamon very carefully.

3 Baking soda is used to help the baking powder leaven the muffins. The baking soda combines with the natural acid in the molasses,

and when the batter is baking, they work together to raise it just as baking powder does.

4. Whole wheat flour only may be used instead of the blend of whole wheat and all-purpose flour shown in the recipe below. If this is done, use 2¼ cups of whole wheat flour and omit the all-purpose flour.

WHOLE WHEAT MUFFINS

INGREDIENTS (*measure carefully*)		HOW TO MIX
sugar	½ cup	Place all the ingredients in the mixing bowl and mix to a smooth paste. Scrape the sides of the bowl and mix the batter until soft.
salt	1 teaspoon	
shortening	½ cup	
molasses	2 tablespoons	
cinnamon	½ teaspoon	
baking soda	½ teaspoon	
eggs	2	Break and check the eggs. Add one egg at a time to the batter and cream each egg in well.
milk	1 cup	Add half the milk and stir it in gently.
whole wheat flour	¾ cup	Sift the flour and baking powder together into the mixing bowl and stir until the flour is absorbed. Add the rest of the milk and the soaked and drained raisins; mix until the batter is smooth.
all-purpose flour	1¾ cups	
baking powder	1¼ tablespoons	
raisins	½ cup	

CHECK POINTS

These are the same as those for plain muffins.

MAKING AND BAKING THE WHOLE WHEAT MUFFINS

Refer to Fig. 2-1.

If the batter is made with whole wheat flour only, the muffin tins should be filled a little more than half full. The muffins will be a little heavier because whole wheat flour does not give you the same volume or lightness as does the all-purpose flour.

VOCABULARY

alternately	cream	gluten	ingredients	protein
combine	curdling	grain	omit	soggy
corn meal	fold in	grease	overmix	whole wheat

Refer to *Glossary* for the meaning of these terms. If some of the words are not in the *Glossary*, check the dictionary for their meaning. Some of these terms have the same meaning in everyday language.

UNIT 3

**VARIETY
LOAF-TYPE
QUICK BREADS**

AIM   To learn how to make a variety of loaf-type quick breads.

THINGS YOU SHOULD KNOW   Loaf-type quick breads are similar to muffins. In fact, the same recipes used for muffins may be used for the loaf quick breads. The only difference is in the loaf shape and the way the breads are portioned for service. Muffin batter baked in a loaf pan (a pan used to bake bread) results in a quick bread with a loaf shape.

There are several advantages to this type of quick bread. A loaf is a large unit. It may take longer than muffins to bake, but it saves time in pan preparation and keeps fresh longer, since the loaf is not sliced until it is ready to be served. In addition, the different shape adds to the variety of quick breads you can bake and serve.

You will remember that Southern corn bread was made in a large, flat baking pan and then cut into square or rectangular pieces when served. The same method could have been used with the whole wheat muffin batter. All the recipes for the variety of muffins that can be made from the basic plain muffin recipe can also be used for making loaf-type quick breads. For example, you may make raisin, date-nut, cheese, or other quick breads by baking the batter in loaf pans rather than muffin tins. The cooled loaves can be sliced and served at mealtime or wrapped and frozen for later use. Certain quick breads are best when made and served in loaf form. Among these, banana bread is one of the most popular.

BANANA   Yield: *1 loaf* (*bread size*) or
BREAD   *2 small loaves* (*cake size*)

NOTES: BANANAS AND BANANA BREAD

1. The bananas supply moisture and take the place of milk. They contain natural sugars and have a special flavor. All these factors improve the flavor and keeping qualities of banana bread. It stays fresh longer than other quick breads, especially if the baked, cooled loaf is wrapped and stored in the refrigerator.

2. Ripe bananas are sweeter and provide better flavor than the green fruit. A green-tipped banana is not fully ripe; it feels firm, even hard. An all-yellow banana has had a large amount of its natural starch changed to sugar (dextrose); it is excellent for eating and cooking. A fully ripened banana is spotted with brown flecks and feels soft to the touch. Almost all of its starch has been converted to sugar, and its flavor is strong. The pulp (inside) of the banana is soft and can be mashed easily. Ripe bananas are best for baking.

3. A peeled banana, like so many other peeled fruits (apples) and vegetables (potatoes) turns brown when exposed to the air. It is affected by the air: it turns brown as a result of *oxidation*. To prevent peeled bananas from turning brown quickly, dip them in, or brush them with, fruit juice. Orange juice, grapefruit juice, pineapple juice, or lemon juice and water may be used. This treatment will keep bananas from discoloring for about two hours.

4. Ripe bananas may be mashed in a bowl with a spoon and then folded into the batter. (Fig. 3-1*a*.) Small lumps or spots on the bananas will not affect the banana bread. If the bananas are firm, force them through a fine strainer with a spoon. (Fig. 3-1*b*.) If you have a mixing machine, place the firm bananas in the mixing machine and mash them as you would boiled potatoes. Mashed bananas should be covered to prevent discoloration if they are not added to the batter as soon as they are mashed.

5. Banana bread batter should be as soft as a plain muffin batter. Some bananas may not have enough moisture. If the batter is too firm, add a little milk to soften the batter. Be sure to add just a small amount at a time until the right consistency (thickness) is reached.

UNIT 3: VARIETY LOAF-TYPE QUICK BREADS   23

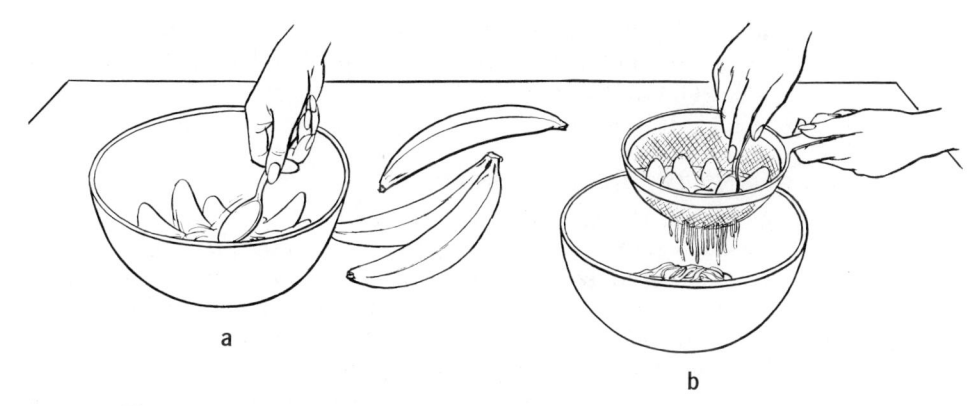

Fig. 3-1 Mashing bananas.

    a Bananas may be mashed in a bowl with a spoon.

    b Or they may be mashed by being pushed through a strainer.

THINGS TO PREPARE Light the oven and set the temperature at 350°. Check the recipe for materials.

mixing bowl and spoon	measuring spoons	loaf pan (paper-lined
worktable and workboard	measuring cups	or greased)
fork for mashing bananas	flour sifter	
rubber bowl scraper	grease brush	

BANANA BREAD

INGREDIENTS (*measure carefully*)		HOW TO MIX
sugar	½ cup	Place these ingredients in the mixing bowl and stir to a smooth paste. Scrape the sides of the bowl and mix until soft and smooth.
salt	1 teaspoon	
baking soda	½ teaspoon	
shortening	½ cup	
eggs	2	Break the eggs and check for freshness. Add one egg at a time and cream well after each addition.
all-purpose flour (sifted)	2¼ cups	Sift the flour and baking powder into the mixing bowl. Stir in lightly. Add the mashed bananas; mix to a smooth batter. *Do not overmix.*
baking powder	1 tablespoon	
mashed bananas	1½ to 2 medium-size ripe bananas	

CHECK POINTS

    1 Check the oven for proper temperature.

    2 Line the loaf pans with paper, or grease and dust them with flour.

3 Check the thickness of the batter again. If overmixed or too stiff, the banana bread will crack on top, rise to a high peak, and have large holes in the grain.

MAKING AND BAKING THE BANANA BREAD

Refer to Figs. 3-1 through 3-4 as you work.

1 Place the batter in the prepared loaf pan. (See Fig. 3-2.) If paper liners are used, try to cut the paper to the exact size of the pan. If no paper liner is used, be sure to grease the entire pan well and then sprinkle the inside with flour. Shake the flour so that it covers the entire pan; then turn the pan upside down to remove the excess flour. The flour acts as a buffer to keep the batter from sticking to the pan during and after baking. Do not fill the pans more than half full. Leftover batter may be placed in muffin tins and baked.

2 Bake the banana bread at 350° for about 40 minutes. After the bread has risen and the top crust is light brown, touch the center

Fig. 3-2 **Preparing a loaf pan.**

a If the loaf-type quick bread is baked without a paper pan liner, grease the pan and dust it with flour.

b Cut the paper to fit the loaf pan.

c Insert the paper liner evenly into the loaf pan.

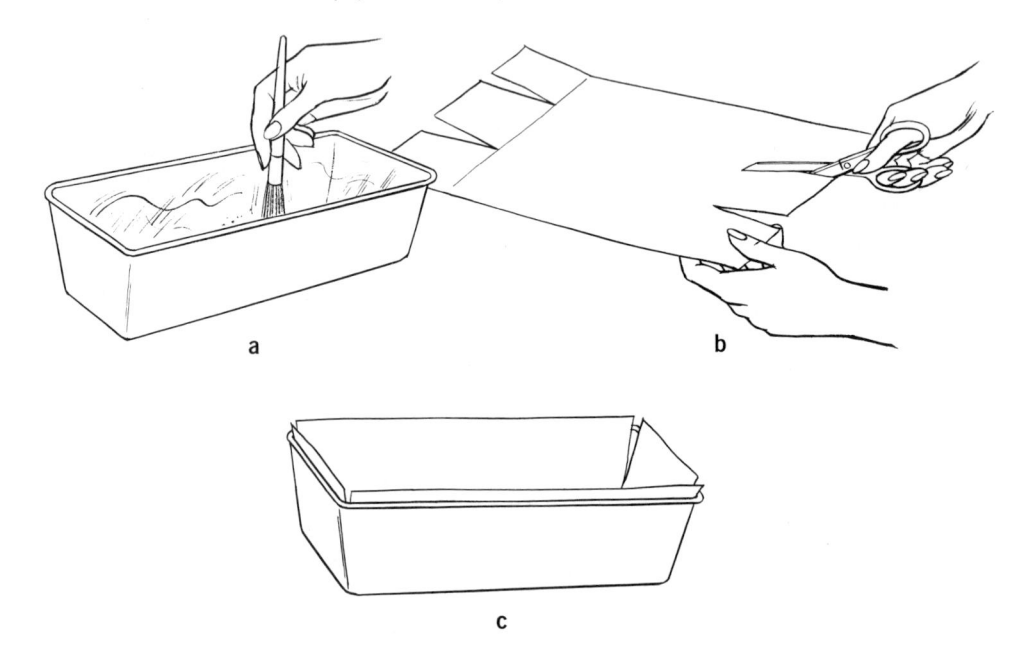

UNIT 3: VARIETY LOAF-TYPE QUICK BREADS 25

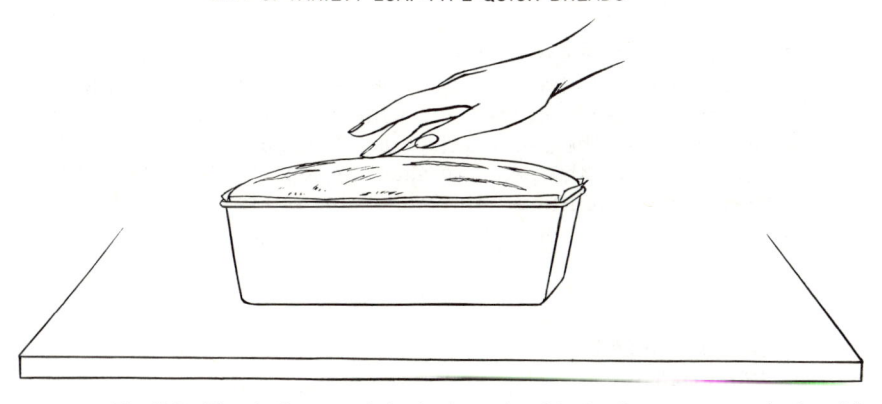

Fig. 3-3   Touch the top of the loaf gently with the finger to test whether it is done.

gently with a finger. If the bread springs back to the touch, it is baked. (Fig. 3-3.) The toothpick test may also be made. Insert a toothpick gently into the center of the loaf and remove it. If the toothpick comes out clean (no sticky batter attached to it), the loaf may be considered done.

NOTE   A higher baking temperature will not speed up the baking process. High oven temperatures will make the crust crack, cause high peaks on the loaf, and possibly burn the loaf.

Fig. 3-4   Divide the baked loaf into 12 or more equal slices. (The picture shows division into 12 slices—3 from each quarter of the loaf.)

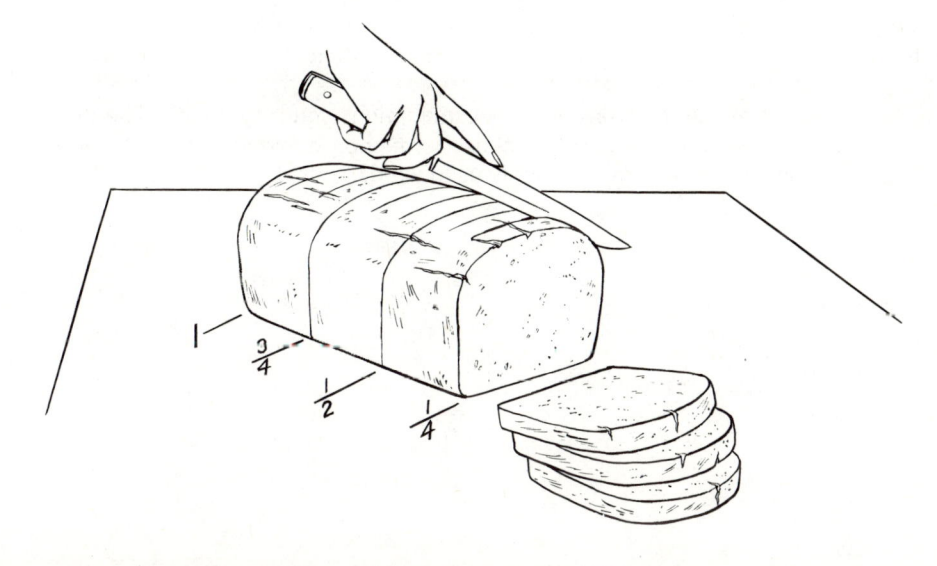

3 Allow the loaf-type quick bread to cool until it is barely warm before removing it from the loaf pan. The bread may stick slightly to pans which have been greased and floured. If this happens, insert a knife between the pan and the quick bread and separate the sticking parts from the pan. To slice the loaf, mark off portions for service before cutting. This will enable you to divide the loaf into equal servings. (Fig. 3-4.)

BANANA BREAD VARIETIES

RAISIN-BANANA BREAD

This variety may be made by adding ½ cup of softened raisins (soaked in warm water for 10 minutes) with the mashed bananas, folding them in gently in the final mixing stage.

BANANA-NUT BREAD

This is made by gently folding in ½ cup of chopped walnuts or pecans with the mashed bananas.

PRUNE BREAD

For this variety, use ¾ cup of cooked, pitted, mashed prunes instead of the mashed bananas. Fold the prunes into the batter after the flour has been lightly stirred.

VOCABULARY

buffer	dextrose	keeping qualities	ripe
consistency	dusting (*review*)	oxidation	starch
converted	insert	pulp	strain

Refer to *Glossary* for any explanations you may need. The dictionary will be helpful for those terms not included in the *Glossary* because they are commonly used words.

UNIT 4

POPOVERS

AIM To learn how to make popovers and popover varieties.

THINGS YOU SHOULD KNOW Popovers are special quick breads. They are different from the usual muffin or biscuit because they are mixed differently and they are leavened (raised) differently. They are not raised by baking powder or yeast but by the natural effects of steam formed during baking and by the natural expansion of eggs during baking.

Popovers look like cream puff shells after they are baked. The batter itself is thin and is called a pour-type batter. In addition to all these differences, the pans that are often used for popovers are special pans. They look like muffin pans but are deeper and not as wide as muffin pans. (Muffin pans may be used, however, with good results.)

A strong bread flour is best for making popovers, although all-purpose flour may be used. The bread flour has a stronger gluten content. (Do you remember that the proteins in flour, when mixed with water, form gluten?) The gluten, with the help of proteins in the eggs, forms the *structure* of the popover. This structure allows the popover to rise without falling back or shrinking after baking.

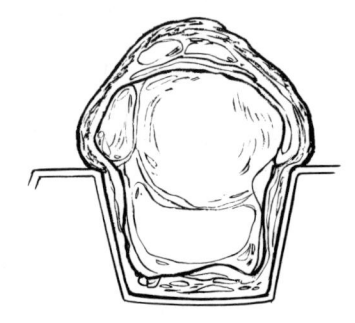

Fig. 4-1 Cross section of the baked popover in the pan.

Generally, after the first 20 minutes of baking the popover has risen fully. Lowering the temperature of the oven then from 450° to 375° for the final 15 minutes of baking enables the gluten to dry completely. This forms a firm structure which supports the popover. However, if the popover is baked too quickly, or if the oven door is slammed or left open during the first stage of baking, the popover will fall back or shrink.

An explanation of how popovers are leavened during baking may be helpful. The gluten in the flour is well developed by mixing to be conditioned for the changes that take place during baking. Part of the water or moisture present in the milk and eggs is changed into steam by the heat of the oven and the hot popover pans. The steam pushes upward since it cannot get out through the sides or bottom of the pan. This upward pressure causes the top crust of the popover to rise. The eggs in the batter start to expand in the oven as they would in a frying pan. This is all part of the natural leavening process. The proteins in the egg, found in the albumen or white of the egg, join the gluten to form the structure of the popover. Together, the gluten and egg proteins support the popover during and after baking. The popover continues to rise until the gluten-protein structure starts to set and dry. The steam continues to rise and evaporate during baking, escaping through tiny cracks in the popover's top crust.

A good popover is high, light, and crisp on the outside, has a shiny, glossy brown color, and is tender on the inside. (See Fig. 4-1.) Popovers are a challenge to make, but it gives you great satisfaction to make them well. Be sure to *read carefully, understand what you read, and follow the instructions exactly.*

BASIC POPOVERS   Yield: *about 12 popovers*

THINGS TO PREPARE   Light the oven and set the temperature at 450°. Prepare the popover pans or muffin pans by cleaning them, greasing them,

UNIT 4: POPOVERS

and warming them before pouring the batter into them. (See Fig. 4-2a, page 30.)   Check the recipe for materials needed.

measuring spoons	mixing machine (if available)	grease brush
measuring cups	ladle or pitcher	oven pads
mixing bowl and spoons	worktable and workboard	flour sifter

POPOVERS

INGREDIENTS (*measure carefully*)		HOW TO MIX
bread flour or	1¼ cups	Sift the flour and salt into the mixing bowl. (Fig. 4-2b.)
all-purpose flour (*not both*)	1½ cups	
salt	1 teaspoon	
eggs	2	Break the eggs and check them. Beat the eggs lightly. Add the milk and shortening to the eggs and beat lightly. Add the liquid mixture to the flour in four stages or parts. Be sure to mix the batter well after each addition. Be careful to prevent lumps; keep mixing until the batter is smooth. To mix the batter properly will take about 6 minutes of mixing by hand. If you use a mixing machine (Fig. 4-2c), it will take about 2 to 3 minutes of mixing on medium speed after all the liquid has been added.
milk	1¼ cups	
melted shortening	2 tablespoons	

CHECK POINTS

1 Check the oven temperature to be sure it is ready at 450°.

2 Be sure the pans are warm and evenly greased.

3 Have the pouring pitcher or ladle ready for use.

4 Have a cloth ready to wipe up any batter which drips on the table or on the pans.

MAKING AND BAKING THE POPOVERS

Refer to Figs. 4-2d and e as you work.

1 Put the batter into a pitcher with a pouring spout. Use a ladle to pour the batter into the tins if a pitcher is not available. Fill each tin ½ full, making sure that all the tins are filled evenly. Wipe up any drippings as you pour the batter.

2 Place the popovers in the oven and bake them for about 20 minutes. Do not move the pans during this baking period. At the end of this first period, the popovers will have risen and should have a light brown crust color. Now, lower the oven temperature to 375° and

Fig. 4-2 Preparation of popovers.

    a Grease the popover or muffin pan with soft fat or shortening.
    b Sift the flour into the mixing bowl.
    c The batter is often mixed in a mixing machine.
    d You may use a ladle to pour out the batter.
    e Or you may use a pitcher to pour the batter.

UNIT 4: POPOVERS

bake the popovers 15 minutes longer. The lower temperature bakes the inside of the popover while the crust becomes brown and glossy.

3 Remove the popovers from the pans soon after baking and serve them while they are warm.

HOW TO MAKE POPOVER VARIETIES

CHEESE POPOVERS

These may be made by adding 1½ tablespoons of grated Parmesan cheese to the batter. It is best to blend the cheese with the flour and salt before adding the liquid.

WHOLE WHEAT POPOVERS

This variety may be made by adding ½ cup of whole wheat flour and omitting ½ cup of the all-purpose flour. A small amount (½ teaspoon) of sugar color (burnt sugar) or 1 tablespoon of dark molasses may be added to give a darker color to whole wheat popovers.

NOTE: COMMON POPOVER FAULTS AND THEIR CAUSES

The popovers are soggy and soft. This is generally due to underbaking. It may also happen when steam is trapped in the popover. It is good practice to puncture each popover with a fork as soon as they are removed from the oven, in order to let the trapped steam escape. Popovers that are left in the pan to cool also tend to become soggy. Popovers should be removed from the pans while they are still quite warm.

The popovers do not rise enough and lack volume. This often occurs when the ingredients are not mixed enough to form a smooth batter with a well-developed gluten. Machine mixing makes it easier to mix the batter smoothly and properly. The same fault may result when the oven temperature is not hot enough because of a faulty control or heat regulator. Check the temperature of the oven with an oven thermometer if you think this may be the cause. (An oven thermometer is also called a *pyrometer*.)

The popovers have tough or hard crusts. This is generally caused by overbaking. It may also come from the use of too much flour, which makes the batter too thick. This causes a thicker crust which requires a longer baking period. Toughness results. To thin the batter, it is advisable to use an extra egg rather than water or milk. The egg may be a little more expensive, but it will make better popovers.

The popovers stick to the pan. This is generally caused by pans which have not been greased enough or have not been greased evenly. Sometimes heating the pan will cause all the grease to settle to the bottom. If this happens, rebrush the pans with the grease at the bottom of the tin. Remember, too, to remove the popovers from the pan while they are warm.

VOCABULARY

albumen	natural leavening	steam	thin down
batter	oven heat	structure	toughness
expand	pyrometer	temperature	volume

Refer to *Glossary* for necessary explanations. The dictionary may be helpful in the case of terms not included in the *Glossary*.

PART TWO ■■ □□□□□□

sweet yeast-raised dough products

INTRODUCTION: HOW YEAST CONDITIONS A DOUGH

The changes that take place in a yeast-raised dough make the dough light and gassy instead of heavy and thick. This is due to the action of the yeast. Let us look at what yeast is and what it does when added to a dough.

1 Yeast is a living, one-cell organism. Many cells are compressed into one cake of yeast. The manufacturer of commercial yeast selects a special "yeast seed" and uses it to grow millions of other cells. These are then processed and made into yeast packages.

2 When you place yeast in water or milk and dissolve it, the yeast cells become free to move about and to grow and multiply when they are added to dough. Dough itself contains food for yeast growth. The starch in the flour, the sugar added to the dough, the water or milk used, the proteins present in the flour—all provide food for the yeast. The yeast cells use only a small part of this food for growth, yet they multiply and grow very quickly, and each cell produces another cell in a chain-like form. As a result of all this activity, a gas is formed and given off. This is called carbon dioxide gas. This gas is trapped inside the dough and absorbed into the cells formed by the structure of gluten and starch in the flour. As the amount of gas increases, the dough rises and expands. The dough becomes light and gassy and stretches easily without tearing.

3 The gluten, formed when you mixed the flour into the dough and then developed in the dough by added mixing, is also conditioned and made to stretch by the yeast's action. The gluten enables the dough to expand without tearing and to hold in the gas. This is very important; the same gluten holds in the gas given off later by the yeast, after the bread or roll is shaped and placed on pans. The gluten also helps the product rise in the oven during baking and keep its structure or shape at the same time. You can now see that the action of the yeast causes chemical changes to take place in the dough which prepare the dough to be made into various units. The yeast also conditions the gluten, enabling it to provide structure for the product.

4 A number of factors control the speed or rate at which the yeast will grow and ferment the dough. If we used more yeast—say, two cakes instead of one—the dough would ferment faster because there would be more yeast cells. When the milk or water used is warm, the yeast grows faster. If the water or milk is cold, the yeast works slowly. You can see that warm temperatures speed fermentation and cool temperatures slow it down. For this reason the dough is placed in a warm place to ferment. *However, yeast must never be*

INTRODUCTION

dissolved in boiling or very hot water or milk. Temperature over 140° will kill or destroy the yeast cells. This is known as the "thermal death point of yeast."

5 Remember, *salt and yeast must never be dissolved together.* Salt, when dissolved in water, forms an acid. This acid solution can destroy the activity of the yeast cells. Salt must be measured very carefully when making a yeast-raised dough. Too much salt will slow down or stop the action of yeast in a dough. Not enough salt will allow the yeast to grow too fast and will cause the gluten to tear and the dough to turn sour because of too much fermentation. It is very important that you *measure salt carefully when making yeast-raised doughs.*

6 Moisture helps the yeast grow faster, thus speeding the rate of fermentation. For this reason you are instructed to place the dough in a warm, moist place to rise. The same rule holds true after the products are shaped and placed on pans: the moisture helps them to rise faster. (The cloth that covers the dough during the period of fermentation prevents air from drying the dough and forming a crust. Once a crust is formed on the dough, it remains and causes tough streaks in the products.)

7 If, after you have made and fermented the dough and have shaped the units, you do not wish to bake them immediately, cover the units with cellophane or freezer wrap and put them in the refrigerator. The refrigerator temperature will keep them from rising quickly or spoiling for a period of 24 hours. Cold keeps yeast cells from growing rapidly. When the units are taken from the refrigerator and returned to room temperature, they will rise normally.

8 Yeast-raised doughs and products made from these doughs can be kept in the freezer for long periods without baking. They must be wrapped well with freezer wrap to keep ice crystals from settling on them. When the units are to be used, remove them from the freezer and allow them to return to room temperature. This will take a few hours. Then place the units in a warm place to rise; bake them as usual.

9 Once the units have risen, they must be baked. This means that the oven should be heated to the proper temperature in advance. If you place the dough or the shaped units near the oven or on top of the oven (if the outside of the oven does not get hot), the dough or units will ferment faster.

10 Dry yeast is yeast from which most of the water or moisture has been removed. This makes the yeast inactive so that it may be kept at room temperature without spoiling. Compressed yeast is also known as fresh yeast. This yeast must be kept refrigerated when not in use. As fresh yeast becomes old and stale, it turns a brownish color. In this condition it is still reasonably good. Yeast that is completely spoiled becomes soft and pasty and develops a nasty odor. The green color of mold may also be noticeable. This yeast should not be used.

NOTE: SPONGE DOUGHS These are doughs which are made by mixing the yeast solution and part of the milk, flour, and sugar together in a soft batter. Since no salt is added, the yeast works rapidly and the soft-batter dough rises quickly. This dough is known as a sponge dough. The sponge is then mixed with the salt and the remaining ingredients into a regular dough. This sponge-dough method is often used in the preparation of bread.

UNIT 5

**BASIC
SWEET
YEAST
DOUGH**

AIM   To learn how to make a sweet yeast dough, understanding the basic facts about yeast and fermentation.

THINGS YOU SHOULD KNOW   Variety in baked products is as important as variety in planned menus. We pointed out in the first unit how many uses biscuits have in addition to replacing bread. Products made from yeast-raised doughs, such as bread, rolls, and the many varieties of baked products related to bread, are the backbone of the baking industry.   Soft rolls or buns, for example, are widely used. Imagine the hamburger without the soft hamburger bun. It would seem strange to serve a frankfurter on any bread other than a soft frankfurter roll.

You can see that the cook has much to gain from being able to make fresh soft rolls and sweet buns. You will take great pride in serving warm, fragrant soft rolls and buns, as well as a variety of quick breads. It is no more difficult to make yeast-raised varieties than to make quick bread varieties. The experience you have gained in making quick breads will be of great help to you.

There is, of course, a distinct difference from making quick breads in the way yeast-raised dough is mixed, then fermented or conditioned before being made up into various units. The dough is *leavened by yeast,* as you have learned, not by the action of baking powder or baking soda. *You must read carefully, understand what you read, and follow instructions exactly.*

THINGS TO PREPARE   Select a warm place for the dough to rise in.

measuring spoons	grease brush	table brush
measuring cups	cloth to cover dough	rubber bowl scraper
mixing bowl and spoon	flour sifter	
small bowl for yeast solution	worktable and workboard	

BASIC SWEET YEAST DOUGH   Yield: *18 soft rolls or buns*

INGREDIENTS (*measure carefully*)		HOW TO MIX
yeast (compressed or dry)	1 package	Dissolve the yeast in the water (Fig. 5-1*a*) and set aside. Dry yeast should be allowed to stand for ten minutes before it is added to the dough.
warm water (110°)	¼ cup	
sugar	⅓ cup	Place the sugar, salt, and shortening in the mixing bowl and mix them to a smooth paste.
salt (*measure accurately*)	1½ teaspoons	
shortening	⅓ cup	
eggs	2	Break the eggs and check them for freshness. Add one egg at a time; blend it in well before the next addition.
milk (warm)	¾ cup	Add the milk and vanilla and stir them in slightly.
vanilla	1 tablespoon	
all-purpose flour	5 cups (approximately)	Sift the flour and put about ½ cup of flour aside to be used if the dough is too soft. Place the rest of the flour in the bowl and stir the mixture for a few turns. Add the yeast solution and mix the dough until it is smooth and does not stick to the sides of the bowl. (Fig. 5-1*b* and *c*.) The dough should be of medium consistency. If the dough feels soft and sticky, add the ½ cup of flour you set aside. *Be sure to mix the dough until it is smooth.*

CHECK POINTS

   1 Is the dough smooth? Does it pull away from the sides of the bowl as you mix it?

   2 Is the worktable ready? Dust the work area with flour so that the dough may be placed upon it.

UNIT 5: BASIC SWEET YEAST DOUGH   39

Fig. 5-1 **Preparation of sweet yeast-raised dough.**
  a Dissolve the yeast in lukewarm water.
  b Add the yeast solution to the flour.
  c Develop the dough well.
  d Knead the dough to make it smooth.
  e Cover the dough while it is rising.
  f The dough will rise above the top of the bowl.

3 Have you selected a warm place to put the dough so that it can rise quickly?

NOTE: DOUGH CONDITIONING

1 Remove the dough to the floured part of the worktable. Knead the dough with the palms of your hands until the flour is worked into the dough and the dough is round and smooth. (Fig. 5-1*d*.)

2 Brush the mixing bowl with a little oil or melted fat and return the dough to the mixing bowl. Cover the dough with a cloth and place it in a warm place to rise. (Fig. 5-1*e*.)

3 When the dough has risen to about twice its original size (Fig. 5-1*f*) and feels soft and gassy to the touch (about 1 to 1½ hours), take it from the bowl and place it on a lightly floured part of the worktable. At this point, the dough is ready to be shaped into the kind of rolls or buns you wish to make. The different kinds will be discussed in Unit 6.

VOCABULARY

acid	ferment	organism	*Review*
carbon-dioxide	fragrant	rate	consistency
chemical	gassy	solution	dusted
crystals	menu	variety	structure
factors	one-cell	yeast-raised	yeast

Refer to *Glossary* for any explanations you may need. The dictionary may be helpful in the case of terms not included in the *Glossary*.

UNIT 6

**VARIETY
SOFT ROLLS
AND BUNS**

**PARKER
HOUSE
ROLLS**   Yield: *approximately 16 rolls*

    AIM   To learn how to make Parker House rolls.

THINGS YOU SHOULD KNOW   A wide variety of sweet rolls and buns may be made from the basic sweet dough you have prepared. Each of the varieties will be explained, with a sketch or diagram for each step of the main part to help you.
    Parker House rolls are delicate rolls that can be opened easily by pulling the two halves apart. They are particularly good to serve with luncheons or snacks because the separated parts can be spread easily before serving with a variety of relishes. They also add variety to the hot breads and biscuits you can make and serve.

THINGS TO PREPARE   Light the oven and set it at 390°.

| worktable | French knife or | table brush | rolling pin | melted fat |
| workboard | other knife | grease brush | baking pan | fermented dough |

41

CHECK POINTS

1 Has the dough risen until it is soft and light?
2 Has the oven reached the proper temperature?
3 Is the worktable or workboard ready and dusted lightly with flour?
4 Is the baking pan greased and ready?

NOTE If the rolls are to be shaped and placed on pans to be baked later, even the following day, make room for them in the refrigerator. If the unbaked rolls are to be frozen, prepare space for them in the freezer.

MAKING AND BAKING THE PARKER HOUSE ROLLS

Refer to Fig. 6-1 as you work.

1 Place the risen dough on the worktable and flatten gently with the palms of your hands to let the gas out and remove large air pockets. If the dough feels sticky, dust it lightly with flour.

2 Roll the dough up into a long roll (like a jelly roll) about 1 inch thick. Be sure the strip of dough is of even thickness. This is necessary to divide the dough into equal parts.

3 Divide the dough into 16 equal pieces as follows (refer to Fig. 6-1*a*):
   Cut the dough exactly in half with the knife.
   Cut each half exactly in half once again. You now have 4 equal pieces of dough.
   Cut each piece of dough in half again. You now have 8 equal pieces.
   Finally, cut each of the pieces exactly in half again and you will have 16 equal pieces.

4 Round each piece of dough in the palms of your hands so that the dough looks like a round ball with a smooth surface. (Fig. 6-1*b*.) Place the round pieces in two rows on a lightly dusted part of the table and flatten them gently. Cover the units with a cloth and allow them to rest for about 10 minutes. (They will become soft and a little gassy again.)

5 Take each piece of dough, flatten it gently, and then roll it with the rolling pin until it is an oval shape about 3 inches long. (Fig. 6-1*c*.) Be sure to use only enough flour while rolling to keep the dough from sticking to the table or the rolling pin. After rolling, place the pieces of dough alongside each other in neat rows. Remove any excess flour from the tops of the dough with a brush. If extra flour is left on the top of the dough and then brushed with melted fat, the inside of the roll will be pasty or sticky after baking.

6 Brush each of the units lightly with melted fat. Fold one edge of the dough over to the other edge so that you form a half circle and

UNIT 6: VARIETY SOFT ROLLS AND BUNS   43

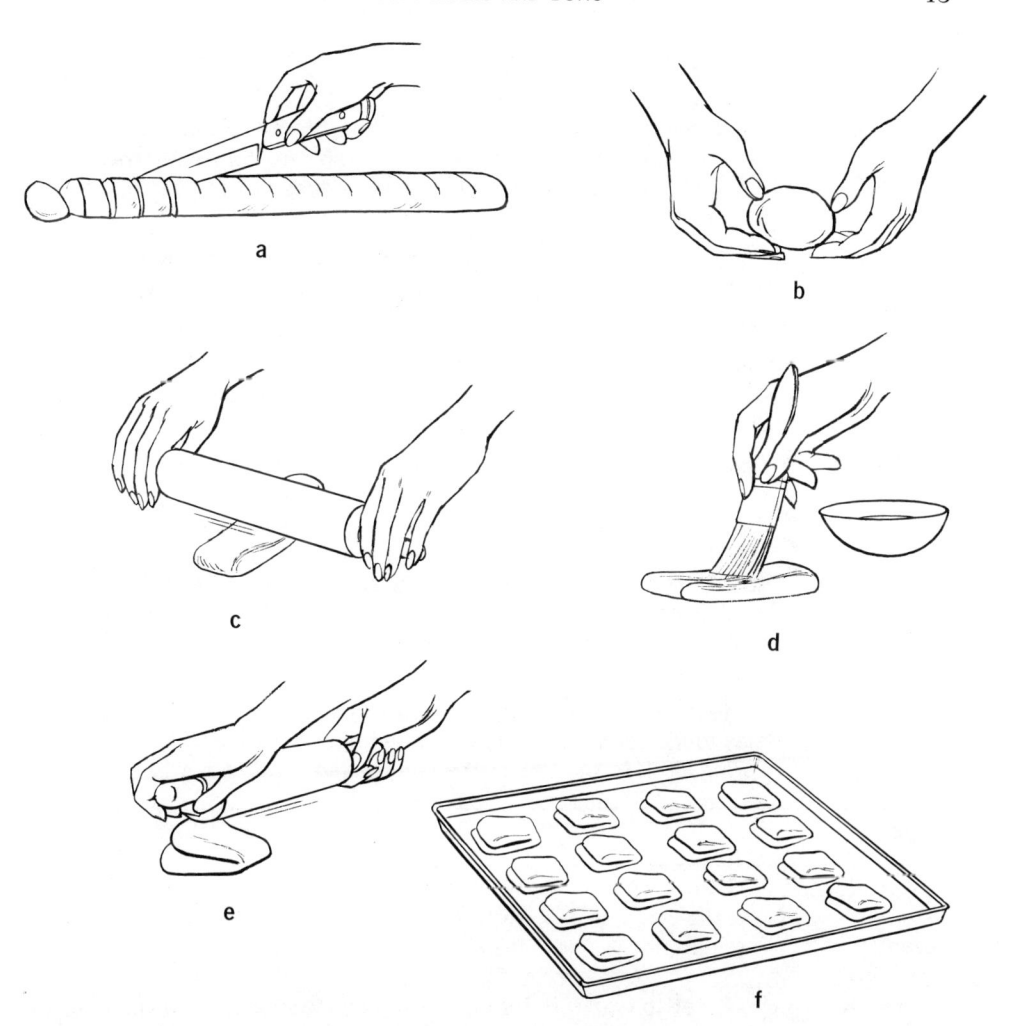

Fig. 6-1 **Parker House rolls.**

  a Roll the risen dough into an even strip 1 inch thick and cut it into 16 equal pieces.

  b Form each piece of dough into a round ball with the fingers or in the palms of the hands.

  c Roll the centers of the dough pieces with a small rolling pin.

  d Brush the centers with melted fat or butter.

  e Fold the ends of each dough piece together. Roll the center fold with a rolling pin to flatten it.

  f Space the rolls about ½ inch apart on the pan. Allow them to rise until almost doubled in size.

the edges meet like two slices of bread in a sandwich. (Figs. 6-1*d* and *e*.)

7 Place the rolling pin over the folded part (not the "sandwich" ends) of the dough. Pressing gently, flatten the fold with the rolling pin. This will cause the two ends or edges to become thicker and to separate slightly.

8 Place the rolls on a lightly greased pan and space them about ½ inch apart. (Fig. 6-1*f*.) Brush the tops of the dough with melted fat or butter.

9 Place the rolls in a warm place (on top of the range or oven) and allow them to rise until they have almost doubled in size. They should feel very soft when gently touched.

10 Place the pan of rolls carefully in the oven and bake at 390° for 12 to 15 minutes, until they have a golden-brown crust color. If the oven bakes unevenly, wait until the rolls have risen fully and have started to show a light crust color before you move the pan from one spot to another. Be sure to check the bottoms of the rolls by lifting a roll lightly with a fork or knife. Shift the rolls from one oven shelf to another if necessary to get an even crust color on the bottoms of the rolls.

11 To test for doneness, in addition to looking at the crust color you may touch the rolls gently with one finger or with a fork. If the rolls spring back to the touch, they are baked.

VOCABULARY

crust color	instructions	sketch
flatten	oval	surface
freezer	refrigerator	thickness

Refer to *Glossary* for necessary explanations. You will find the dictionary helpful for commonly used words or terms that are not included in the *Glossary*.

CLOVERLEAF ROLLS (MUFFIN-TYPE) Yield: *approximately 16 to 24 rolls*

AIM To learn how to make cloverleaf rolls from the basic sweet yeast dough.

THINGS YOU SHOULD KNOW Cloverleaf rolls are soft rolls that are shaped into the cloverleaf form as they are put into prepared muffin tins. They look like muffins when they are baked. With the experience you

UNIT 6: VARIETY SOFT ROLLS AND BUNS 45

have had making other rolls and biscuits, you should be able to make good-looking, good tasting cloverleaf rolls from the basic sweet yeast dough you have prepared.

THINGS TO PREPARE   Light the oven and set the temperature at 390°.   Prepare the worktable or the workboard for the dough.

| properly fermented dough | egg wash or | wash brush for eggs | French knife |
| greased muffin pans | melted margarine | table brush for flour | dusting flour |

CHECK POINTS

1 Is the dough properly fermented?   Has it risen well?

2 Are the muffin pans greased evenly and completely?

3 Is the egg wash or melted fat ready?

4 Is the oven set at the proper temperature (390°)?

MAKING AND BAKING THE CLOVERLEAF ROLLS

Refer to Fig. 6-2 (page 46) while you work.
1 Place the risen dough on the worktable or workboard which has been dusted with flour to prevent the dough from sticking.

2 Flatten the dough with the palms of your hands and shape it into an even roll or strip as you did for the Parker House rolls.

3 Divide the dough into 16 *equal* pieces.   Follow the same cutting procedure as you did for the Parker House rolls.   (Fig. 6-1*a*.)

4 Then take each piece of dough and divide it into 3 equal pieces. Round each small piece of dough into a ball with your fingers. (Fig. 6-2*a*.)   Place the 3 small balls of dough into each cup of the muffin tin.   (Fig. 6-2*b*.)   (If there are 12 cups in the muffin tin, and each cloverleaf roll is made up of 3 small balls of dough, there should be 36 small balls of dough.   There are 8 cups in some muffin tins and 6 cups in others.   Prepare enough muffin tins to hold the number of rolls you make.)

NOTE   If the muffin tins are smaller than usual, you must divide the dough into smaller pieces.   For example, if the muffin pans are about two-thirds the regular size, divide the dough into 24 pieces.

---

5 Place the filled muffin tins in a warm place to rise, and cover the rolls with a cloth to prevent the formation of a crust on the roll dough.   Then allow the rolls to rise to the top of the muffin tin. Brush the tops of the rolls very gently with egg wash if you wish them to have a shiny crust color when baked.   Use melted margarine or butter to brush the tops for a homemade-looking, dull-colored crust.

6 Place the muffin tins gently into the oven, which has been heated to

PART TWO: SWEET YEAST-RAISED DOUGH PRODUCTS

Fig. 6-2 **Cloverleaf rolls (muffin-type).**

    a Divide each of the 16 dough pieces again into 3 equal parts. Shape the pieces into round balls with the fingers.

    b Place 3 round balls in each cup of the greased muffin tin.

    c The rolls will rise to the edge of the pan.

    d A baked cloverleaf roll.

390°, and bake them about 15 to 18 minutes until they are golden brown. Shift the pans in the oven if the oven heat is uneven and the rolls bake unevenly. Do not shift the pans until the rolls have risen and have taken on a light crust color. When this occurs, it means that the rolls are set and will not fall back when the muffin tins are turned or moved from one shelf to another.

7 Remove the rolls from the oven carefully and allow them to cool

UNIT 6: VARIETY SOFT ROLLS AND BUNS   *47*

until they feel mildly warm. Then tap the pan gently and turn it on its side so that the rolls may drop out. If a roll should stick, cut around the sides of the roll with a spatula or knife and remove it. If the rolls are allowed to remain in the tins after they have cooled, the rolls will become moist or soggy at the bottom because of the steam or moisture that is released while the rolls are cooling. (This is called "sweating.") It is advisable to remove the rolls, allow them to cool completely, and then return them to clean muffin tins. This will prevent your cloverleaf rolls from drying out, and you may easily warm them again later if you wish to.

VOCABULARY

| advisable | brown evenly | equal | muffin shape | sweating |
| basic | divide | margarine | release | trapped |

Refer to *Glossary* for an explanation of any words you do not know. The dictionary will be helpful for those terms not included in the *Glossary* because they are frequently used.

BUTTERFLAKE ROLLS (MUFFIN-TYPE)   Yield: *16 rolls*

AIM To learn how to make butterflake rolls from the basic sweet yeast dough.

THINGS YOU SHOULD KNOW Look at the picture of the butterflake roll (Fig. 6-3*f*) and you will note the layers or flakes of dough in a roll shaped like a muffin. The muffin tin provides the shape and the flakes are formed by layering strips of dough with layers of melted butter or other fat. This procedure not only changes the appearance of the roll but also makes the roll richer. Your past experience with biscuits and rolls will be helpful in making these attractive rolls. Be sure to look at the sketches as you read the instructions carefully. It is pleasing and exciting to see these rolls rise and flake during baking.

THINGS TO PREPARE Light the oven and set the oven temperature at 390°. Grease enough muffin tins for 16 regular-size rolls. (Smaller muffin pans require more and smaller pieces of dough. Use judgment in cutting the dough to suit the capacity of your muffin tins.)

| worktable or | fermented dough | rolling pin | melted fat |
| workboard | dusting flour | French knife | grease brush |

CHECK POINTS

1 Is the dough properly fermented?   Has it risen well?
2 Are the muffin pans properly prepared (greased well)?
3 Has the butter or fat been melted?
4 Is the oven at the proper baking temperature (390°)?

MAKING AND BAKING THE BUTTERFLAKE ROLLS

Refer to Fig. 6-3 as you work.

1 Place the risen dough gently on the flour-dusted worktable or board and flatten it gently with the palms of your hands. While doing this, try to form the dough into a rectangular shape.

2 Dust the top of the dough lightly with flour and roll the dough gently with the rolling pin into a rectangular shape about ¼ inch thick. The dough should be about 18 inches long and 12 inches wide. Be sure to check the bottom of the dough to see that there is enough flour so that the dough will roll easily without sticking. Keep the dough of even thickness when rolling it out in order to get equal-size rolls.

3 Allow the rolled-out dough to rest for about 5 minutes on the table. Remove any excess flour from the top of the dough.

4 Brush the top of the dough with melted butter or other melted fat. Be sure you cover the entire surface. Then let the dough relax; this will prevent shrinking when you cut the dough into strips.

5 Cut the dough into strips about 1½ inches wide. (Fig. 6-3*b*.) This should give you 12 strips. It is advisable to measure and mark off the strips before you cut them. A pastry wheel or pastry knife is the correct tool to use for cutting the strips, but you can also use a French knife.

6 Place 6 strips of dough on top of each other so that you now have a piece of dough with 6 layers, about 1½ inches high. (Fig. 6-3*c*.) If you layer all the strips, you will have 2 such pieces. Mark off sections on each piece about 1½ inches wide. Together, both pieces will give you 16 markings. Now cut down evenly with the French knife at each mark. (Fig. 6-3*d*.) Be careful while cutting. Each cut will give you one roll. *Look at the sketches while working.*

7 Place each cut piece into the muffin tin with the cut side and the layers pointing up. (Fig. 6-3*e*.) This will allow the cut strips to rise and fan out during the rising period and when they are baking.

8 Place the filled muffin pans in a warm place to allow the rolls to rise. Cover the rolls with a cloth to prevent the formation of a crust. (This will also make the rolls rise a bit faster than they would if uncovered.)

UNIT 6: VARIETY SOFT ROLLS AND BUNS   49

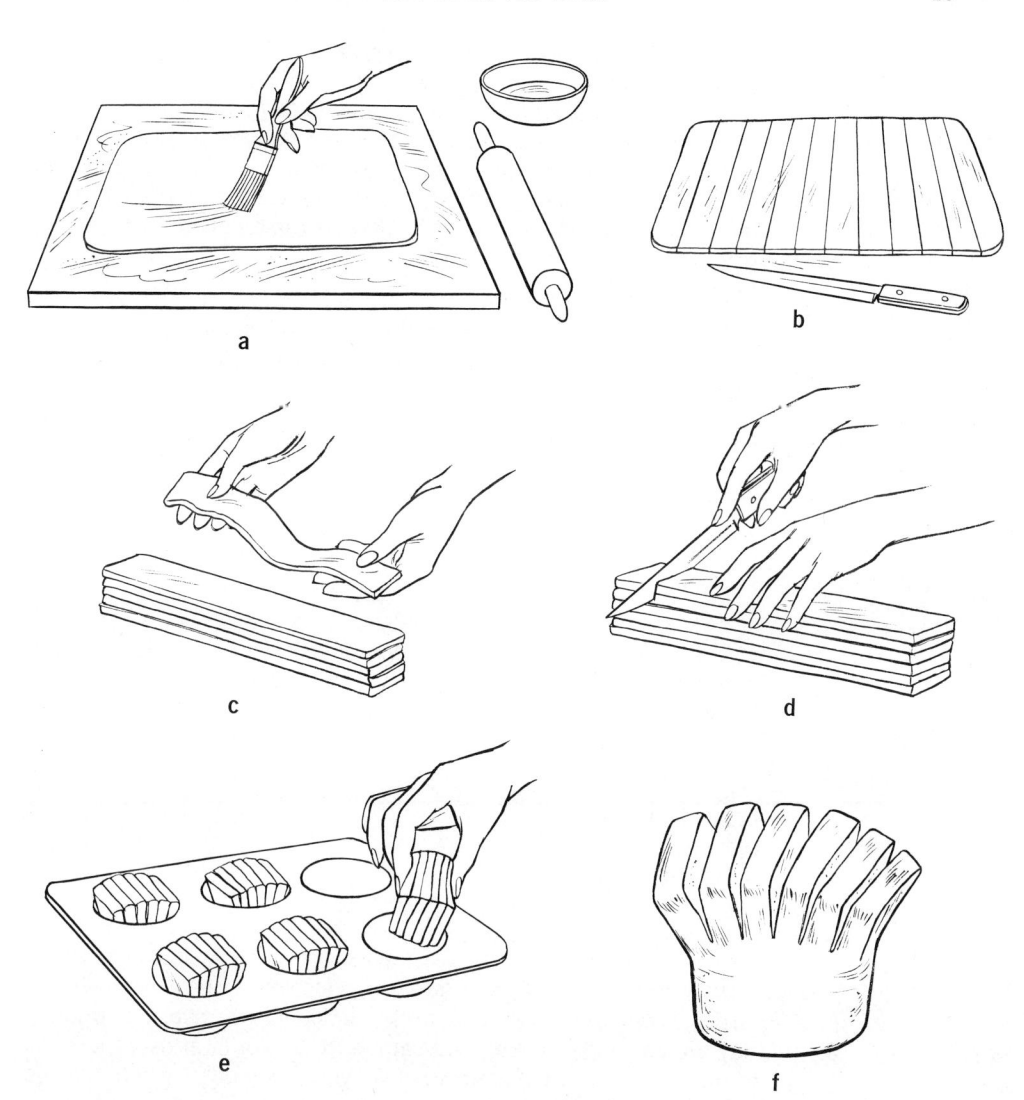

Fig. 6-3 **Butterflake rolls (muffin-type).**

- **a** Roll the dough out about 18 inches long, 12 inches wide, and ¼ inch thick; then brush the top of the dough with melted fat.
- **b** Cut the dough into strips about 1½ inches wide.
- **c** Place 6 strips of dough evenly on top of each other.
- **d** Cut the layered piece of dough into sections 1½ inches wide.
- **e** Place the cut pieces into greased muffin pans with the cut end facing up.
- **f** The baked butterflake roll.

9 Allow the rolls to rise until they reach the top of the pan or slightly above. Then place them gently into the oven and bake them about 15 to 18 minutes until they are golden brown. If the oven bakes unevenly, shift or move the pans after the rolls have risen and have started to take on a light brown crust color. When you think the rolls are baked, you may press them gently with a fork while they are still in the oven. If they spring back after the touch of the fork, they are baked.

10 Allow the rolls to cool until they are slightly warm. Remove them gently from the pans, and cover the rolls until you are ready to serve them. These rolls may be returned to the muffin pans and reheated before serving.

VOCABULARY

appearance	flakes	lukewarm	shape	surface
attractive	knowledge	rectangle	skill	(*review*)
capacity	layers	relax dough	strips	

Refer to *Glossary* for any explanations of words you do not know. Frequently used words not included in the *Glossary* may be found in the dictionary.

HAMBURGER ROLLS AND FRANKFURTER ROLLS

Yield: *16 regular rolls or*
12 large rolls or
24 small rolls

AIM To learn how to make hamburger and frankfurter rolls.

THINGS YOU SHOULD KNOW These rolls are very popular. They are used for parties, cook-outs, picnics, and quick-service meals. Although they are easily purchased and can be frozen for later use, there will be times when you will want to make your own rolls. There may be times, for example, when the store does not have any in stock. Or you may wish to serve these rolls in miniature (small) form for tiny franks and hamburgers. They can be made easily from the basic sweet yeast dough. *Read the instructions carefully, be sure you understand them, and look at the sketches while you are making the rolls.*

THINGS TO PREPARE Light the oven and set the oven temperature to between 395° an 400°.

basic sweet yeast dough
  properly fermented
baking pans

French knife
worktable or workboard
brush for egg wash

grease brush
dusting flour

melted fat
table brush

CHECK POINTS

1 Is the dough properly conditioned and ready for use?
2 Is the table or board dusted with flour?
3 Is the oven lighted and at the proper temperature (395°–400°)?
4 Are the pans greased?
5 Have you decided how many rolls you need or want?

MAKING AND BAKING THE HAMBURGER ROLLS

Refer to Fig. 6-4 (page 51) while you work.

1 Dust the worktable or board lightly with all-purpose flour and place the risen dough gently on the table. Flatten the top of the dough lightly with the palms of your hands. This will let the gas out of the dough and remove any large air or gas pockets.

2 Roll the dough up into an even roll about 1 inch thick. Be sure it is of even thickness throughout so that the rolls will be equal in size.

3 Divide the dough into 16 equal pieces for regular hamburger rolls. Follow the same procedure as you did when you made Parker House rolls (Fig. 6-1a). For larger rolls, divide the dough into 12 pieces. For small rolls, divide the dough into 24 equal parts.

4 Pick up each piece of dough with the fingers of both hands. Pinch and fold the bottom half of the dough underneath the dough until a tight, round ball of dough is formed. (Fig. 6-4a.) You may then roll the dough firmly in the palms of your hands to further round and tighten the dough. You will learn to do this quickly with experience. If the dough is sticky during the rounding, dust your fingers or palms with a little flour as you shape the ball of dough.

5 Place the round balls of dough on a lightly greased baking pan, spacing them about 1 inch apart. Let the pieces of dough rest or relax about 10 minutes to soften them. Then flatten them gently with the palms of your hands.

6 Place the rolls in a warm place to rise, covering them with a cloth. They should rise until they have almost doubled in size and feel soft and gassy when touched gently with a finger. Brush the tops of the risen rolls very lightly with egg wash or with melted fat before baking. Be careful and gentle when brushing to prevent the rolls from falling back.

7 Place the rolls gently into the oven and bake until they have a light brown crust color. The regular rolls should take about 15 minutes to bake. Larger rolls will take about 18 minutes to bake, and the small rolls should take about 12 minutes. If the oven bakes unevenly, shift the pans, but wait until the rolls have risen and show a light crust color. This will prevent the rolls from falling back. Hamburger rolls and frankfurter rolls should be baked to the just-

PART TWO: SWEET YEAST-RAISED DOUGH PRODUCTS

Fig. 6-4 **Hamburger rolls.**
    a Shape or round the pieces of dough with the fingers.
    b Space the rounded rolls on the pan 1 inch apart.
    c Brush the tops of the dough with egg wash or milk.
    d Use oven pads when turning the hot pans or taking pans from the oven.

UNIT 6: VARIETY SOFT ROLLS AND BUNS 53

done stage because these rolls are usually toasted before serving. The rolls are done when they feel soft and spring back if touched gently with a fork.

MAKING AND BAKING THE FRANKFURTER ROLLS

Refer to Fig. 6-5 (page 54) as you make the rolls.

1 Be sure to prepare the same things that you did for hamburger rolls. Check the same factors listed in *Check Points*.

2 Place the risen dough on the flour-dusted part of the table or workboard and flatten the dough with the palms of your hands to remove large gas pockets.

3 Form the dough into an even roll about 1 inch thick. Be sure the strip is of even thickness so that the buns will be of equal size.

4 Divide the dough into 12 equal pieces as follows: Divide the dough in half. Divide each half again so that you now have 4 equal pieces of dough. Divide each of the pieces into 3 equal parts so that you now have 12 rolls. *Mark the sections* to be sure the dough is equally divided before you cut the pieces with the French knife.

5 Round the pieces of dough as you did when you made the hamburger rolls. Let the rounded pieces rest or relax about 10 minutes to soften. Cover the pieces with a cloth while they relax.

6 Now place the palm of your hand over a piece of dough and press down gently. Roll the dough forward, and then backward, using gentle pressure. (Fig. 6-5*a*.) You will note that the dough forms a strip with the ends sticking out beyond both sides of your palm. If the dough feels sticky, dust the worktable and the palm of your hand with a little flour. Now place both palms on the longer strip and press down as you roll the dough forward and backward until it is about 6 inches long and of even thickness. (Fig. 6-5*b*.)

7 Place each roll, as you shape it, on a lightly greased baking pan and flatten the roll gently with the fingers or palm of the hand. This will press the roll into the grease or fat on the pan and keep the roll from shrinking. Space the rolls about 1 inch apart on the pan. (Fig. 6-5*c*.)

8 Place the pan of rolls in a warm place to rise. Cover the rolls with a cloth. This will prevent a crust from forming and allow the rolls to rise faster. Let the rolls to rise until they have almost doubled in size and feel soft and gassy to a gentle touch. Brush the rolls very gently with a little water or milk before baking.

9 Place the pans gently in the oven (395° to 400°) and bake about 12 minutes until the rolls are golden brown. Touch the rolls gently with the back of a fork to test for doneness. The rolls should spring back lightly to the touch if they are baked. (Be careful when removing the rolls from the oven. Use oven pads.)

54   PART TWO: SWEET YEAST-RAISED DOUGH PRODUCTS

Fig. 6-5 **Frankfurter rolls.**

   a Roll the piece of dough with the palms of the hands.

   b Use the fingers of both hands to roll the strip of dough evenly to a length of 5 or 6 inches.

   c Space the rolls about 1 inch apart on the pan and flatten them gently with the palm of the hand.

   d When the rolls have risen, brush them with water.

   e A baked frankfurter roll.

UNIT 6: VARIETY SOFT ROLLS AND BUNS

VOCABULARY

airy	popular	roll the dough	shape (*review*)	space evenly
double	pressure	rounding	shrink	sticky
miniature				

Refer to *Glossary* for the explanations you need. The dictionary may be helpful for terms not included in the *Glossary* because they are frequently used words.

TWISTED SOFT ROLL VARIETIES

AIM To learn how to make a variety of twisted rolls (single-knot, double-knot, braided figure-8, and three-braid rolls).

THINGS YOU SHOULD KNOW The basic yeast-raised sweet dough can be used to make many roll varieties. Some of the most popular soft rolls are those varieties which are twisted and shaped with the hands and fingers. They are shaped or molded like many other things you have learned to make. For example, you make a single knot first when you tie your shoelaces. Some girls and women braid their hair with a three-braid twist. These same skills are used in making twisted rolls. Each shape offers another variety of roll. The more of these you know how to make, the greater the variety of rolls you can make and serve. With practice, you will be able to make all the rolls listed above in the *Aim* of this unit. *Read carefully and follow instructions.*

THINGS TO PREPARE Light the oven and set it at 395°.

properly risen and conditioned dough	French knife	flour sifter	melted shortening
grease brush	dusting flour	baking pans	egg wash brush
	egg wash		

CHECK POINTS

1 Is the dough properly conditioned (soft and gassy)?

2 Is the oven lighted and set at the correct temperature?

3 Is the worktable or board ready and dusted with flour?

4 Are the pans and tools ready?

SINGLE-KNOT ROLLS   **Yield:** *16 regular rolls; or 24 small rolls*

MAKING AND BAKING THE SINGLE-KNOT ROLLS

Refer to Fig. 6-6 while you work.

1. Place the risen dough on the flour-dusted part of the worktable. Flatten the dough gently with the palms of your hands to remove large air pockets. Roll the dough up into a tight roll about 1 inch thick as you did when you made hamburger rolls. Check the strip of dough for even thickness to ensure that, when divided, the pieces of dough will be equal. Use a little dusting flour if the dough feels sticky.

2. Measure and mark off the dough for division into 16 regular-size rolls or 24 small-size rolls. Cut the pieces of dough evenly and dust them with a little flour to keep the raw sides of the dough units from sticking to each other.

3. Roll out each piece of dough with the palms of your hands to about 5 inches in length. Small rolls may be about 4 inches long. *Try to make the strips of even thickness.* When rolling the strips, use a gentle pressure with the palms of your hands. If the dough sticks, use a little dusting flour on your hands and on the worktable.

4. Line up each strip of dough in a neat row on the worktable. Dust them with a little flour to keep them separated.

5. Start with the first strip of dough you rolled out. *Refer to Fig. 6-6 as you perform each step.* Pick up the strip of dough holding it with your fingers at each end. Now, as if you were making the first tie with your shoelaces, pull one end of the strip of dough through the loop formed by crossing the ends over each other. Pull the end through just enough to have each point of the strip show through about ½ inch and so that there is no hole showing any more. *Be careful not to pull the ends of the strip too tightly so that the points stick out too much.*

6. Place all the knot rolls on a clean part of the table in neat rows. When all the rolls have been twisted and shaped, flatten them gently with the palms of your hands; then brush them with egg wash (one beaten egg mixed with 2 tablespoons of water). (The egg wash will be applied again after the rolls have risen and before they are placed in the oven.)

7. Place the rolls on a lightly greased baking pan, spacing them about 1 inch apart so that they may rise without touching each other. The rolls will probably touch slightly during baking.

8. Place the rolls in a warm place to rise. Cover them with a cloth to prevent a crust from forming. Allow the rolls to rise until they have almost doubled in size and feel soft and gassy to a light touch. Brush the rolls gently again with egg wash.

UNIT 6: VARIETY SOFT ROLLS AND BUNS   57

Fig. 6-6 **Single-knot rolls.**

    a Sprinkle the cut pieces of dough lightly with flour.

    b Roll the pieces of dough into 6-inch strips and line them up next to each other.

    c Roll the strips out a little longer, keeping them even.

    d Cross the ends of the strip of dough with the fingers, forming a loop. Pull one end of the strip through the loop so about ½ inch of the end shows.

    e The made-up single-knot roll.

    f Place the rolls on the pan so that there are 3 rolls down and 5 rolls across.

PART TWO: SWEET YEAST-RAISED DOUGH PRODUCTS

   9 Place the rolls carefully into the oven (395°) and bake for 15 to 18 minutes. Smaller rolls will take about 12 to 14 minutes. Test for proper bake by looking at the crust color (it should be golden brown), lifting a roll gently with a fork to see if the bottom is baked, and touching the roll gently on top with a fork. If the roll is fully baked, it will spring back when touched with the fork. Remove the pans of rolls from the oven with oven pads. (If the oven bakes unevenly, shift or turn the pans in the oven after the rolls have risen and show a light brown crust color. Shifting the rolls too soon causes the rolls to fall back because the internal structure of the roll has not set.)

NOTE: SERVING THE ROLLS It is best to serve the rolls while they are freshly baked and still warm. For service later, let the rolls cool and then put them into plastic bags with a top seal. These rolls should be refrigerated and then reheated quickly before serving. The rolls may also be wrapped and stored in the freezer. Allow the rolls to defrost *before* reheating them in the oven.

DOUBLE-KNOT ROLLS   Yield: *16 regular rolls; or 24 small rolls*

THINGS TO PREPARE Prepare the same things as you did for single-knot rolls.

CHECK POINTS Check the same things you did for single-knot rolls.

MAKING AND BAKING THE DOUBLE-KNOT ROLLS

   Refer to Fig. 6-7 while you work.
   1 Place the risen dough on the floured table or workboard and flatten it gently with the palms of your hands to remove any large air pockets that were formed during fermentation (action of the yeast).

   2 Roll the dough up into a strip about 1 inch thick. Be sure the strip is of even thickness in order to get equal size rolls.

   3 Measure and mark off sections on the strip before you cut the dough. Measure carefully so that the rolls will all be the same size. Cut the dough into 16 equal pieces for regular rolls or 24 equal pieces for small rolls. Dust the pieces of dough lightly with flour to keep them from sticking to each other.

   4 Roll out each of the dough strips to about 7 inches in length and line them up on the table. *Refer to Fig. 6-7 as you twist and shape the rolls.* Starting with the first strip of dough, cross the ends as you did for single-knot rolls, but pull both ends more so that their points extend about 2 inches on each side (Fig. 6-7*a*).

   5 Fold one point over outside the ring of dough and pull it up through the center so that only a small part of the point shows. (Fig. 6-7*b*.) Take the other point or end and pull it through the center, letting the point remain at the bottom of the roll (Fig. 6-7*c*).

UNIT 6: VARIETY SOFT ROLLS AND BUNS   59

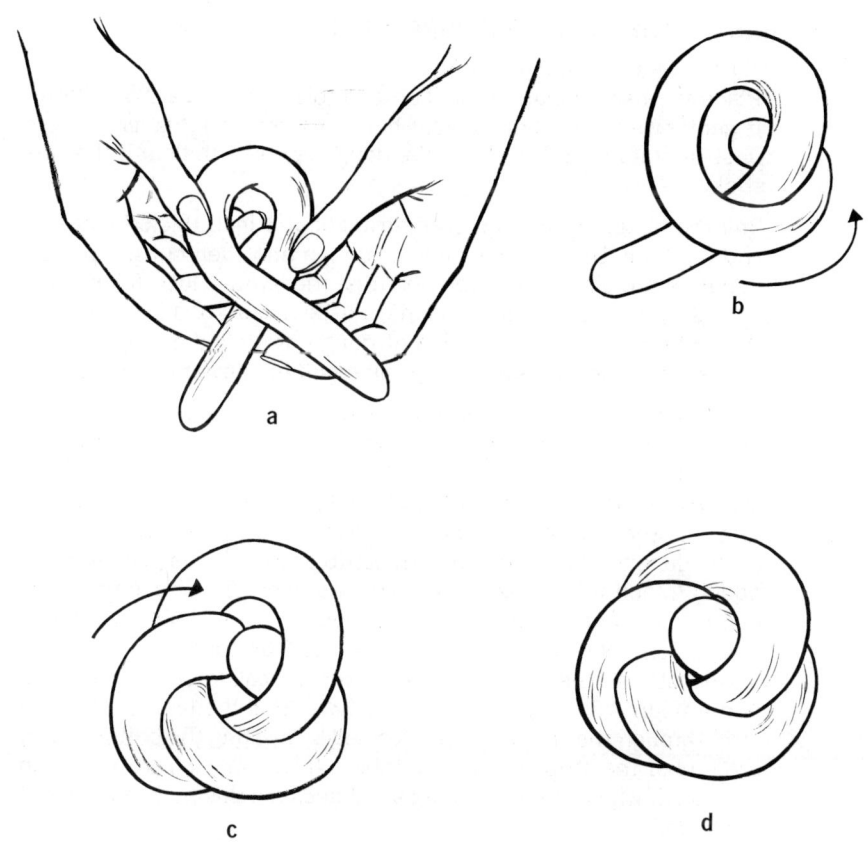

Fig. 6-7 **Double-knot rolls.**

    a Roll each strip out about 7 inches long and fold the ends over each other to form a small hole in the center.

    b Fold the ends through as for the single knot roll, but with ends sticking out about 2 inches.

    c Fold one end *over* and up through the center. Fold the other end *under* and up through the center.

    d The double-knot roll.

    6 Line up the rolls on the table, egg-wash them, place them on the pan, allow them to rise, and bake them as you did the single-knot rolls.

BRAIDED FIGURE-8 ROLLS   Yield: *16 rolls*

THINGS TO PREPARE   Prepare the same things as you did for single-knot rolls.

CHECK POINTS   Check the same things you did for single-knot rolls.

MAKING AND BAKING THE BRAIDED FIGURE-8 ROLLS

Refer to Fig. 6-8 while you work.

1. Place the risen dough on the floured table or workboard and flatten it gently with the palms of your hands to remove large air pockets. Dust the table and the top of the dough lightly with flour if they are sticky.

2. Roll the dough up into an even strip about 1 inch thick. Measure and mark off 16 equal sections of dough and then cut the pieces. Separate the pieces of dough and dust them with a little flour. Roll each strip out about 8 inches long, a little longer than for knot rolls. (Fig. 6-8*a*.) Be sure the strips of dough are rolled evenly. Strips that are uneven (thick and thin) will result in unevenly shaped rolls.

3. Place the strip of dough on the table in a vertical position so that one end of the strip is pointing toward you and the other away from you. *Refer to Figs. 6-8b through f for guidance as you read the instructions that follow.* Take the point or end closest to you and fold it to the right to form a loop. Place the point about two-thirds of the distance from the top of the strip and press the point into the dough (pinch it). It now looks like a number "6." Take the other point or end and pull it through the loop so that it looks like a lasso. (Fig. 6-8*c*.) Now take the bottom of the loop (bottom of the "6") and twist it to the left so that you have a small loop at the bottom and a figure "8" is formed. (Fig. 6-8*d*.) Pull the lasso end of the strip through the small loop you formed by twisting the bottom. Let the end of the strip show just a little. (Fig. 6-8*e*.) (Do not stretch the dough when you are making a roll because this pulls the roll out of shape.)

4. Line up the rolls on the table as you make them, placing them next to each other. Flatten them gently after you have made them all. Brush them with egg wash, place them on pans, and allow them to rise until they have almost doubled in size. Brush them gently with egg wash again and then bake them at 395°, as you did the single-knot rolls.

VOCABULARY

applied	egg wash	mark and divide	practical	touch
conditioned	internal	molding	prevent	twisting
crossing	knot	points	structure (*review*)	vertical

Refer to *Glossary* for an explanation. The dictionary may be helpful for those terms not included in the *Glossary* because they are commonly used words.

UNIT 6: VARIETY SOFT ROLLS AND BUNS   61

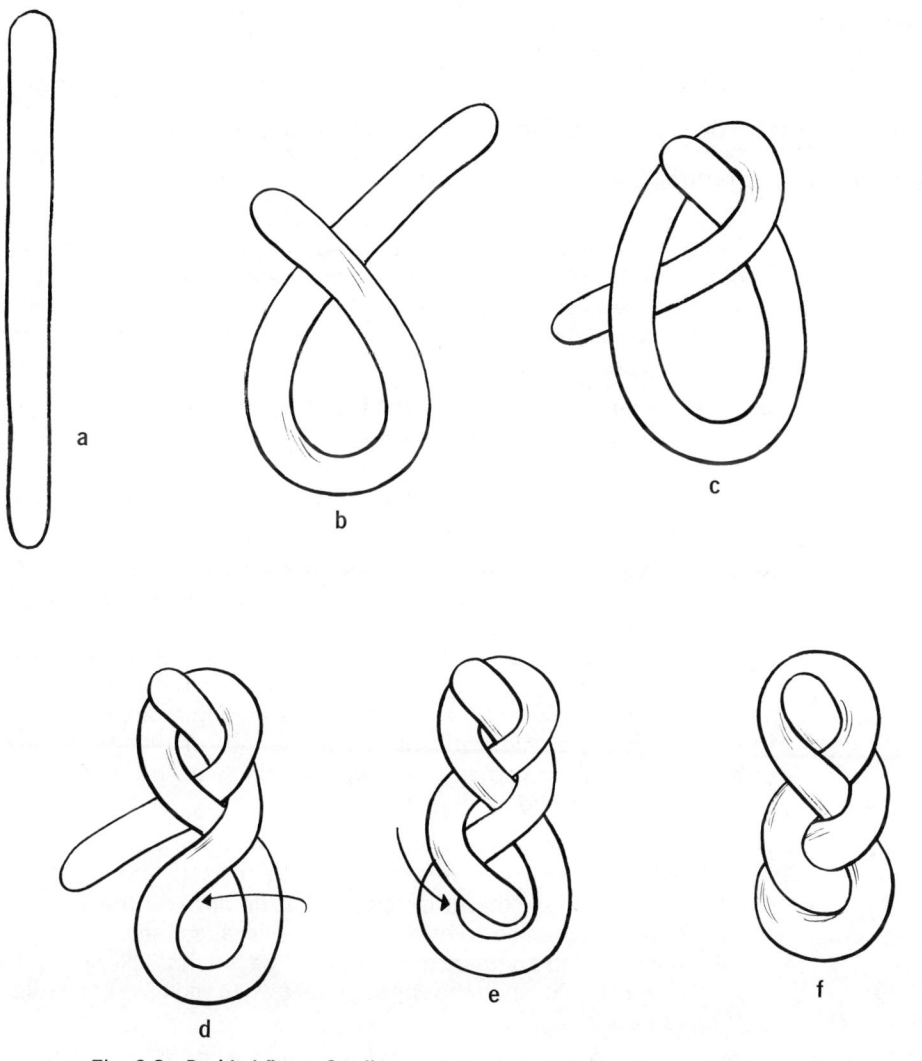

Fig. 6-8 **Braided figure-8 rolls.**

    a Roll each strip out about 8 inches long. Keep the strip in a vertical (up and down) position.

    b Form a loop so that the strip looks like a "6."

    c Pull the top edge through the loop to form the shape of a lasso.

    d Twist the bottom part of the lasso loop to the left so that the figure "8" is formed.

    e Pull the loose end through the bottom loop of the "8."

    f The braided figure-8 roll.

PART TWO: SWEET YEAST-RAISED DOUGH PRODUCTS

THREE-BRAID ROLLS   Yield: *12 rolls*

THINGS TO PREPARE   Prepare the same things as you did for single-knot rolls.

CHECK POINTS   Check the same things you did for single-knot rolls.

MAKING AND SHAPING THE THREE-BRAID ROLLS

Refer to Fig. 6-9 while you work.

1. Divide the dough into 12 equal pieces after you have rolled a strip of dough 1-inch thick, as you did for the other twisted varieties. Then divide each piece of dough into 3 equal pieces. Be careful when cutting the dough. Dust the smaller pieces of dough with flour and place them to one side of the work area.

2. Take 3 small pieces of dough at a time to shape a roll. Roll each of the small pieces into a strip about 5 inches long. When you have rolled out each of the 3 pieces, dust them lightly with a little flour to keep the strips from sticking. *Try to have the strips of equal thickness.*

3. Line up the 3 strips in front of you in a vertical position (up and down). Start by taking the outside strip on the right and folding it over the center of the strip next to it. Now take the strip on the left and fold it over the center of the first strip. (Fig. 6-9*c*.) Next, fold the middle strip over the center of the second (left) strip. (Fig. 6-9*d*.) You will now see a braid effect beginning to appear. Continue to fold or braid until you reach the ends of the strips; then pinch the ends together. Pick up the pinched end and turn it completely over and away from you.

4. You now have the 3 loose, unbraided ends in front of you. Continue to braid these strips. (Refer to Fig. 6-9*c*, *d*, and *e* for guidance in braiding.) Braid the strips snugly but do not pull the strips of dough when you come to the end. This will cause the braid to curl out of shape, and one part of the roll will be much thicker than the other. Be sure to pinch the ends together when you have completed the braiding.

5. Place the braided rolls close together on the table, flatten them gently, and brush the tops with egg wash. Place them about 1½ inches apart on the pans so that they may rise without touching. Let the rolls rise until they have almost doubled in size and feel soft and gassy to the touch. Brush them very lightly with egg wash again. If you wish, you may sprinkle poppy seeds or sesame seeds on the tops of the rolls after you have brushed them with egg wash. This will add richness and variety to their appearance.

6. Bake the rolls at 395° about 3 to 5 minutes longer than the other varieties of twisted rolls. These rolls are a bit larger and should take a little longer to bake.

UNIT 6: VARIETY SOFT ROLLS AND BUNS 63

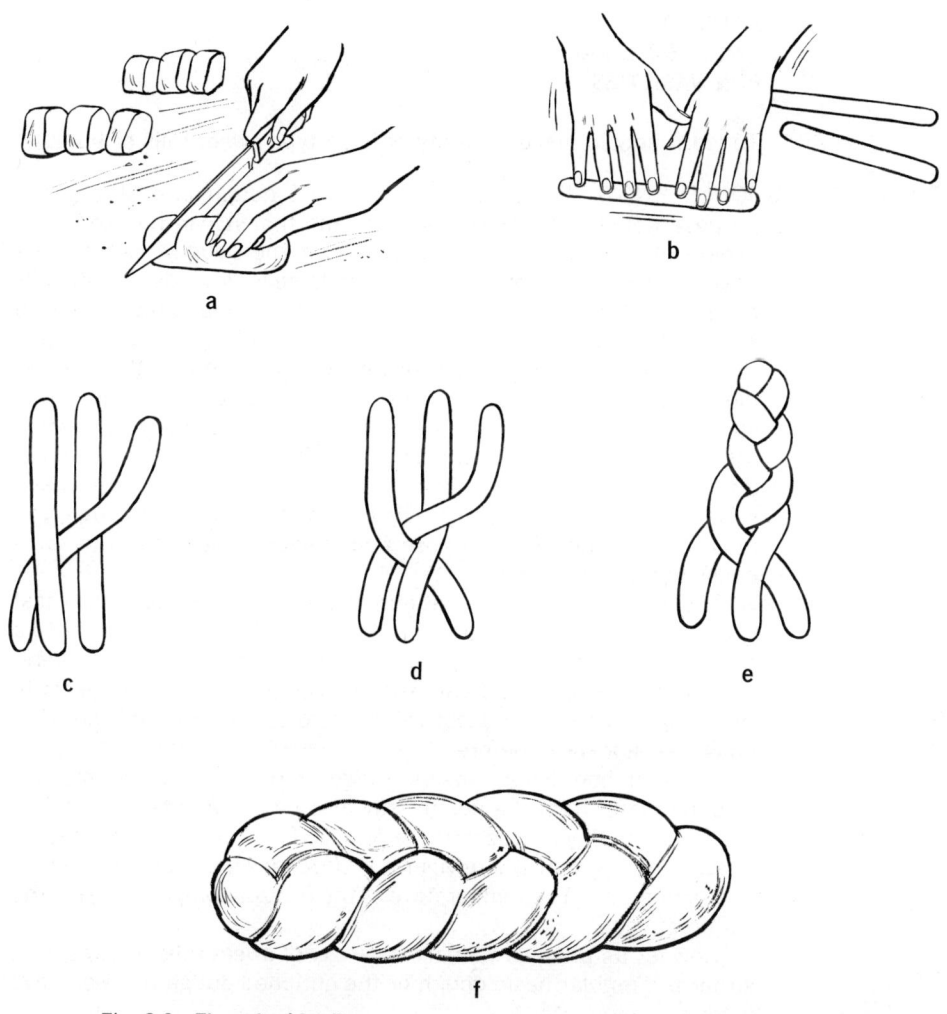

Fig 6-9 **Three-braid rolls.**

    a Divide each piece of dough into 3 equal pieces.

    b Roll each piece into a strip of even thickness 5 to 6 inches long.

    c Place 3 strips next to each other in a vertical position. Take the strip on the right and fold it over the middle strip and under the strip on the left.

    d Place the strip on the left under the center strip and pull the end gently to the right. Return to the outside strip and fold it over into the center, forming the braid.

    e Fold the braid over when half the strips are braided; continue to braid as before. Be sure to start with the strip furthest away from the center.

    f A three-braid roll.

FILLED-TYPE SWEET ROLL AND BUN VARIETIES

AIM To learn how to make a variety of filled-type sweet rolls or buns.

THINGS YOU SHOULD KNOW Basic yeast-raised sweet dough is a sort of all-purpose dough. The term *basic* means that it can be used for a variety of products. It also means that the dough itself may be changed. For example, you have made several kinds of soft rolls from the basic dough and in this unit, we are going to make an even softer roll or bun. The dough will be changed from the basic recipe to one that is richer. To do this, we will add more of those ingredients which enrich a dough. An additional egg, an extra ¼ cup of sugar, and another ¼ cup of shortening added to the basic recipe will enrich it. (If you add an extra egg without adding any flour, the dough will be too soft. Remember, when making sweet yeast-raised doughs, that for every egg you add to enrich the dough, you must add ¼ cup of all-purpose flour to keep the dough the same consistency or thickness.)

The added ingredients that enrich the dough will make the yeast work harder to raise the dough. It is like adding extra weight to a package you are carrying: you need more effort to carry it. Therefore, it is advisable to add an extra package of dry or fresh yeast to the dough so that the yeast will be able to ferment and raise the dough as quickly as before.

The enriched dough may be refrigerated or frozen. Sweet rolls or buns made from the dough may also be refrigerated and baked the following day or frozen to be removed and baked when needed. The temperature of the refrigerator slows down the action of yeast to a minimum. The temperature of the freezer completely halts the action of yeast.

Now let us proceed to make a variety of sweet rolls or buns from either the regular basic dough or the enriched dough that you have made.

CINNAMON BUNS Yield: *12 to 16 buns*

THINGS TO PREPARE Light the oven and set the temperature at 390°. Be sure the dough is properly conditioned (well risen).

cinnamon sugar	melted shortening	soaked and drained raisins	French knife
syrup wash	greased baking pan	worktable or workboard	dusting flour
simple icing	grease brush	wash brush for eggs	
egg wash	rolling pin	and syrup	

NOTE: SPECIAL PREPARATIONS

Cinnamon sugar is prepared by blending 1 teaspoon of cinnamon with ½ cup of granulated sugar. Be sure to blend the sugar and

UNIT 6: VARIETY SOFT ROLLS AND BUNS   65

cinnamon together thoroughly by stirring well. You may increase the cinnamon slightly to make the flavor stronger. You may weaken the flavor by increasing the sugar to ¾ cup. Keep the cinnamon sugar in a closed jar when not in use. You may use cinnamon sugar for other foods, too, such as French toast, cinnamon toast, or rice pudding.

Syrup wash is made by bringing 1 cup of granulated sugar and ½ cup of water to a boil. Add a little lemon juice (¼ teaspoon) and 2 tablespoons of pancake syrup and boil about 2 minutes longer. The lemon juice and pancake syrup will keep the boiled syrup from crystallizing when it cools.

Simple icing is prepared by mixing 1 cup of sifted confectioners' sugar with 2 tablespoons of hot water to make a thick paste. Stir in 2 drops of vanilla flavor. If the icing is too thick, add 1 teaspoon of the simple syrup and stir in well. If the icing is too thin, add a little confectioners' sugar to thicken it. It is best to make the icing quite thick and keep it in the top of a double boiler or over a pot of hot water. As the icing is warmed by the hot water, it becomes softer. The icing should be warmed to about 110° (just slightly above body temperature). The warm icing will dry when it cools after having been spread on the buns. If the icing is cool or too thin, it will remain sticky or tacky.

CHECK POINTS

1 Is the oven lighted and set at the proper temperature?

2 Is the dough properly fermented (well risen)?

3 Is the worktable ready and dusted with flour?

4 Is the cinnamon sugar ready? Are the syrup, simple icing, and egg wash ready?

MAKING AND BAKING THE CINNAMON BUNS

Refer to Fig. 6-10 (page 66) while you work.

1 Place the risen dough on the flour-dusted table or workboard and flatten it with the palms of your hands to remove large air pockets.

2 Dust the top of the dough and the rolling pin lightly with flour. Roll the dough into a rectangular shape 12 to 15 inches long, 6 inches wide, and about ¼ inch thick. Feel the dough with your fingers to check the thickness. If it is too thick in spots, roll it gently with the rolling pin. If it is too thin here and there, push the dough together gently with your fingers or roll the thick parts to the thin parts to get an even thickness. If the dough should feel sticky or does not roll smoothly, dust the table and rolling pin lightly with flour.

3 Remove any flour from the top surface of the dough; then brush the dough with vegetable oil or melted shortening, taking care to cover the entire surface of the dough.

PART TWO: SWEET YEAST-RAISED DOUGH PRODUCTS

Fig. 6-10 **Cinnamon buns.**

- **a** Roll the dough into a rectangular shape. Brush the top of the dough with melted fat and sprinkle it with raisins and cinnamon sugar.
- **b** Roll the dough up and brush the top of the rolled-up dough with melted fat.
- **c** Cut the roll into buns of equal size, or thickness.
- **d** Place the buns on a pan about ¼ to ½ inch apart. The buns should be 4 down on the pan and 4 or 5 across. Be sure the buns are placed with the cut side up.
- **e** Brush the hot, baked buns with hot simple syrup, using a brush or the back of a spoon.
- **f** Apply simple frosting or icing to the buns while they are still warm. Do this with a spoon.

UNIT 6: VARIETY SOFT ROLLS AND BUNS

4 Sprinkle the top of the dough with ¼ cup of raisins which have been soaked for about 10 minutes and then drained. Sprinkle the entire top of the dough with cinnamon sugar. (Sprinkle evenly. Too much cinnamon sugar in any one spot will cause the sugar to melt into the bun and may burn or cause the bun to stick after baking.)

5 Fold over the top of the dough so that you form a hem about 1 inch thick, as you did when you made cinnamon biscuits. Roll the dough up into a tight roll about 1½ to 2 inches thick. (Fig. 6-10b.) If the roll of dough is too thick, lift it gently and stretch it. If it is too thin, push the roll together to thicken it. If the ends are thin and tapered, unroll the dough slightly, fold the edge of the dough in, and roll it up again to make the roll of even thickness throughout.

6 Brush the top of the roll with vegetable oil or melted fat. (It is this fat or oil which enables the buns to bake into each other and yet be taken apart easily without tearing.) Measure the roll of dough into 4 sections. (Do not cut it yet.) Then mark off each quarter into 3 pieces for 12 buns, or 4 pieces for 16 buns. When you are satisfied that the dough is marked off evenly, cut the buns out carefully.

7 Place the buns on the greased pan with the spiral layers showing. Space the buns about ½ inch apart and flatten them gently. Brush them with egg wash and place them in a warm place to rise. You may cover them with a cloth to prevent crust formation and cause them to rise faster. Allow the buns to rise until they have almost doubled in size and feel light and gassy to the touch. Egg-wash them very gently again and put them into the oven (390°).

8 Bake the buns about 18 to 20 minutes until they have a golden-brown crust color. If the oven bakes unevenly, shift the pan of buns after the buns have risen and show a light brown crust color. The buns may be considered done when they spring back quickly to a gentle touch with a fork.

9 Remove the buns from the oven and brush them immediately with hot or warm syrup. (Fig. 6-10e.) This will make the top crust shine. Allow the buns to cool until they are lukewarm; then apply the warm simple icing. (Fig. 6-10f.)

CRESCENT ROLLS OR HORNS (CINNAMON-FILLED) Yield: *12 to 16 rolls*

   AIM To learn how to make crescent rolls or horns.

THINGS YOU SHOULD KNOW Soft crescent rolls, which are horn-shaped sweet rolls, come in several varieties. The varieties are based upon the ways the rolls are shaped and the different types of filling used. You will find, in making these rolls, a different approach in rolling the dough and in shaping the horns or crescents. They are attractive rolls and they are fun to make. *Be sure to read carefully and follow the instructions exactly.*

68   PART TWO: SWEET YEAST-RAISED DOUGH PRODUCTS

THINGS TO PREPARE   Prepare the same things as you did for the cinnamon buns, including the raisins if you wish to use them as part of the filling.

CHECK POINTS   These are the same as those for cinnamon buns.

MAKING AND BAKING THE CRESCENT OR HORN-SHAPED ROLLS

Refer to Fig. 6-11 as you work.

1. Place the risen dough on a floured section of the worktable and flatten it gently to remove the large air pockets which form during fermentation. Try to keep the dough in a round shape like that of a pizza.

2. Check the bottom of the dough to see if there is enough flour to prevent sticking. Dust the top of the dough and the rolling pin lightly with flour and roll the dough into an even circle about 12 inches in *diameter* (the distance across the center of the circle of dough from one side to the other). If the dough shrinks after you have rolled it, let it relax for a few minutes and roll it again. Be sure the dough is of even thickness (¼ inch) throughout. If the dough is not completely round, push it into circular shape with your fingers.

3. Remove any flour from the top surface of the dough and brush it with vegetable oil or melted shortening. Sprinkle the surface

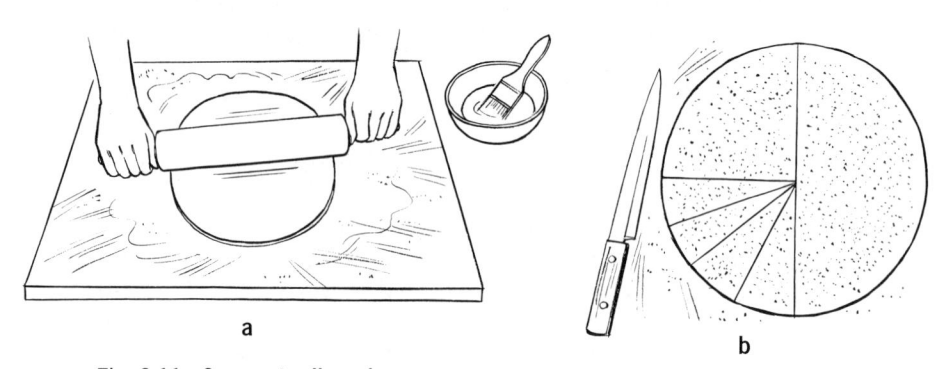

Fig. 6-11   **Crescent rolls or horns.**

    a Roll the dough into a round shape like a pizza.

    b Brush the dough with melted fat and cinnamon sugar, and then cut it into 16 equal wedge-shaped pieces.

    c Starting at the base of the wedge (triangle) of dough, roll the dough up tightly.

    d Place the horns, with the ends curled in, on a greased or paper-lined pan. Space them about 1 inch apart.

    e When making larger amounts of crescent rolls, roll the dough out into a rectangular shape and cut as illustrated. Be sure to brush it with melted fat and sprinkle with cinnamon sugar *before* cutting out the wedges.

    f A baked crescent or horn roll.

UNIT 6: VARIETY SOFT ROLLS AND BUNS 69

evenly with cinnamon sugar. (Avoid using too much sugar.) Raisins may be used as added filling.

4 Let the dough relax about 5 minutes before cutting it into sections. Cut the dough exactly in half with the French knife or pastry wheel. Then cut the dough in half again so that you have 4 equal sections. If you are going to make 12 rolls, cut each quarter section into 3 equal parts. If you are going to make 16 rolls, cut each quarter section in half and you will have 8 equal pieces. Cut each of these pieces in half again and you will have 16 equal sections of dough. Try not to move the dough as you cut so that when you are through you still have a full circle with all the cut sections in it.

5 Take one piece of dough from the circle (like a wedge from a pizza). Starting at the bottom, or base, of the triangle of dough, fold the dough over about ½ inch to form a hem, or seam. Now roll the piece of dough up tightly to the point of the triangle. Be sure the point is placed under the horn or crescent you have shaped. (If you want a longer crescent-shaped roll, spread the base of the dough a bit before you start to roll the dough up to form the horn. You will have more layers if you stretch the dough as you roll it up.)

6 Place the crescents or horns on the table next to each other. Flatten them gently and brush the tops with melted butter or fat for a dull, homemade-looking finish. (The crescents may also be egg-washed.) Place the rolls on a greased baking pan, leaving the short

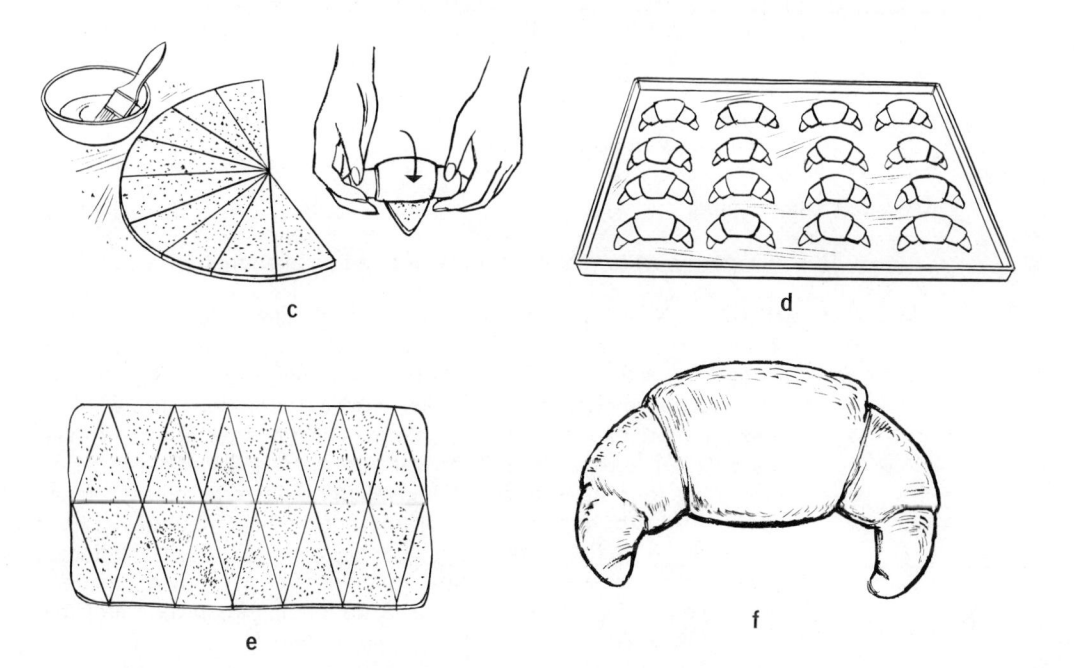

c

d

e

f

horns straight, and curving the longer rolls into a crescent shape. Space the rolls about 1 inch apart on the pan.

7 Place the rolls in a warm place to rise. They may be covered with a cloth. Let them rise until they are almost double in size. If the rolls are egg-washed, brush them again very gently with egg wash before placing them in the oven to bake. Bake the rolls at 390° for 18 to 20 minutes until they are golden brown. Remember that larger rolls take longer to bake than smaller rolls. Test for doneness by pressing the center (the thickest part of the roll) gently with a fork. If it springs back to the touch, the rolls are done. Rolls brushed before baking with melted butter or fat may be brushed again with melted butter as soon as they are taken from the oven. Rolls that have been egg-washed should be brushed with heated syrup, then iced with simple icing after they have cooled.

If you wish to make larger amounts of crescent or horn rolls (30 to 32 rolls), prepare twice as much dough or even more. The larger piece of dough should be rolled out on the table in a rectangular shape (see Fig. 6-11e), rather than a round shape. Brush the dough with melted fat, cinnamon sugar, and raisins if desired. Then roll the dough lightly again until it is about 12 inches wide and as long as its ¼-inch thickness will allow. The dough must be of even thickness to get equal-size rolls.

Cut the dough in half horizontally (from left to right) and then cut each half into triangular pieces, with their points facing alternately away from and toward you. Twice the basic dough recipe should give you about 16 rolls from each half section of dough. Half of the triangles of dough will have the points facing you after you have cut the wedges. Turn these around so that the wide base of each triangle faces you, then roll up the pieces into tight horn or crescent shapes as you did in step 5.

FILLED SNAIL-SHAPED BUNS   Yield: *16 buns*

AIM   To learn how to make a variety of filled snail-shaped buns.

THINGS YOU SHOULD KNOW   The basic sweet yeast-raised dough, enriched slightly with extra sugar, egg, and shortening, makes an excellent base for these buns. If the buns are made properly—and by this time you have enough experience to make them well—they will look like the more expensive Danish pastries, which are made in a similar manner. The different fillings you use create great variety. Thus, if you use four different fruit fillings, jam toppings, or jellies, you can make 4 buns of one variety, 4 of another, and so on, until you have filled all 16 of the snail buns. Each variety will have a different appearance because of the different color of each topping, and each will have a different taste and flavor depending upon the filling you used. *Read carefully and follow instructions.*

UNIT 6: VARIETY SOFT ROLLS AND BUNS

THINGS TO PREPARE Set the oven at 390°.

properly fermented and risen dough	simple syrup	wash brush and syrup brush
a variety of jams and jellies	simple icing	rolling pin
	egg wash	teaspoon
cinnamon sugar	melted shortening	worktable or board
	French knife or pastry wheel	

CHECK POINTS

1 Is the oven lighted and set at the proper temperature (390°)?
2 Is the dough properly risen and ready for use?
3 Is the worktable ready?
4 Are all the tools and fillings handy?

MAKING AND BAKING THE SNAIL-SHAPED BUNS

Refer to Fig. 6-12 (page 72) while you work.

1 Place the dough on the flour-dusted worktable and flatten it gently with the palms of your hands to remove any large air pockets. Roll the dough gently with the rolling pin into a rectangular shape about 15 inches long, 12 inches wide, and ¼ inch thick. Check the dough with your fingers to see that it is of even thickness. This is important in order to get buns of equal size. If the dough should stick while you are rolling it, roll up the dough gently on the rolling pin and dust the table with flour. Dust the top of the dough if the rolling pin sticks.

2 Remove any excess flour from the top surface of the dough and brush the dough evenly and completely with vegetable oil or melted fat or butter. Now draw a very light line with one finger across the center of the dough from left to right. Sprinkle that half of the dough closest to you with cinnamon sugar. Sprinkle the sugar evenly and completely. Fold the upper half of the dough over the half sprinkled with cinnamon sugar. You now have two layers of dough with a cinnamon sugar and melted fat filling. Next, roll the dough gently with the rolling pin to seal the layers of dough and make the strip about 8 inches wide (it was formerly about 6 inches wide).

3 Measure and mark off the dough into 16 equal parts by dividing the dough in half, then in quarters, and lastly, cutting each quarter into 4 strips (Fig. 6-12c). Be careful to cut the units evenly.

4 Pick up one piece of dough at a time in the fingers of each hand and stretch it gently an extra inch or so. Then twist the strip of dough so that several spirals are made with the cinnamon sugar filling showing like the spiral stripes on a barber pole.

5 Take one end of the twisted strip and roll it up along the strip of dough as if you were coiling a rope. Tuck the outside end of the

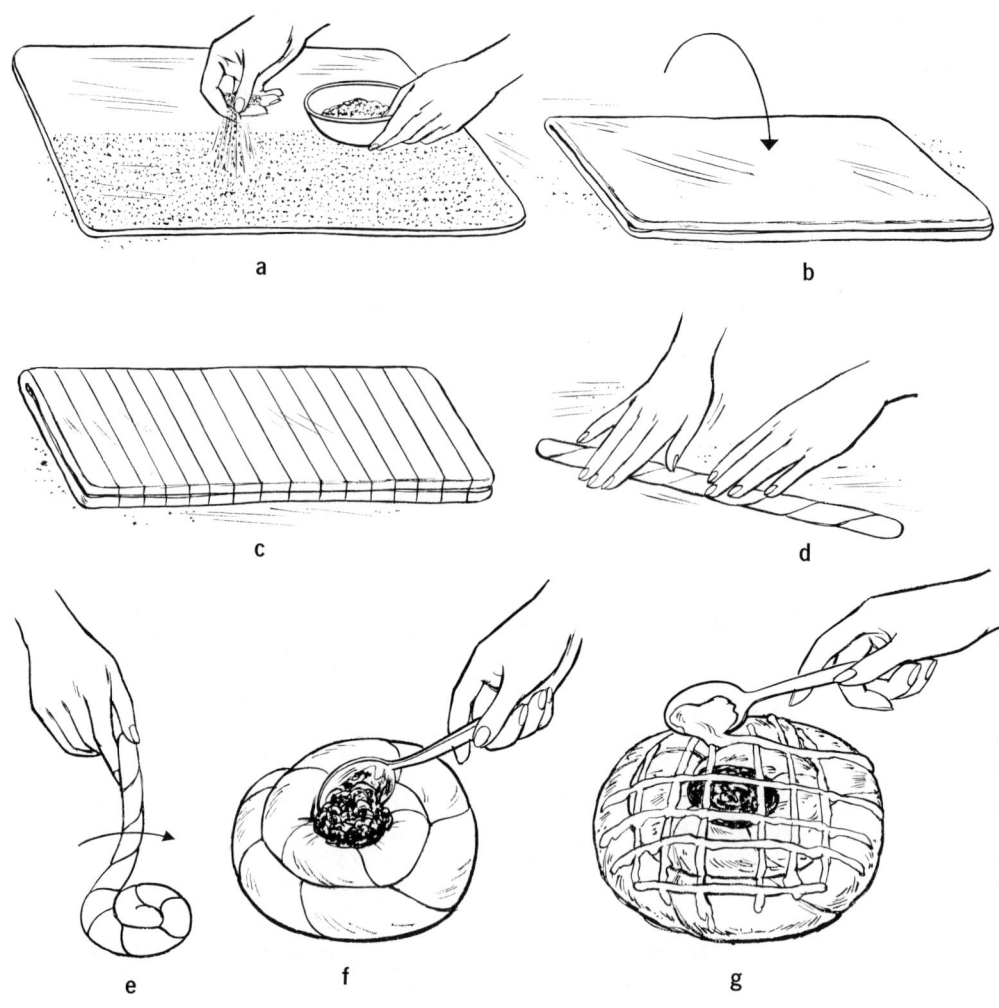

Fig. 6-12 **Filled snail-shaped buns.**

- a Roll the dough to a rectangular shape. Brush the top with melted fat. Sprinkle *half* of the dough with cinnamon sugar.
- b Fold the unsprinkled half of the dough over the half that has been sprinkled with cinnamon sugar.
- c Cut the folded dough into 16 equal strips.
- d Twist each strip of dough gently and roll out evenly with the palms of the hands.
- e Shape the rolled strip of dough into a coil or snail shape.
- f Fill the center of the risen bun with filling. Press the center down gently with fingers to make a hollow and use a spoon to place the filling in the center.
- g Stripe the baked buns with simple frosting while they are still warm.

strip under the snail you have made and pinch it together with the bun. Roll the strip of dough closely but do not pull it. Place the buns on the greased baking pan as you shape them, spacing them about 1 inch apart.

6 When all the buns are made and on the pan, flatten them gently with the palms of your hands and brush the tops with egg wash. Place the buns in a warm place to rise. Allow them to rise until they are almost double in size and feel soft and gassy to a gentle touch.

7 Brush the buns very gently with egg wash again. Press the center of each bun lightly with two fingers of each hand to make an impression for the filling. (Do not press so hard that you tear through the dough. If you do, the filling will cause the bun to stick to the pan after baking.) Now fill the centers of the buns with the fillings you have ready. Use a teaspoon to put the filling into the bun and place an equal amount of filling into each bun.

NOTE You may sprinkle the buns with cinnamon sugar and chopped nuts instead of using fruit or jam fillings.

8 Place the pan of buns carefully into the oven and bake at 390° about 15 minutes. These buns are flat and therefore bake faster than thicker buns do. If the oven bakes unevenly, shift the pans after the buns have risen and show a light brown crust color.

9 Bake the buns until they are golden brown and the tops spring back gently when touched lightly with a fork. Brush them with warm syrup wash as soon as you remove them from the oven. (Be careful not to smear the filling in the center.) When the buns have cooled until they are barely warm, place a little simple icing in their centers. You may stripe the top of the bun by letting the icing drip from the spoon. (Fig. 6-12g.)

CRUMB BUNS Yield: *16 buns*

AIM To learn how to make crumb buns.

THINGS YOU SHOULD KNOW Crumb buns are a very popular breakfast treat. Served fresh and warm as a snack, they are always welcome. They may be made in advance and frozen, and because the buns are placed close together on the pan, they take up little space in the freezer. The buns are made from the basic sweet yeast-raised dough. The recipe for the crumb topping follows.

CRUMB TOPPING Yield: *enough for 16 buns*

INGREDIENTS (*measure carefully*)		HOW TO MIX
brown sugar	¾ cup	Place these ingredients in the mixing bowl and
salt	¼ teaspoon	blend together until soft and smooth.

CRUMB TOPPING (*Continued*)

INGREDIENTS (*measure carefully*)		HOW TO MIX
shortening	½ cup	
cinnamon	¼ teaspoon	
vanilla	½ teaspoon	
all-purpose flour (sifted)	1¼ cups	Sift the flour into the bowl and fold it into the shortening mixture until lumps are formed. Then, rub the topping between the palms of your hands until it forms small lumps the size of green peas. (See Fig. 6-13a.)

NOTE If the topping feels dry and sandy, add a tablespoon or two of vegetable oil or melted fat to it, rubbing it in with the palms of your hands. If the topping feels moist and forms very large lumps, add 2 or 3 tablespoons of sifted flour and rub together until small lumps of topping form. Store leftover crumb topping in a covered jar for later use.

THINGS TO PREPARE Light the oven and set the temperature at 390°. Be sure the dough is well risen. Have the crumb topping ready. Prepare the same things as for hamburger rolls.

CHECK POINTS Check the same things as for hamburger rolls.

MAKING AND BAKING THE CRUMB BUNS

Refer to Fig. 6-13 while you work.

1 Place the risen dough on the flour-dusted worktable or board and flatten it gently with the palms of your hands to remove any large air pockets formed during fermentation.

2 Roll the dough up into a tight, even roll about 1 inch thick. Be sure the strip of dough is of even thickness to get equal-size rolls.

3 Divide the strip of dough into 16 equal pieces, as you did for the hamburger rolls. Separate the pieces of dough, dust them very lightly with flour, and place them neatly in rows on the table. Allow them to rest for 5 to 10 minutes.

4 Pick up each piece of dough with both hands and stretch it gently until it is about 4 inches long and 1½ inches wide. Be careful not to tear the dough while stretching it. Place each stretched bun on the greased pan, spacing them about ¼ inch apart. These buns will touch and bake into each other.

5 Place the buns in a warm place to rise until they are about 1½ times their original size. Brush the tops lightly with egg wash, then sprinkle the buns with the crumb topping you have prepared. Be sure the topping is spread evenly so that the entire bun is covered.

Fig. 6-13 **Crumb buns.**

- **a** In the last stage of mixing the crumb topping, rub the flour and sugar-shortening paste to small lumps between the palms of the hands.
- **b** Roll the dough into a tight roll about 1 inch thick and divide the roll of dough into 16 equal pieces.
- **c** Stretch the pieces of dough evenly after the cut pieces of dough have relaxed.
- **d** Place the pieces of dough on a greased pan, spacing them about ½ inch apart.
- **e** Brush the partially risen buns with egg wash or milk and then sprinkle the tops of the buns with crumb topping.

6 Return the buns to the warm place and allow them to rise until they have almost doubled in size and feel soft and light to a gentle touch.

7 Put the buns gently into the oven. Jarring or banging the pan may cause the buns to fall back. Bake them at 390° about 20 minutes. These buns will take a bit longer to bake because they are close together and bake into each other. *Do not touch the crumb topping with your fingers to test for doneness or proper bake.* Use a fork and press the center gently after the buns have risen and the crumb topping has turned golden brown. If the bun in the center springs back to a light touch, the buns are baked.

8 Remove the buns from the oven carefully and allow them to cool until they are mildly warm. To make the buns look more attractive, dust the tops lightly with confectioners' sugar by placing the sugar in a sifter and shaking it over the crumbs.

ROUND FILLED BUNS Yield: *16 buns*

AIM To learn how to make round filled buns.

THINGS YOU SHOULD KNOW These buns are simple to make after you have had some experience with hamburger rolls. They are like hamburger rolls in shape and differ because the centers are filled and the buns are glazed and iced after being baked. Their variety comes from the kinds of fillings you use in the centers. You may use various fruit fillings, jams, jellies, cheese, or other types. Each different filling will add variety to the color, flavor, and general appearance of the baked bun. *Read carefully and follow the instructions exactly.*

THINGS TO PREPARE Prepare the fillings you are going to use. Make the same preparations you did for hamburger rolls, with the addition of the simple syrup glaze and the simple icing.

CHECK POINTS Check the same things you did for the other soft rolls or buns.

MAKING AND BAKING THE ROUND FILLED BUNS

Refer to Fig. 6-14 as you work.

1 Place the risen dough on the flour-dusted part of the worktable or workboard. Flatten it gently with the palms of your hands to remove any large air pockets. Then roll the dough up into a tight roll about 1 inch thick, making sure the thickness is even.

2 Mark off the dough into 16 equal sections and cut them after checking the accuracy of the measurements once more.

3 Round up the pieces of dough with your fingers as you did for the hamburger rolls. Place the rounded pieces neatly to one side, cover them with a cloth, and let them relax about 10 minutes.

4 When the units feel soft and a little gassy, place them on the

UNIT 6: VARIETY SOFT ROLLS AND BUNS   77

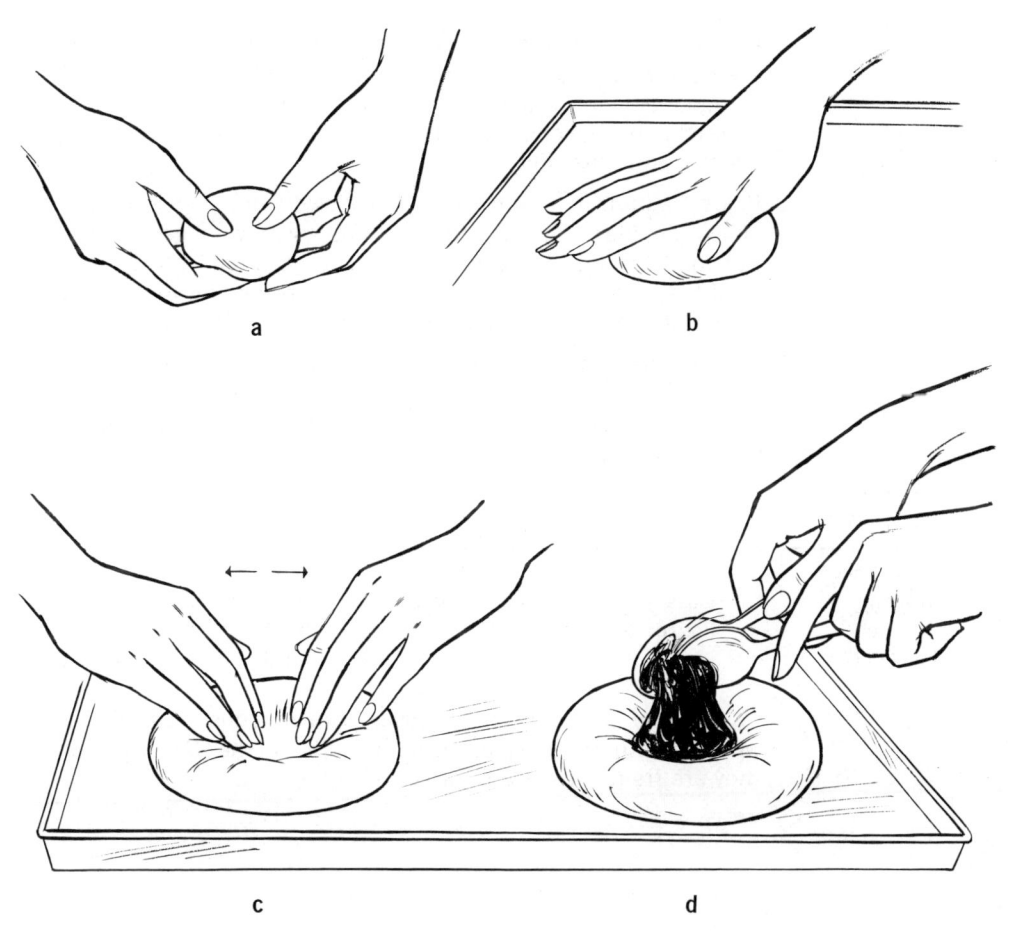

Fig. 6-14 **Round filled buns.**

    a Round the pieces of dough with the fingers as for hamburger rolls.

    b After the round buns have rested and softened on the pan, flatten them with the palm of the hand.

    c When the buns have risen and are soft, hollow the centers gently with the fingers.

    d Fill the centers or hollows, using a spoon. Use an equal amount of filling in each bun.

greased pan, spacing them about 1 inch apart. Flatten the units with the palms of your hands and allow the buns to relax again about 10 minutes to permit the buns to rise slightly on the pan. Now press the centers of the buns with your fingertips, making a hollow in the center of the bun. Be careful not to tear the dough as you press the centers down.

5 Brush the tops of the buns with egg wash. Using a teaspoon, fill the centers of the buns with the fillings you have selected. Place an equal amount of filling in the center of each bun. You may use jam, jelly, fruit slices (such as apples mixed with cinnamon sugar), cheese, and other fillings.

6 Place the buns in a warm place and allow them to rise until they are almost double in size and feel soft and gassy when gently touched. Put the buns into the oven at 390° and bake for 18 to 20 minutes until they are golden brown. If the oven bakes unevenly, shift the pans after the buns have risen and have a little color.

7 Remove the buns from the oven and brush them gently with heated syrup wash. Be careful not to burn yourself or smear the filling. Allow the buns to cool until they are mildly warm; then stripe them with warm simple icing.

VOCABULARY

				Review
confectioners'	drain	melted	sprinkle	consistency
crescent	gloss	minimum	syrup	sticky
diameter	horizontally	soak	thicken	surface
double boiler	icing	spirals	weight	

Refer to *Glossary* for necessary explanations. The dictionary will be helpful for those terms not included in the *Glossary* because they are frequently used words.

PART THREE ■■■☐☐☐☐

fried products (doughnuts & crullers)

UNIT 7

**VARIETY
YEAST-RAISED
DOUGHNUTS**

AIM   To learn how to make a variety of yeast-raised doughnuts.

THINGS YOU SHOULD KNOW   Doughnuts are very popular with most people. Think of the many times and places where you have purchased doughnuts or had doughnuts served to you. Doughnuts are favorites for breakfast, enjoyed at coffee breaks, make wonderful snacks, and are often served at special holiday parties such as Hallowe'en. Their popularity has led to the establishment of special doughnut shops. But doughnuts that are homemade are particularly appreciated by those who eat them. Just as you have made other baked products, you can learn to make a variety of doughnuts with great success.

Doughnuts, unlike products that are baked in the dry heat of the oven, are cooked in heated fat or vegetable oil. You place the made-up doughnuts into fat that is heated to approximately 375°. Like the heat of the oven, the heat of the hot fat cooks the doughnuts, giving them a golden-brown crust.

This unit of fried products will show you how to make a variety of the most popular doughnuts. You will see that the variety comes

UNIT 7: VARIETY YEAST-RAISED DOUGHNUTS   *81*

from the type of dough used; for example, raised doughnuts are made from a yeast-raised dough. Jelly doughnuts are among the most popular of the yeast-raised variety.

JELLY
DOUGHNUTS   Yield: *16 to 20 jelly doughnuts*

The basic sweet yeast dough used for soft rolls and buns is an excellent dough for making jelly doughnuts. It is neither too lean and firm, nor too rich and soft. To understand this statement better, let us discuss the usual question asked about jelly doughnuts: "How do you put the jelly into the center of the doughnuts?" The answer is that the jelly is forced into the doughnut after it has been fried and cooled. This means that the doughnut must have a light, soft inside texture, or grain, which keeps the jelly in and prevents it from running out again. The inside of the doughnut must have the characteristics of a sponge. Products made from the basic sweet yeast dough do have these characteristics; you will recall the soft, sponge-like texture of the soft rolls and buns you made.

THINGS TO PREPARE   An electric fryer and basket, like that used for French fried potatoes, is ideal; but a wide-bottomed saucepan, an iron skillet, or a deep frying pan may be used in place of the electric fryer. Fill the pan you use with about 2 inches of melted shortening, vegetable oil, or equal amounts of each. Heat the fat to 375°.

properly conditioned (well-risen) sweet yeast dough	confectioners' sugar	dusting flour
cookie press with small, pointed nib	absorbent paper	French knife
worktable or workboard	flour-dusted pan	simple icing
wooden mixing spoon	cinnamon sugar	smooth jelly
	pastry bag and small nib	slotted spoon
		sieve

CHECK POINTS

    1 Is the dough properly conditioned?

    2 Is the fat being heated properly and *safely?* (Use a small, controlled gas flame so that the fat is not overheated.)

    3 Are all the tools and equipment ready?

MAKING, FRYING, AND FINISHING THE JELLY DOUGHNUTS

    Refer to Fig. 7-1 (page 82) while you work.
    1 Place the risen dough on the flour-dusted part of the worktable or workboard and flatten it gently with the palms of your hands to remove the large air pockets. Roll the dough up into a tight roll about 1 inch in diameter (thickness). Be sure it is of even thickness throughout in order to get doughnuts of equal size. (You must

Fig. 7-1 **Jelly doughnuts.**

    a Roll the dough into a tight roll 1 inch thick and divide the dough into equal pieces.

    b Turn the doughnuts carefully with a long wooden spoon as they fry.

    c Drain the doughnuts and place them on absorbent paper.

    d For pan-frying, gently place the risen doughnuts on a slotted spoon and lower softly into the fat.

    e The doughnuts may be filled with a pointed pastry bag and tube.

    f Dust the jelly doughnuts by sifting confectioners' sugar over them.

UNIT 7: VARIETY YEAST-RAISED DOUGHNUTS 83

remember this because larger doughnuts take longer to fry than smaller doughnuts, and placing them together in the same fryer at the same time will cause problems for you. They will not be done at the same time.) Measure and mark off the dough into 16 or 20 units as you did when you made the hamburger rolls; then cut the units evenly. (Fig. 7-1*a*.)

2 Shape the doughnuts as you did the hamburger rolls by rounding each piece of dough with your fingers. Place the rounded pieces of dough on a flour-dusted pan, spacing them about 1½ inches apart. Cover the units of dough with a cloth and place them in a warm place to rise. While you wait for them to rise, double-check the heated fat and the other things you will need to make sure they are ready for use. Allow the units to rise until they are *not quite* double in size but still feel soft and gassy to the gentle touch. *You will have to lift the units of dough in order to place them into the hot fat. If you allow them to rise too much, they will fall back when you lift them.*

3 Check the frying fat to see that it is at the proper temperature. A word of caution must be given about using washed frying pans that are still damp or wet when the fat is put into them. *The moisture will cause the hot fat to splatter when almost ready for use. Be sure frying equipment is dry before placing fat or oil into it.*

NOTE: TESTING THE TEMPERATURE OF THE FRYING FAT OR OIL The electric fryer has a thermostat which automatically controls frying temperature. The thermostat turns up the heat when the temperature starts to drop and lowers the heat when the desired temperature is reached. A frying thermometer may be used to test the temperature of the fat when you are frying in a deep saucepan or skillet. Be careful, in using a frying thermometer, to avoid breaking it when you are placing it into the hot fat and to avoid splattering the fat.

When there is neither an electric fryer nor a frying thermometer available, you may *very carefully* place *one* drop of water into the hot fat with a spoon. If there is a quick, crackling sound, you may consider the fat ready for frying. You may also test the temperature of the frying fat by putting one uncooked doughnut into it and checking the time it takes to develop a golden-brown color on each side. If the doughnut takes from 1 to 1½ minutes to turn a golden-brown color on each side, the fat is ready for frying. If the crust turns dark very quickly, of if the fat starts to smoke even before you fry the test doughnut, lower the flame and add more fat or oil to the hot fat. *Do this very carefully.*

4 Try to have the fat heated to just the right temperature at the same time the doughnuts have risen to the point where they are ready for frying. The timing is important; you will learn to do this with a little experience. Place 4 to 6 doughnuts (depending on their size) very gently into the wire basket of the electric fryer. Lower the basket

into the hot fat. Allow the doughnuts to brown and then turn them gently with a long wooden mixing spoon. (Fig. 7-1b.) *Do not use a metal spoon because metal conducts heat rapidly and you may burn your fingers.* Allow the doughnuts to brown evenly on the other side before lifting the wire basket from the fat. Let the doughnuts drain for a few seconds over the pan before you drop them from the basket onto the absorbent paper. Shake the doughnuts on the paper so that it absorbs most of the excess fat. (Fig. 7-1c.) Carefully lift the doughnuts to a clean pan and let them cool.

If you are frying in a skillet or saucepan, lift the risen doughnuts very gently, one at a time on a slotted spoon. (Fig. 7-1d.) Lower each doughnut gently into the hot fat as quickly and as *safely* as you can to avoid splattering the fat. The size of the saucepan or skillet will determine how many doughnuts you can fry at one time. Try to turn the doughnuts in the order you placed them into the fat because the first one in will brown first. Remove the doughnuts very carefully, one at a time. Try to take them out in the order you put them in, as this will control their crust color.

5 After all the doughnuts have been fried, allow the fat to cool to about 125° (still warm) before you move the skillet. Strain the fat through a very fine strainer to remove any particles of dough or flour. These particles burn and turn black, and if they are left in the fat, they will stick to the food you fry next time. (Cheesecloth makes an excellent strainer for warm fat. The cloth should be washed and dried after each use.) Straining the fat is especially important if the fat has started to smoke before frying. Smoking means that the fat has been overheated which tends to break down some of the fat particles into black carbon.

6 Be sure the doughnuts are completely cool before you fill them. Mix the jelly or jam in a bowl until it is smooth and has no lumps. Check the pastry bag and nib or tube to see that the nib fits tightly. This will prevent the jelly from leaking out the sides when the pastry bag is squeezed. Use a fine-pointed nib or tube. The cookie press should also have a fine-pointed nib or tube. (You may make a bag from a piece of freezer or parchment paper, cutting a small hole in the end with scissors.)

Fill the bag or cookie press with the smooth jelly. Pick up one doughnut at a time and stick the point of the nib or tube into the center-line of the doughnut. (Fig. 7-1e.) This line runs around the middle of the side of the doughnut where the crust colors of the top and bottom meet. This line is usually much lighter than the crusted top and bottom. It is also much softer, so that it is simple to insert the point of the tube here. Insert the tube 1 inch or slightly more into the doughnut. Gently squeeze the cookie press or bag so that you force jelly into the doughnut. When you have inserted enough jelly, stop squeezing and remove the point from the doughnut. (Do not squeeze too hard. This will force too much jelly into the doughnut and cause it to run out. With a little experience, you will quickly

UNIT 7: VARIETY YEAST-RAISED DOUGHNUTS 85

learn to control the amount of jelly you squeeze into the doughnuts.) Set the doughnuts on a pan next to each other with the hole made for the jelly tilted slightly upward. This will keep the jelly from running out until it sets.

7 The jelly doughnuts may be finished or decorated as follows:
   a. Dust the tops of the jelly doughnuts with confectioners' sugar. Put the sugar into a strainer of a flour sieve and shake it gently over the doughnuts until they are all dusted evenly with sugar. (Fig. 7-1f.)
   b. The doughnuts may be rolled in cinnamon sugar. Shake the excess sugar off after rolling the doughnuts.
   c. The doughnuts may be dipped in warm simple icing, then drained.

GLAZED RING DOUGHNUTS　　　　　　　　　　　　　Yield: *16 to 20 doughnuts*

AIM　To learn how to make glazed ring doughnuts from yeast-raised dough.

THINGS YOU SHOULD KNOW　Glazed doughnuts are as popular as jelly doughnuts. You have probably seen a variety of these doughnuts on your visits to shopping centers, grocery stores, and doughnut shops. The variety most preferred are the glazed doughnuts made from a yeast-raised dough. The basic sweet yeast dough used for soft rolls and buns is an excellent dough for glazed doughnuts. It rises well before frying and almost doubles in size when it is fried. It has the additional advantage of not absorbing much fat during frying. (You can prepare some glazed doughnuts at the same time that you are making jelly doughnuts. If you wish to, you can make a complete variety, all from the basic dough.) Let us see how the glazed doughnuts are made.

THINGS TO PREPARE　Prepare the same things that you did for jelly doughnuts. (You will not need jelly filling or the pastry bag and nibs.) Prepare the simple icing. Prepare a grate to permit the icing to drain from the doughnuts.

CHECK POINTS　Check the same things as you did for the jelly doughnuts. Make sure the icing glaze is ready and keeping warm in a double boiler.

MAKING, FRYING, AND FINISHING THE GLAZED RING DOUGHNUTS
　　　Refer to Fig. 7-2 (page 86) as you work.

NOTE　The usual method of making ring doughnuts for glazing is given in Steps 1 and 2.

PART THREE: FRIED PRODUCTS (DOUGHNUTS & CRULLERS)

Fig. 7-2 **Glazed doughnuts.**

   a To make ring doughnuts by hand, wrap a rolled-out strand of dough around the palm of the hand and join the ends by rolling them on the table.

   b Ring doughnuts may be cut out with a doughnut cutter.

   c Dip the warm doughnuts into the icing glaze.

   d Place the glazed doughnuts on a wire rack to drain after they have been dipped into the icing.

  1 Place the risen dough on a floured part of the table and flatten it gently. Check the bottom of the dough to see that there is enough flour so the dough will not stick when rolled. Dust the top of the dough and the rolling pin lightly with flour. Roll the dough out until it is a little less than ½ inch thick. Check the thickness of the dough with your fingers to see that it is even all over.

  2 Cut out the doughnuts with a doughnut cutter. (Fig. 7-2*b*.) A 3-

UNIT 7: VARIETY YEAST-RAISED DOUGHNUTS 87

inch cutter will give you about 16 doughnuts. A 2½-inch cutter will give you 20 doughnuts. Cut the doughnuts out as close together as you can to reduce the amount of scrap dough. Knead the scrap dough together into a smooth-surfaced round or rectangular shape. Allow it to relax about 10 minutes and then roll it out again. Cut out as many doughnuts from this dough as you can. Repeat these steps until all the dough has been used. You may set aside the centers of the doughnuts as you cut the doughnuts out. The centers can be fried separately and served as little doughnut specialties. Place the cut-out doughnuts on a flour-dusted pan, spacing them about 1 inch apart to give them room to rise without touching. Cover the units with a cloth and place the pan in a warm place so that the doughnuts may rise until they are slightly less than doubled in size. They should feel soft and gassy to the touch.

NOTE The method for making doughnuts given in Steps 3 and 4 avoids having to cut out the doughnuts and eliminates the need to rework scrap dough and roll it again. It is like making a bagel or ring of dough by hand and is a challenge as well as being fun to do.

3 Place the risen dough on a flour-dusted part of the worktable or workboard and flatten it with the palms of your hands. Roll the dough into a tight roll about 1 inch in diameter, making sure that it is of even thickness throughout so that you get equal-size pieces of dough. Divide the dough into 16 or 20 equal pieces.

4 Dust the pieces of dough lightly with flour and separate them. Roll each piece of dough out about 5 inches long. Be sure each strip of dough is of even thickness. Wrap the dough around your hand with the ends meeting in your palm. Place one point a little (½ inch) over the other and pinch the dough together. Then roll the pinched ends on the table to seal them properly. (Fig. 7-2a.) Place the rings of dough on a flour-dusted pan, cover them with a cloth, and allow them to rise until they are almost double in size.

5 Check the fat to see if it is ready as you did when making jelly doughnuts. Try to have the fat ready when the doughnuts are ready for frying. Fry the doughnuts as you did the jelly doughnuts. Be careful when you are placing the doughnuts into the hot fat and when you are removing them.

6 Be sure the doughnuts are well drained on the absorbent paper. Greasy doughnuts do not lend themselves to glazing; the icing does not stick. Have the simple icing glaze warm so that the doughnuts can be dipped easily.

7 Dip the doughnuts into the icing while they are still quite warm. (Fig. 7-2c.) The heat of the doughnut plus that of the icing will cause the icing to run or melt and form a glaze. You may use a fork to dip the doughnuts into the icing and to remove them. Place the

doughnuts on a wire rack or roasting rack set over a pan so that the icing will run off the doughnut into the pan. (Fig. 7-2d.) Remove the doughnuts from the rack as soon as the glaze runs off and allow them to dry on another pan. You may scrape up the icing in the pan and return it to the double boiler for reheating; you may need it to glaze other doughnuts.

8 Ring doughnuts may be finished or decorated without glazing. Their variety may be increased as follows:
   a. The ring doughnuts may be left plain, with just the golden-brown color of freshly fried doughnuts.
   b. The doughnuts may be dusted with confectioners' sugar when they are cool.
   c. They may be rolled in cinnamon sugar to make cinnamon doughnuts.

TWIST AND BOW-TIE DOUGHNUTS   Yield: *16 to 20 doughnuts*

AIM   To learn how to make twist and bow-tie doughnuts from the basic sweet yeast dough.

THINGS YOU SHOULD KNOW   These two types will add to the variety of doughnuts you can make from the basic sweet yeast dough. Their names tell you that the difference between them lies in the way these doughnuts are shaped. Your experience in shaping various twist rolls and buns should make it very easy for you to shape these doughnuts. You must *read carefully and follow instructions.* If, for example, you do not seal the ends of the twist doughnuts securely, they will unwind while frying and lose their appearance. On the other hand, making these doughnuts properly will add to the variety of your accomplishments.

THINGS TO PREPARE   Prepare the same things as you did for glazed doughnuts. You will not need the simple icing since these doughnuts are not glazed.

CHECK POINTS   Check the same things as you did for jelly doughnuts.

MAKING, FRYING, AND FINISHING TWIST DOUGHNUTS

Refer to Fig. 7-3 as you work.

1 Place the dough on a flour-dusted part of the worktable and flatten it with the palms of your hands to remove the large air pockets. Roll the dough up into a tight roll about 1 inch thick and divide the roll into 16 to 20 equal pieces. Separate the pieces and dust them lightly with flour.

UNIT 7: VARIETY YEAST-RAISED DOUGHNUTS   89

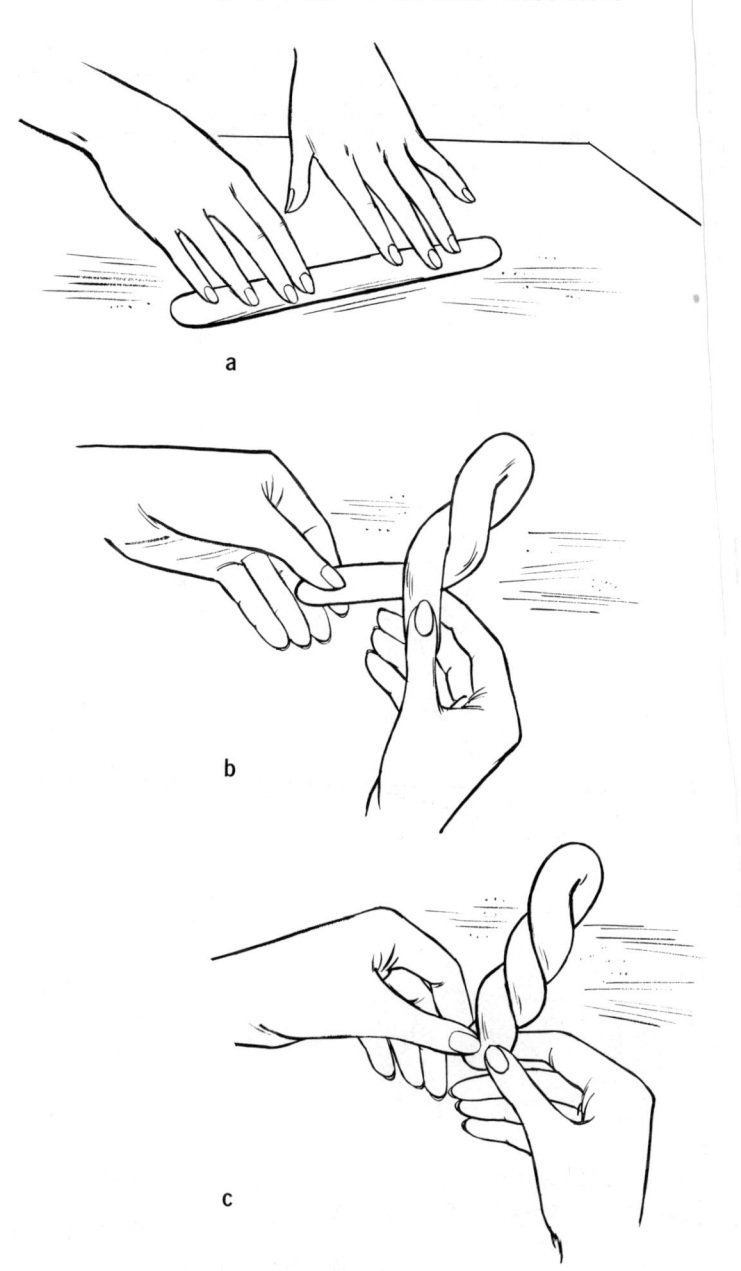

Fig. 7-3 **Twist doughnuts.**

    a Roll out each piece of dough about 6 or 7 inches long.

    b Fold the strip of dough in half and twist three or four times.

    c Pinch the ends of the twisted strip together tightly.

PART THREE: FRIED PRODUCTS (DOUGHNUTS & CRULLERS)

2 Roll each piece of dough out about 6 or 7 inches long, keeping it of even thickness, as you did when you made twisted soft rolls. Place both ends of the strip of dough together, pinching them tightly. Pick up the pinched end in one hand and twist the other looped end three times to form a spiral or twist.

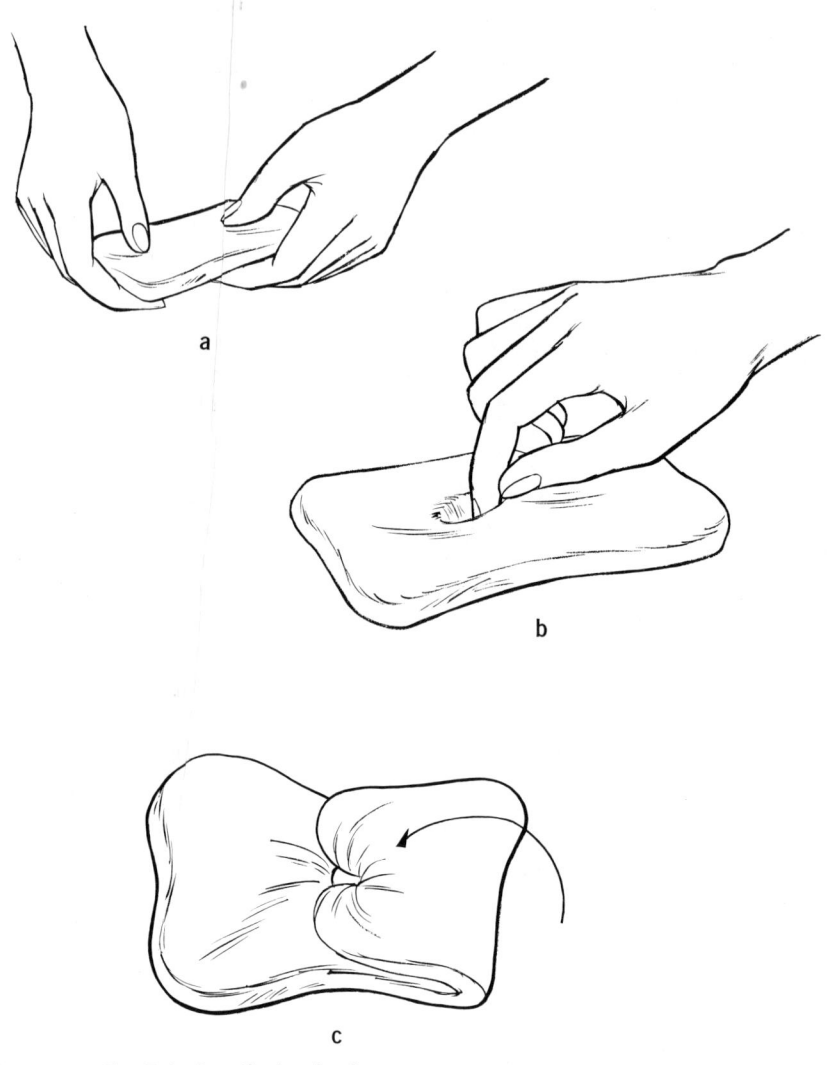

Fig. 7-4 **Bow-tie doughnuts.**

    a Stretch each piece of dough with the fingers.

    b Make a small hole in the center of the dough.

    c Pull one end of the dough through the hole and stretch slightly to form a bow-tie shape.

UNIT 7: VARIETY YEAST-RAISED DOUGHNUTS

3 Place the twisted doughnuts on a flour-dusted pan and flatten them with the palms of your hands so that they do not unravel or open. If they do unravel, allow them to relax and twist them again.

4 Let the units rise until they have almost doubled in size; then fry them as you did the glazed doughnuts. Be careful when you are placing the doughnuts into the hot fat and when you are removing them.

5 Twist doughnuts may be finished by dusting them with confectioners' sugar when they are cool. For variety, they may instead be rolled in cinnamon sugar.

MAKING, FRYING, AND FINISHING BOW-TIE DOUGHNUTS

Check Fig. 7-4 while you work.

1 Place the risen dough on a floured part of the worktable and flatten it with the palms of your hands. Roll the dough into a tight, even roll about 1 inch thick. Be sure the roll's thickness is even throughout to get equal-size doughnuts. Cut the strip into 16 or 20 equal pieces. Dust them lightly with flour and place them in rows next to each other on the table. Allow the units of dough to rest about 10 minutes to soften.

2 Pick up each piece of dough and stretch it with your fingers until it is about 3 inches long and 1½ inches wide (as you did for crumb buns). (Fig. 7-4*a*.) Push one finger (preferably your thumb) through the dough to make a hole in the center. (Fig. 7-4*b*.) Then take one end of the dough and pull it through the hole. If the dough does not go through, make the hole a bit larger. Pull the ends slightly so that the unit has an even bow-tie shape.

3 Place the units on a flour-dusted pan, cover them with a cloth, and place them in a warm place to rise until they have almost doubled in size. Fry these doughnuts as you did the other doughnuts. Remember to be careful when you are placing the doughnuts into the hot fat and when you are removing them.

4 Allow the doughnuts to cool and then finish them by dusting them with confectioners' sugar or rolling them in cinnamon sugar.

VOCABULARY

absorbent	fry	inject	pressure	saucepan	snack
appreciation	glaze	lean	(review)	serve	specialty
carbon	holiday	particles	purchase	skillet	unravel
fact					

Refer to *Glossary* for any explanations you may need. The dictionary may be helpful for those terms not included in the *Glossary*.

UNIT 8

**VARIETY
CAKE-TYPE
AND COMBINATION
DOUGHNUTS**

AIM To learn how to make variety cake-type and combination doughnuts.

THINGS YOU SHOULD KNOW The cake-type doughnut (or *cruller*) is considered the most popular kind of doughnut. Perhaps this is influenced by the fact that this type of doughnut is easily mass-produced and the consumer has therefore a great selection from which to choose. In addition, prepared doughnut mixes are available so that the cook is able to make the doughnuts quickly at home. As a matter of fact, most of the doughnut shops use prepared doughnut mixes. It is also important that cake-type doughnuts can be made much more quickly than the yeast-raised varieties. When doughnuts are made at home or in the kitchens of eating establishments, the cook may prefer to use a personal recipe. We give special recipes for these doughnuts below.

NOTE: COMPARISON OF CAKE-TYPE AND YEAST-RAISED DOUGHNUTS Cake-type doughnuts are leavened or raised primarily by the action of baking powder. (Some special doughnuts, such as whole wheat doughnuts or chocolate doughnuts, are made with baking soda as

UNIT 8: VARIETY CAKE-TYPE AND COMBINATION DOUGHNUTS 93

well as baking powder.) The cake doughnut differs from the yeast-raised variety, therefore, in that it is not necessary to allow the dough to rise. We have learned that yeast-raised doughnuts are made from a well-risen dough and require a period of fermentation for the yeast to raise the dough. The baking powder in the doughnut releases the same gas (carbon dioxide) as the yeast does when it makes the dough rise. When the cake-type doughnut is placed into hot fat, the baking powder becomes active and the gas it releases causes the doughnut to expand. These doughnuts have the shortness and texture of cake and are not as light and porous (open grained) as the yeast-raised variety. Thus, you can see that cake-type doughnuts are not only made differently but look and taste different from the yeast-raised variety.

CAKE-TYPE DOUGHNUTS OR CRULLERS

Yield: *16 to 20 cake-type doughnuts*

THINGS TO PREPARE   Prepare the fat for frying and heat it to 375°. Check the recipe for the ingredients needed.

CAKE-TYPE DOUGHNUTS (CRULLERS)

INGREDIENTS (*measure carefully*)		HOW TO MIX
sugar	½ cup	Place these ingredients in the mixing bowl and blend them together to a smooth paste.
salt	1½ teaspoons	
shortening	⅓ cup	
vanilla	1 teaspoon	
eggs	2	Break the eggs, check for freshness, add to the paste above, and blend in well.
milk	1 cup	Add the milk to the batter and stir it in slightly.
(*Be sure to sift the flour before measuring.*)		
all-purpose flour	3½ cups	Sift the flour and baking powder into the bowl. Stir the mixture well until a smooth dough is formed.
baking powder	2 tablespoons	

CHECK POINTS

1 Is the fat being heated?

2 Is the worktable ready for the dough?

3 Are the necessary tools ready (for example, the doughnut cutter)?

MAKING, FRYING, AND FINISHING THE DOUGHNUTS

(*Look back at Fig. 7-2.*)

1. Place the dough on a floured part of the worktable or board. Knead the dough slightly and form it into a rectangular shape. Check the bottom of the dough and dust the table with flour if necessary to prevent stickiness. Sprinkle the top of the dough as well with some dusting flour.

2. Allow the dough to relax about 10 minutes; then roll out the dough gently with the rolling pin about ½ inch thick. *Check the dough with your fingers to see that it is of even thickness all over.* Roll out the thicker parts or push the dough together where it is thin.

3. Cut out the doughnuts as you did when you made ring doughnuts. (See Fig. 7-2*b*.) Be sure to cut them close to each other to avoid extra scrap dough. You may separate the centers and fry them for doughnut balls. Knead the scrap dough into a smooth, rectangular shape and allow it to rest for a few minutes before rolling it out again. Repeat this process until all the dough is used.

4. Place the doughnuts on a pan that has been lightly dusted with flour. The doughnuts may be placed close to each other since these doughnuts do not have to rise. *Check the frying fat at this point to see if it is ready.* Let the doughnuts rest 10 minutes and then fry them as you did the yeast-raised variety.

NOTE As the doughnuts are put into the hot fat, they will expand; and their crusts will tend to crack slightly as the doughnuts fry. This is caused by the gas which the baking powder gives off in the presence of the hot fat. Large cracks or openings in the doughnuts may be caused by not letting the doughnuts rest for 10 minutes before frying. They may also be caused by a dough containing too much flour or by scrap dough that has been overmixed. Cracks may also be caused by frying fat that is too hot. You may note that the packaged doughnuts you buy have a smoother top without many cracks. This is because these doughnuts are made from a soft batter dough rather than the stiffer dough you made. The soft batter doughs are dropped into the hot fat by machine and are not rolled and cut out as your doughnuts were.

---

5. Be sure to turn the doughnuts so that the same light golden crust color results on both sides. Be careful when turning them to avoid splashing the fat.

6. Drain the doughnuts and then place them on absorbent paper.

7. If the doughnuts are to be glazed, dip them into warm simple icing while they are still warm. (Fig. 7-2*c*.) Place them on the grate and allow them to drain well. (Fig. 7-2*d*.) For greater variety, the doughnuts may be left plain, rolled in cinnamon sugar when they have cooled, or dusted with confectioners' sugar.

CRULLER VARIETIES

TWISTED CRULLERS

These may be made easily from this dough by dividing it into 16 or 20 equal pieces and shaping them as you did the twist doughnuts you made from the yeast-raised dough. (Refer to Fig. 7-3 as you make them.) These doughnuts may be finished as you did the yeast-raised variety.

BOW-TIE CRULLERS

These are made in the same way as those you made from the yeast-raised dough. (Refer to Fig. 7 4.) Finish or decorate these as you did the others made from the yeast dough.

SPECIALTY CAKE-DOUGHNUT DROPS

These are usually made by frying the centers of the cut-out doughnuts. They are better if made from a softer dough. Add 1 egg and ¼ cup of milk to the cake-type recipe to soften it. Spoon small drops of this batter directly into the hot fat, working quickly and safely. Turn the drops with a wooden spoon as they fry. Try to see that they all have an even crust color. These miniature doughnuts may be dusted lightly with confectioners' sugar or rolled completely in confectioners' sugar or cinnamon sugar. These doughnuts, added to the larger ones, will make a pretty display of greater variety.

COMBINATION DOUGHNUTS

Yield: *16 to 20 doughnuts*

AIM To learn how to make a variety of doughnuts from a combination doughnut dough.

THINGS YOU SHOULD KNOW The term *combination* refers to the mixture of leavening agents used to raise the dough. Baking powder and yeast are both used in this recipe. The dough is only partially fermented; then the leavening is completed by the baking powder. This gives combination doughnuts characteristics of both the yeast-raised and the cake-type doughnuts. They will be soft and tender like cake doughnuts and yet be lighter in volume and a little more open in texture. This doughnut dough lends itself very well to the making of all the varieties listed. It is not recommended, however, for jelly doughnuts (although it can be used) because the texture of the doughnuts is not sufficiently open or spongy to hold the jelly filling. These doughnuts may be shaped like jelly doughnuts and fried. Then, after cooling, they may be cut through about halfway and filled with chilled custard or whipped cream.

PART THREE: FRIED PRODUCTS (DOUGHNUTS & CRULLERS)

THINGS TO PREPARE   Dissolve the yeast in advance. Remember that dry yeast needs at least 10 minutes to dissolve completely before being used. Prepare the same things as you did for cake doughnuts and yeast-raised doughnuts. Check the recipe for the ingredients you will need.

COMBINATION DOUGHNUTS

INGREDIENTS (*measure carefully*)		HOW TO MIX
dry yeast or compressed yeast	1 package	Dissolve the yeast in the milk and place the mixture to one side.
milk (warm)	½ cup	
sugar	3 tablespoons	Place the ingredients into the mixing bowl and blend until smooth.
salt	1½ teaspoons	
shortening	½ cup	
eggs	2	Break, examine, and add the eggs to the mixing bowl batter; blend in well
milk (warm)	½ cup	Add the liquid to the batter and stir it in slightly.
vanilla	1½ teaspoons	
(*Be sure to sift the flour before measuring.*)		
all-purpose flour	4 cups	Sift the flour and baking powder into the bowl. Stir slightly, add the yeast solution, and mix to a smooth dough.
baking powder	2 teaspoons	

CHECK POINTS
 1 Is the fat being heated?   Is the thermostat control set at 375°?
 2 Are the necessary tools and pans ready for use?
 3 Is the worktable dusted with flour?

MAKING, FRYING, AND FINISHING THE COMBINATION DOUGHNUTS
Refer back to Fig. 5-1 on making the yeast-raised dough.
 1 Leave the dough in the mixing bowl after you have mixed it, covering it with a cloth and putting it in a warm place to relax and to rise slightly. This resting period should take about 20 minutes when the dough should feel soft and slightly gassy.

 2 Place the dough gently on a floured part of the worktable and shape it into a rectangle. Dust the table with additional flour if necessary to prevent the dough from sticking to the table when it is rolled out.

 3 Roll the dough out about ½ inch thick, checking that it is of even thickness all over. Cut out ring doughnuts. Or you may wish to divide the dough into 16 or 20 equal pieces, as you did for soft rolls, and shape the pieces into twist or bow-tie doughnuts. (See Figs. 7-2, 7-3, and 7-4.)

UNIT 8: VARIETY CAKE-TYPE AND COMBINATION DOUGHNUTS

4 Check the temperature of the fat and fry these doughnuts in the same way you did the yeast-raised doughnuts.

5 Finish or decorate these doughnuts, using any of the methods you learned for the yeast-raised doughnut varieties.

VOCABULARY

active	display	flour	porous	shrink
combination	doughy	gluten	purposes	solution
comparison	establishment	(*review*)	scrape	tenderness
crack	examine	partially	shortness	

Refer to *Glossary* for the explanation of any words you do not know. Use the dictionary for any terms not included in the *Glossary*.

PART FOUR ■■■■□□□□

variety pies

UNIT 9

PIE CRUST
AND FRUIT FILLINGS
FOR PIES

PIE   Yield: *enough dough for two 9-inch pies*
CRUST   *or three 8-inch pies.*

AIM   To learn how to make pie crust for fruit-filled pies.

THINGS YOU SHOULD KNOW   Pie is still America's most popular dessert, and a cook who has the ability to make a good pie is highly regarded. Often the dessert—in this case, the pie—makes the difference between a good meal and one that is just ordinary. Most people still feel that homemade pie is the best kind, and they are usually right. You can learn to make excellent pies. All you need is to understand the principles of pie making and to acquire the practical skills that go with understanding. Your prior experience in baking will be very helpful to you.

    The crust is an important part of the pie; it contains or holds the pie filling. No matter what the filling may be, most people look first for a tender crust. When you eat pie, the first thing your fork touches is the crust. If the crust gives way to the fork with a short and tender crumbling effect, you know it is well made. In learning

UNIT 9: PIE CRUST AND FRUIT FILLINGS FOR PIES   *101*

to make pies, the first thing you will learn to prepare will be the pie crust.

NOTE: PIE CRUST AND THE INGREDIENTS USED TO MAKE IT   The *flour* for pie crust dough should be the soft variety. That is, it should have less gluten than all-purpose or bread flour. Pastry flour is the flour to use, as it is softer than all-purpose flour but stronger than cake flour. A blend of cake flour and all-purpose flour, shown below in the recipe for pie crust, may be substituted for pastry flour if you do not have pastry flour on hand. When you are mixing cake and all-purpose flour, be sure to sift them together about three times in order to get a complete blend.

The *fat* or *shortening* provides the shortness and tenderness in pie crust dough. Shortening, because it is quite firm at room temperature, because it mixes easily with other ingredients, and because it is neutral in flavor, is the most popular fat for making pie crust. Some cooks and homemakers prefer lard because of its special flavor. Butter is seldom used because of its low melting point, which makes it hard to handle at room temperature when mixing the dough. Butter can be used if it is chilled and chopped in with the flour, but the cost must also be considered.

Salt provides the taste in pie crust, which would be flat without it. Salt also brings out the flavor of the other ingredients used in the pie. It is especially important when the pie crust is to be used for pot pies and similar dishes. It is best to dissolve the salt in the water before adding it to the other ingredients; this ensures more thorough distribution.

Water in pie crust dough should be chilled or cold because the cold keeps the fat particles firm during the mixing of the dough. This is especially important if you must use the dough as soon as you have made it. The water also serves to dissolve the salt and sugar.

Sugar is usually not used in most pie crust recipes, but it does have value. Let us see why this is true. Sugar, when dissolved in water, becomes a syrup, and the syrup adds a measure of tenderness to the dough. It also enables the crust to brown faster when the pie is baking. (Pie is often kept in the oven longer than necessary because the crust does not brown fast enough, and this causes the fruit filling to boil over and run out of the pie.) Sugar also helps pie crust to brown faster and better on the bottom of the pie, which eliminates the rawness and sogginess found in some pies. Sugar should be dissolved with the salt in the water before adding it to the dough.

Toughness is the most common fault of pie crust. If the crust does not break easily when a fork is applied to the pie, it is a sure indication that the dough is tough. A lean dough may also be somewhat tough. Toughness will result if the pie crust tends to shrink after you have rolled out the dough. It is evident in pies whose crusts shrink away from the edge of the pie pan while baking. *All of this is due to improper mixing or overmixing of the dough. It is also due to improper handling of the dough while you are making the pie.*

Pie crust dough should be mixed very gently and handled with tenderness while it is being made up. *When the water is added to the flour at the time of mixing, fold or toss the flour over very lightly until the dough is formed.* The water is quickly absorbed. If you see that the dough is too dry or firm, sprinkle a tablespoon or two of water over it and fold it over gently until the water is incorporated. If the dough seems to be too moist or soft, sprinkle a little flour over it and fold it over a few times until the flour is absorbed. You must let your own judgment be your guide. A properly mixed pie crust dough is lumpy, sticky, and medium soft.

By chilling the pie crust, as the recipe advises, you keep the fat particles in the dough firm. This makes rolling out the dough easier because it will be less sticky. It also means that you will need less flour to dust the worktable and the rolling pin. Even if you roll the dough without flour, sandwiched between two pieces of waxed paper, it will be easier to roll out.

THINGS TO PREPARE   Check the recipe for the necessary ingredients.

measuring spoons	flour sieve	pie pan	worktable or board
measuring cups	space in the	mixing bowl	rubber bowl
pastry blender	refrigerator	and spoon	scraper

PIE CRUST DOUGH

INGREDIENTS (*measure carefully*)
pastry flour (sifted)   5 cups
shortening   1½ cups
Note: A blend of 2½ cups of cake flour and 2½ cups of all-purpose flour can be used instead of the pastry flour.

HOW TO MIX (*See Fig. 9-1.*)
Place the flour in the mixing bowl. Chop the shortening or fat into the flour with a pastry blender or 2 knives until small lumps are formed.

salt   1½ teaspoons
sugar   2 tablespoons
cold water   1 cup

Form a hollow in the flour and fat mixture. Dissolve the sugar and salt in the water and pour this solution into the hollow. Toss or fold the flour and fat mixture gently with the water. Fold lightly from the bottom of the mixing bowl to the top. A few such overhand folds with your hands or with the mixing spoon will be enough to form a sticky, lumpy dough. At this point you should decide whether the dough needs more water or flour. If it is right, place the dough on a floured pan or on waxed paper and chill it in the refrigerator before rolling it out.

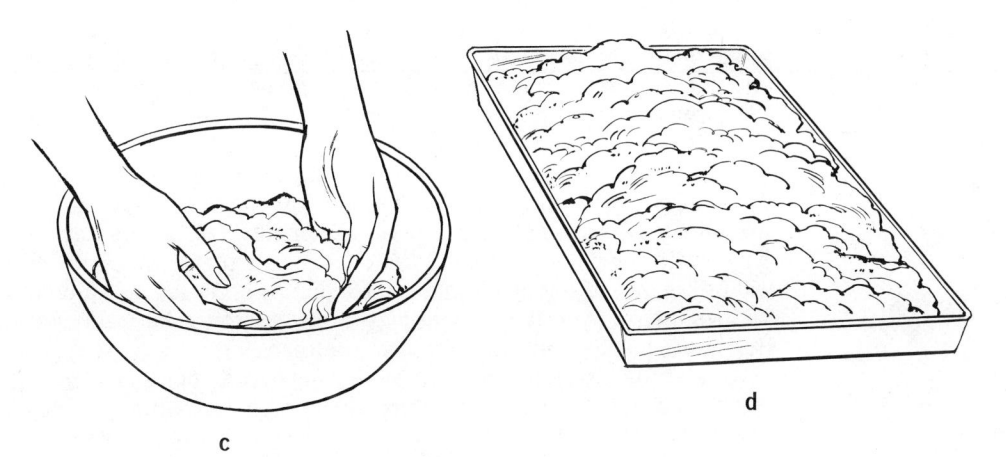

Fig. 9-1 **Making pie crust dough.**

    a Use a pastry blender to cut the fat into the flour.

    b Make a hollow in the center of the flour-shortening mixture.

    c Fold the water gently into the flour-shortening mixture.

    d The pie crust dough should be refrigerated before use, in a floured pan or on waxed paper.

FRUIT FILLINGS

AIM To learn how to prepare variety fruit fillings for fruit pies.

THINGS YOU SHOULD KNOW Most people are attracted to a pie whose fruit filling looks natural and inviting. To look this way, the pie filling should be soft and tender and flow or run a little on the plate. Most people turn away from a fruit filling that looks dull and starchy, because the tender, soft filling is usually the one that tastes good. You should be able to prepare good-looking and good-tasting fruit fillings as easily as you prepare other pudding-type desserts.

Fruit fillings for pies can be made from fresh fruits, canned fruits, or frozen fruits. Each of these fruit types requires a special preparation. The recipes for the various fruit fillings in this unit will explain how they are to be prepared. *Read carefully and follow the instructions exactly.*

FRESH APPLE PIE FILLING Yield: *filling for two 9-inch pies*

NOTE: THE USE OF FRESH APPLES FOR PIE FILLING Fresh apples vary in type, consistency, sweetness, and firmness. Apples that are soft and sweet fall apart easily in baking. Apples that are firm and tart tend to keep their shape, as apple slices should when baked in a pie. These apples are the best for pie making. You will have to be the judge of the proper apple to use and the amount of sugar to use in addition to that given in the recipe if the apples are very tart or sour. Try to bake and prepare the pies so that the baked slices of apple are soft but still keep their appearance.

Apples tend to release part of their natural juices during baking. When apple slices are mixed with sugar, the sugar is dissolved by these juices in the apple and a syrup is formed. The apples may be baked with the sugar syrup, but the chances are that the pie bottom will be soggy and the filling will look like lumpy applesauce. (Some recipes instruct you to mix flour with the sugar to thicken and bind the syrup, but this does not improve the taste.)

One of the best ways to combine the sugar and apples is to drain the syrup formed when the raw apple slices are mixed with the sugar and cinnamon, cook it, and thicken it with cornstarch. As soon as the baked pies are taken from the oven, you add equal amounts of the hot syrup to each pie through a round hole you cut out of the top crust before covering the pie. You may add the syrup with a funnel or pour it from a creamer dish with a spout.

THINGS TO PREPARE Check the recipe for the ingredients.

| measuring spoons | apple peeler and corer | refrigerator space | saucepan |
| measuring cups | mixing bowl and spoon | paring knife | workboard |

FRESH APPLE PIE FILLING

INGREDIENTS (*measure carefully*)

apples (about ~~12~~ medium) [9]	~~3~~ lbs
sugar [36]	~~2~~ [6] cups (approximately)
lemon juice	~~1~~ [3] tablespoon
cinnamon	[4.5] 1½ teaspoons
butter	~~2~~ [6] tablespoons

HOW TO PREPARE

Peel, core, and slice the apples. Mix the apple slices with the sugar, lemon juice, and cinnamon. Toss them gently to avoid breaking the slices. Let the apples and sugar stand about 20 to 30 minutes. Drain off the syrup which forms into a separate saucepan and place it to one side. Now fill the pie tin (which is lined with the bottom crust) with the apple slices. Be sure to cut a round hole in the top crust of the pie before you place the crust over the heaping sliced apples. Dot 1 tablespoon of the butter over the apples before putting the top crust on each pie.

CHECK POINTS

1. Are the apples sliced into equal pieces?
2. Is the bottom pie crust in the pie tins?
3. Have you drained the syrup for cooking and thickening?

PREPARATION OF THE SYRUP FOR APPLE PIES

INGREDIENTS (*measure carefully*)

drained syrup	1 cup

HOW TO PREPARE

Add water to the syrup, if necessary, to make 1 cup. Bring the syrup to a boil in the saucepan.

syrup or water	¼ cup
cornstarch	3 tablespoons

Dissolve the cornstarch in the syrup or water, and add it to the boiling syrup in a steady stream. Stir well until thick. The syrup should boil again. Try to have the syrup ready before taking the pies from the oven so that you can pour the hot syrup into the hot pies. The syrup will cool and thicken, or bind, the apple slices as the pie cools.

NOTE If *frozen apple slices* are used, let the slices defrost and then prepare them in the same way as you did the fresh apples.

PART FOUR: VARIETY PIES

CANNED APPLE PIE FILLING Yield: *filling for two 9-inch pies*

Canned apples are usually packed in #10 cans. There are enough apples in a #10 can to make six or seven 9-inch pies. Therefore, take out about ⅓ of the apples and juice for two 9-inch pies, put the rest of the apples in jars, and refrigerate them. These apples can always be used for more pies or other apple products.

Canned apples are precooked, or steamed, before they are canned. The brands vary in sweetness and firmness. Some contain added sugar and more syrup than others. The best canned apples for pies are those that are firm and packed with little syrup. You will have to taste the different brands to find out which apples are the best.

CANNED APPLE PIE FILLING

INGREDIENTS (*measure carefully*)		HOW TO PREPARE (*See Fig. 9-2.*)
juice drained from the apples (add water if necessary)	1 cup	Place all the ingredients into the saucepan, stir them well to dissolve the sugar, and bring to a boil on the stove.
sugar	1 cup	
cinnamon	1½ teaspoons	
salt	pinch	
lemon juice	1 tablespoon	
juice or water	¼ cup	Dissolve the cornstarch in the water or juice and add to the boiling syrup in a steady stream. Bring the syrup to a boil again. Add the butter and stir it in well. Remove the syrup from the stove. Fold the apples gently into the hot syrup.
cornstarch	¼ cup	
butter or margarine	2 tablespoons	
drained canned apples	⅓ of a #10 can	

Let the filling cool before filling the pies. Warm or hot filling causes the fat in pie crust dough to melt and the bottom crust of the pie will be soggy after it is baked. If the apple filling is to be refrigerated for later use, let it cool first. Be sure it is covered to keep it from absorbing the odors of other ingredients of foods in the refrigerator.

You will note that the apples are not cooked with the syrup. They have been precooked before canning. These apple slices will not shrink during baking so the pie does not have to be filled above the rim of the pie. Fresh apple slices do shrink and the pie should be filled with fresh apples well above the level of the rim. *Refer to Fig. 9-2 while you prepare the apple filling or fruit fillings for pies.*

Fig. 9-2 **Canned apple pie filling.**

- **a** The canned apples should be drained to separate the juice or syrup from the fruit.
- **b** Pour the cornstarch solution into the boiling syrup in a steady stream while stirring.
- **c** Fold the apples or other drained fruit into the thickened syrup.
- **d** Pour the filling into a shallow pan to cool before filling the pies.

108   PART FOUR: VARIETY PIES

PINEAPPLE PIE FILLING　　　　　　　　　　　　　　　　Yield: *two 9-inch pies*

　　　　AIM　To learn how to prepare pineapple pie filling.

THINGS YOU SHOULD KNOW　Pineapple pie filling is usually made from crushed pineapple or pineapple bits. Sometimes the broken pieces of the better quality pineapple slices are finely chopped and used for the filling. But in most cases the pineapple used for pie filling is a coarser and whiter-colored pineapple, shredded or crushed into very fine pieces and packed in very little juice. This grade of pineapple is cheaper and has to be improved in taste and quality. Crushed pineapple not packed in light or heavy syrup is commonly packed in large #10 cans. The net weight of these cans is usually about 6½ to 7 pounds.

　　The cook does not often need that much fruit at one time and therefore generally buys the #2½ can. This size can contains crushed pineapple or pineapple bits packed in light syrup. Because the fruit is of better quality, adjustments have to be made in the recipe for pineapple pie filling. You will have to read the can label for information about the contents and then make the necessary adjustments.

　　You may have to chop the pineapple into smaller pieces for the filling. If the pineapple you use has been packed in syrup, you may have to reduce the amount of sugar in the recipe for the filling. The recipe given here is based on using practically unsweetened pineapple (the kind that usually comes in a #10 can). Remember to taste the pineapple you use for sweetness to see if you should adjust the recipe. It takes about 1 pound of pineapple cooked into filling to make enough for one well-filled 9-inch pineapple pie. This is about ⅓ of the #10 can, as was mentioned. If you are using a different size can, be sure to figure out how much of that can makes 1 pound. (The unused pineapple from the #10 can should be refrigerated in jars for later use.)

THINGS TO PREPARE　Check the recipe for ingredients.

| measuring cups | saucepan | mixing bowl | can opener |
| measuring spoons | strainer | worktable | refrigerator space |

PINEAPPLE PIE FILLING

INGREDIENTS (*measure carefully*)		HOW TO PREPARE
crushed pineapple	⅓ of a #10 can or 2 #2½ cans (each can weighing about 1¼ lb)	Taste the fruit for sweetness. Drain the fruit and place the syrup in the saucepan.

PINEAPPLE PIE FILLING (*Continued*)

INGREDIENTS (*measure carefully*)		HOW TO MIX
sugar	1¼ cups (If the pineapple is packed in light syrup, use only ¾ cup of sugar.)	Measure the drained syrup or juice in the saucepan and add water if needed. Add the correct amount of sugar, stir well, and boil.
juice or syrup	1 cup (Add water if there is not enough drained juice and syrup.)	
juice or water	¼ cup	Dissolve the cornstarch in the juice or water. Add this mixture to the boiling syrup in a steady stream, stirring well. Bring the syrup to a boil again until it is thickened. Be careful to avoid splattering. Turn off the gas, remove the pan from the stove, and stir the drained pineapple into the thickened syrup. You may add 1 tablespoon of lemon juice to increase the tartness, or two or three drops of yellow food color to deepen the yellow shade of the pineapple filling. (Stir the color in well to be sure it is evenly distributed.) Allow the filling to cool before placing it into the pie shell. For faster cooling, pour the filling into a broad, shallow pan so that more of it is exposed to the air.
cornstarch	¼ cup	

CHERRY PIE FILLING   Yield: *two 9-inch pies*

AIM   To learn how to prepare cherry pie filling.

THINGS YOU SHOULD KNOW   This filling is made from sour, pitted cherries that are packed in water. These cherries are not packed in syrup; you must sweeten them as you prepare the filling. These are the only cherries used for pie, other than frozen cherries that are especially packed for pie fillings. Other types of cherries, such as Royal Anne cherries or maraschino cherries, should not be used. They are too expensive, and in addition, Royal Anne cherries have pits in them. Cherries for pie have their pits removed before they are canned. The cherries are packed in #10 cans and in #2½ cans.

PART FOUR: VARIETY PIES

THINGS TO PREPARE Check the recipe for the necessary ingredients. Prepare the same things you did for pineapple pie filling.

CHERRY PIE FILLING

INGREDIENTS (*measure carefully*)		HOW TO PREPARE
sour, pitted cherries	⅓ of a #10 can or 2 #2½ cans	Drain the fruit, and measure the water in which the cherries were packed. Add water to make one full cup. (Save any leftover cherry water.) Place the water and sugar into the saucepan and boil.
sugar	1½ cups	
cherry water	1 cup	
water or juice	¼ cup	Dissolve the cornstarch in the water and add this to the boiling syrup in a steady stream. Bring the syrup to a boil again, continuing to stir until the stock is clear and thickened. Remove the saucepan from the stove and stir in the drained cherries gently. A few drops of red food color may be added with the cherries to improve the color of the filling. Let the mixture cool before filling the pie shell.
cornstarch	¼ cup	

If you use frozen cherries, allow the cherries to defrost completely before you use them to make filling. This will enable you to drain their juice or syrup and measure it accurately. Frozen cherries are usually precooked with water and sugar, so these cherries may already be sweetened. Red color and cherry flavor may have been added to the cherries before freezing. You should know these things in order to make the necessary adjustments in the sugar, color, or flavor. Prepare these cherries, after they have been defrosted, just as you did the canned cherries.

BLUEBERRY OR HUCKLEBERRY FILLING

AIM To learn how to prepare blueberry or huckleberry pie filling.

THINGS YOU SHOULD KNOW Canned blueberries or huckleberries used for pie fillings are packed in water, generally in #10 cans. As you did with other fruits packed in #10 cans, use only one-third of the can. (Be sure to measure one-third of the juice or water as well as one-third of the fruit.) Most cooks prefer to use fresh or frozen blueberries, if available, to prepare pie filling. Recipes using both the canned and the fresh or frozen berries will be given.

THINGS TO PREPARE Prepare the same things you did for the pineapple pie filling.

UNIT 9: PIE CRUST AND FRUIT FILLINGS FOR PIES *111*

CANNED BLUEBERRY PIE FILLING Yield: *two 9-inch pies*

Measure one-third of a #10 can of blueberries packed in water. This is equal to approximately 1 full quart, or 4 full cups, of fruit and water or juice.

INGREDIENTS (*measure carefully*)		HOW TO PREPARE
blueberries or huckleberries drained juice or water sugar	⅓ of #10 can 1 cup 1¼ cups	Place the sugar and juice in the saucepan and boil.
cornstarch water or juice	¼ cup ½ cup	Dissolve the cornstarch in the juice and add it to the boiling syrup in a steady stream, stirring well. Bring the syrup to a boil again. Continue to stir until the stock thickens and becomes clear. Remove it from the stove and gently fold in the drained blueberries with ⅛ teaspoon of cinnamon. Allow the filling to cool before using it to fill the pie shell.

FRESH OR FROZEN BLUEBERRY PIE FILLING Yield: *one 9-inch pie*

Measure 1 pint of fresh berries for each pie. If you use frozen berries, use 2 cups. Defrost the frozen berries and drain off the juice or water to use in preparing the filling.

INGREDIENTS (*measure carefully*)		HOW TO PREPARE
water or drained juice fresh or defrosted blueberries sugar	1 cup 1 pint 1¼ cups	Place the fruit, water, and sugar in the saucepan; stir them together and bring to a boil. Allow the fruit to boil for two minutes.
cornstarch water or juice	¼ cup ½ cup	Dissolve the cornstarch in the water. Add it to the fruit mixture in a steady stream and bring to a boil. Stir until the stock is clear and thick. Remove it from the stove.
fresh or defrosted blueberries	1 cup	Fold the berries gently into the fruit mixture. To improve the flavor, add ¼ teaspoon cinnamon or you may use 1 tablespoon of lemon juice in place of the cinnamon. (Use one or the other, *not both*.) Allow the filling to cool before putting it into the pie.

PART FOUR: VARIETY PIES

VOCABULARY

appear	dessert	funnel	quality	*Review*
canned	distribute	lard	spout	fold in
clear	filling	melting point	tart	shortness
core	flavor	neutral	tasteless	tender
defrost	frozen	peel	thorough	tough

Refer to *Glossary* for the explanation of any terms you do not know. The dictionary will be helpful for commonly used terms not included in the *Glossary*.

MAKING AND BAKING FRUIT-FILLED PIES

AIM To learn how to make and bake fruit-filled pies.

THINGS YOU SHOULD KNOW You have prepared a pie crust dough which you have then chilled. You have also prepared a fruit filling which you have allowed to cool. Now you are ready to finish the pie, the most enjoyable part of making it. Certain things will determine whether you have a really attractive pie or one with several obvious faults. For example, your pie may taste delicious but not look as good as it tastes. Too much filling will run over the sides of the pie and cause the baked pie to have a sloppy appearance. Putting the correct amount of filling in the dough is an example of the importance of following instructions.

Rolling the pie crust dough on a cloth that has been dusted with flour will keep the dough from absorbing too much flour. It will also keep the dough from sticking easily, and you will not have to reroll the dough. Rerolling the dough causes toughness. *Read the instructions carefully and look at Fig. 9-3 while making the pies.*

THINGS TO PREPARE Set the oven temperature at 425° to 435°.

egg wash or melted butter	greased pie tins	rolling pin	dusting flour	table knife
cooled fruit filling	chilled pie crust	worktable	French knife	fork
small cookie cutter	floured cloth	table brush	wash brush	cup

CHECK POINTS

1 Is the oven lighted and at the proper temperature?

2 Are the necessary tools and greased pie tins ready?

3 Have you chilled the pie crust and the fruit filling?

UNIT 9: PIE CRUST AND FRUIT FILLINGS FOR PIES   *113*

MAKING AND BAKING THE PIES

1 Place the chilled pie crust dough on the flour-dusted cloth and gently shape it into a roll about 3 inches in diameter. *Do not knead the dough to shape it. This will toughen it.*

2 Carefully measure the dough and cut it at a point about two-thirds of its length, or slightly less. (See Fig. 9-3*a*.) Divide the larger piece in half; these 2 pieces will be used for the bottom crusts of two 9-inch pies. Since the bottom crust must cover both the bottom and sides of the pie tin and be slightly thicker than the top crust to support the fruit filling, it should be larger than the dough for the top crust. Divide the smaller third of dough in half for the top crusts. You now have 4 pieces of dough for the tops and bottoms of the two pies you will make. If you make only one pie, use only half the dough. Return the rest to the refrigerator.

3 Starting with the bottom crust piece, flatten each piece of dough on the floured cloth. (Fig. 9-3*b*.) Dust the top of the dough and the rolling pin lightly with flour. Check the bottom of the dough to see that there is enough flour to keep the dough from sticking when rolled. Roll the dough out in a circle slightly larger than the top rim of the pie tin. (Fig. 9-3*c*.) Place the pie tin over the crust when it is rolled out to check that the dough has been rolled out enough to cover the bottom and sides of the greased pie tin. *The dough should be of even thickness.* Check it with your fingers by pressing gently. Fold the dough in half, lift it gently, and place the folded edge of the dough in the center of the pie tin so that half of the tin is covered with dough. Now unfold the other half of the dough so that the entire pie tin is covered. Press the dough gently against the sides of the tin, pressing firmly where the dough is thick to force it up. (Fig. 9-3*d*.)

4 Remove any excess flour from the rim of the crust and then brush the rim with water or egg wash before you fill the pie. This will make a better seal when you place the top crust on the pie and close the edges; this prevents the filling from running out of the pie during baking.

5 Fill the pie almost to the brim with fruit filling. (Fig. 9-3*e*.) Fresh apple filling shrinks during baking. With this filling, therefore, fill the pies above the level of the rim to allow for the shrinkage. Canned apple filling expands least of all the fruit fillings. The pie can be filled almost to the brim with this filling.

With pineapple filling, the pie should be filled about seven-eighths full. Since cherry and blueberry pie fillings contain more natural fruit acids and have more sugar to sweeten them, they expand or run more than other fillings. These pies should be filled about three-quarters full to allow for expansion during baking. Pies that are filled too much will run over during baking, and pies that are not filled enough will look thin and skimpy after baking. *Avoid getting*

PART FOUR: VARIETY PIES

Fig. 9-3 **Putting the pie together.**

a Divide the crust dough into 2 pieces for the bottom and top crusts of the pie—about 60 percent for the bottom and 40 percent for the top.

b Shape each piece of dough very gently into a ball.

c For the bottom crust, roll out the larger ball gently with a small rolling pin to an even thickness slightly larger than the pie tin.

d Place the bottom crust in the pan. Be sure the entire pie tin is covered with crust.

fruit filling on the rim of the bottom crust. It will prevent the top crust from sticking properly to the bottom crust, which is often one of the reasons that fillings run out.

6 Roll the top crust out slightly thinner than the bottom crust and only as large as the top rim of the pie tin. You may hold the tin over the crust and check. Use enough dusting flour to keep the crust from

UNIT 9: PIE CRUST AND FRUIT FILLINGS FOR PIES 115

Fig. 9-3 **Putting the pie together (continued).**

    e Fill the pie almost to the brim with fruit filling.

    f Place the top crust on top of the pie so that the entire pie is covered.

    g The edges of the pie may be sealed by pressing with the fingers.

    h The edges of the pie may also be sealed with a fork.

sticking to the cloth or the rolling pin. Try to keep the crust in a round shape while you are rolling out the dough.

7. Cut a hole in the center of the top crust with a small, round cookie cutter. You may also make some cuts or slits in the top crust with a French knife or other sharp knife. (Observe safety practices when using the knife to cut the dough.) The hole, or the slits made with the knife, are very important. They act as vents for the steam formed during baking. The steam is created by moisture in the

fruit filling which reaches almost 212° during baking. If the steam cannot get out of the pie, it will cause the sides of the pie to open and the fruit filling to run out while the pie is baking.

8 Fold the top crust in half. Lift it gently and place it over the pie so that half the filling is covered. (Fig. 9-3*f*.) Now unfold the other half so that the entire pie is covered. Try to center the hole or the slits on the pie; it makes the pie look more attractive. If you can lift the whole, unfolded crust without tearing it, do so, and cover the entire pie that way. This is difficult to do with large pies, however.

9 To seal the edges of the pie crusts, squeeze them or pinch them together firmly. (Fig. 9-3*g*.) The most common method is to seal them by pressing the tines of a fork against the rim of the tin. (Fig. 9-3*h*.) This makes a ridged border design and seals the pie at the same time. Remove any excess dough from the pie rim by cutting it off carefully with a knife. Fold the dough trimmings together without flour, to avoid toughening. The trimmings may be used for pie bottoms at some later time.

10 Brush or wash the tops of the pies with egg wash to give them a shiny brown crust color when baked. For a non-shiny, homemade effect, brush the tops of the pies with melted butter, margarine, or shortening. Milk will also give a dull finish.

11 Be sure to check the oven temperature to see that it is correct before placing the pies in the oven. A high temperature is important when baking fruit pies, in order to bake the pie crust and give it a pleasing crust color before the fruit filling starts to boil over. Since pie crust contains little or no sugar, a hot oven is required to bake it through and give a brown crust color. A low baking temperature will bring the fruit filling to the boiling point (212°) before the crust is either baked or browned. The filling will boil and run out of the pie while you are waiting for the crust to bake and brown.

12 A 9-inch pie takes approximately 35 minutes to bake at 425°. It is advisable to shift the pie in the oven after it has been baking for about 20 minutes. This will move the pie into an area of fresh heat and will ensure a properly baked pie bottom. Often the pie absorbs the heat of the space in which it sits during the first stage of baking, and the remaining heat may not be enough to bake the crust through properly. This will not be necessary if your baking oven is well insulated and the heat is distributed evenly throughout. You will soon get to know how your oven bakes.

13 The pie is considered baked when the crust is browned and feels crisp to the touch. At this point, some cooks gently shake the pie by holding the rim to see if the pie moves in the tin. If it does, it is a sure sign that the pie bottom is baked; otherwise it would not be possible for the pie to move freely. Do this gently to avoid spilling the filling and perhaps burning yourself.

UNIT 9: PIE CRUST AND FRUIT FILLINGS FOR PIES

14. Remove the pies carefully from the oven and place them on a rack or grate to cool. Allow the pies to cool and the filling to set before cutting and serving them.

15. In the case of the fresh apple pies or pies made from fresh-frozen apples, remember to have the syrup heated and ready to pour into the round hole in the top crust as soon as the pies are taken from the oven. This will allow the hot syrup to spread through the hot pie, permitting the spices and flavor to be absorbed by the apple filling. Apple pies may be reheated before serving.

CRUMB-TOPPED FRUIT-FILLED PIES

Apple crumb and blueberry crumb pies are very popular, and they add greater variety to pie making. These pies are prepared just like the others except that a *crumb topping is placed on the fruit filling instead of a pie crust top.* The topping is the same as that used for crumb buns. Be sure the top of the pie is covered evenly and completely with crumb topping. These pies are baked at the same temperature as crust-topped pies and are considered done when the crumb topping is browned and the pie has baked for the same length of time as the others. Dust these pies with confectioners' sugar when they have cooled and are ready to be served.

VOCABULARY

acid-type	cloth	ridged	tines	*Review*
area	design	skimpy	topping	diameter
boiling point	determine	slits	trim	knead
brim	obvious	support	unfold	

Refer to *Glossary* for the explanation of any words you do not know. The dictionary will be helpful for most terms not included in the *Glossary.*

UNIT **10**

**SOFT-FILLED
PIES AND
TURNOVERS**

**CUSTARD-TYPE
BAKED VARIETY**

AIM   To learn how to make soft-filled pies of the baked variety. (*a*) Preparation of the pie dough for soft-filled pies. (*b*) Preparation of the custard filling for the pies. (*c*) Making and baking the pies.

THINGS YOU SHOULD KNOW   Soft-filled pies are pies with a soft, custard-like filling. They may be made in two ways. In some, an uncooked filling is poured into the pie shell and baked in the oven like a baked pudding. In others, the filling is precooked and then poured into prebaked pie shells. Learning to make both types and the varieties made from each type will add to your ability in pie making.

Of those pies that are filled with the custard and then baked, the plain custard, coconut custard, and pumpkin pies are the most popular. These pies are quite different from the fruit-filled variety. For one thing, the kind of pie crust made for the shell is different. This crust does not have as much shortening and is not as rich as the crust for the fruit-filled pies. The dough is not refrigerated before use. Warm water, rather than iced or chilled water, is used to make

UNIT 10: SOFT-FILLED PIES AND TURNOVERS

the dough. The warm water allows the dough to dry quickly and form a skin, or crust, on the pie shell. The filling (uncooked puddings) are put into the raw shells and the entire pie is baked. Because these are not covered pies, you can see the change taking place in the filling while the pie is baking.

As mentioned above, this type of crust has less fat than regular pie crust. This enables the dough to contain the baked filling or pudding without falling apart. Letting the pie shell dough dry and form a crust after fitting it into the pie tin will keep the filling from soaking through the crust. You may also brush the crust with the white of an egg which forms an extra crust and keeps the filling from soaking through.

PIE CRUST DOUGH FOR SOFT-FILLED PIES　　　　　　Yield: *2 or 3 pie shells*

THINGS TO PREPARE　Check the recipe for the required ingredients.

worktable and workboard	measuring spoons	flour sieve	rolling pin
mixing bowl and spoon	measuring cups	table brush	pie tins
pan grease or fat	grease brush	French knife	

PIE CRUST FOR SOFT-FILLED PIES

INGREDIENTS (*measure carefully*)		HOW TO MIX
cake flour (sifted)	4 cups	Blend all these ingredients together in the bowl to a smooth paste.
sugar	3 tablespoons	
salt	2 teaspoons	
shortening	¾ cup	
water (warm)	¾ cup	Add the water to the above mixture and mix well to a smooth dough.

CHECK POINTS

　　1 Is the work area dusted lightly with flour?

　　2 Are the pie tins greased?

　　3 Are all the work tools ready?

MAKING THE PIE SHELLS FOR SOFT-FILLED PIES

　　Refer to Fig. 10-1 (page 120) as you work.
　　1 Place the dough on a floured part of the worktable. Knead the dough gently into a roll about 3 inches round. Divide the dough into 3 equal parts. (If you plan to make only one pie, wrap 2 pieces in freezer paper and place them in the freezer. To keep them for shorter periods, wrap the dough in waxed paper and refrigerate it.)

　　2 Shape the pieces of dough gently into round balls. Place one of the balls on a floured part of the worktable (or better, on a floured cloth) and roll out the dough into a round circle about ⅛ inch thick. (Fig.

PART FOUR: VARIETY PIES

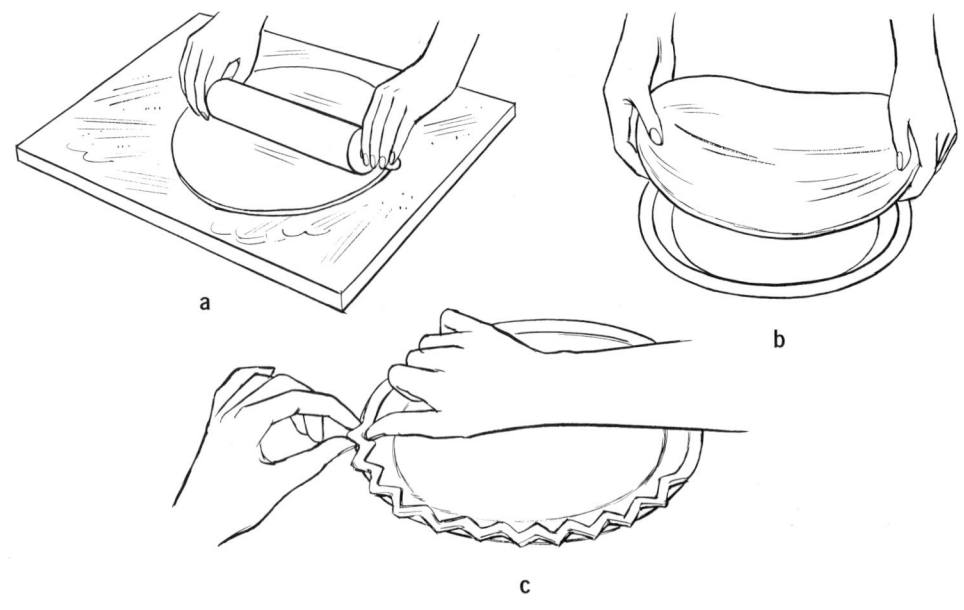

Fig. 10-1 **Crust for soft-filled pie.**

   a Roll out the dough on a floured surface.

   b Gently place the dough in a greased pie tin.

   c After you have pressed the dough into the pan and trimmed the excess away from the rim, flute the rim as shown here. Using two fingers of one hand and the thumb of the other, pinch the dough at regular spaces for an even appearance.

10-1a.) Now measure the circle of dough with the top of the pie tin. The dough should be about 1 inch larger than the top rim of the pie tin.

  3 Place the dough into the greased pie tin, as you did when you made the bottom crust for fruit-filled pies. (See Fig. 10-1b.) Press your fingers gently over the bottom crust of the pie, forcing some of the crust to the sides of the tin. This will make the bottom dough a little thinner and the sides a little thicker. Now press the sides of the tin gently to force some of the dough to the top of the rim. At this point, you should have a high ridge of dough around the rim.

  4 Cut some of the excess dough from the edge of the rim as you did when you trimmed the edge of the finished fruit pie. Now look at Fig. 10-1c and *flute* the rim (make dents or ridges around the rim of the pie by pressing the dough together between two fingers of one hand and the thumb of the other). Space the dents regularly so the rim has an even appearance. This will raise the rim of the pie

UNIT 10: SOFT-FILLED PIES AND TURNOVERS *121*

dough so that it can hold the soft filling when it is poured into the shell. An even rim that is well made also gives the baked pie a nice appearance.

5 Allow the pie shell to dry for about 30 minutes before filling it. When it dries, a crust will form on the dough. As you learned, this crust will keep the soft filling from soaking through the bottom dough during baking.

FILLING FOR BAKED CUSTARD PIE Yield: *one 9-inch pie*

AIM To learn how to prepare custard for baked custard pie.

THINGS YOU SHOULD KNOW You are probably familiar with various puddings and fillings prepared for desserts. Some of these are cooked fillings; others are made simply by mixing the ingredients together in a cold process without any cooking. Both types thicken because of thickening agents used in the prepared pudding mixes.

The filling for baked custard pie must be heated in order for the thickening agents to be able to work. This happens during the baking of the pie. As the oven heat reaches the filling, the cornstarch or tapioca flour you use expands and absorbs the milk. Tapioca flour binds, or thickens, a filling faster than cornstarch. Both have to be stirred into the filling very well to dissolve them. If the filling is allowed to stand before being poured into the pie shell, it must be stirred again because cornstarch tends to settle to the bottom and remain there.

Eggs are a natural thickening agent. If more eggs are used in the custard, less cornstarch (or other thickening) is needed. If the recipe called for four eggs instead of two eggs, there would be no need at all for cornstarch or tapioca flour. There would be enough eggs to thicken all the liquid during the baking period.

THINGS TO PREPARE Refer to the recipe for the ingredients needed. Set the oven temperature at 425°.

saucepan	measuring cups	mixing bowl
handwhip beater	measuring spoons	prepared pie shells

CUSTARD PIE FILLING

INGREDIENTS (*measure carefully*)		HOW TO MIX
sugar	½ cup	Place all the dry ingredients into a mixing bowl and blend them together.
salt	pinch	
tapioca flour	1 tablespoon	
or		
cornstarch	1½ tablespoons	
(*not both*)		

PART FOUR: VARIETY PIES

CUSTARD PIE FILLING (*Continued*)

INGREDIENTS (*measure carefully*)		HOW TO MIX
eggs	2	Break the eggs into a separate dish and examine them for freshness and quality. Stir the eggs together to combine the yolks and whites. Blend the eggs well into the above mixture.
milk (warm) vanilla	2 cups 1 teaspoon	Combine the milk and vanilla. Add to the eggs and sugar in a steady stream, stirring while adding.
melted butter	1 tablespoon	Stir the butter into the filling.

CHECK POINTS

    1 Is the oven heated to 425°?

    2 Is the pie shell ready? Does it have a crust?

    3 Do you have coconut ready for coconut pie?

FILLING AND BAKING THE CUSTARD PIE

    Refer to Figs. 10-2 and 10-3.

    1 Place the prepared pie shell near the oven and pour in the custard filling until it is three-quarters full. (See Fig. 10-2.) Put the pie carefully into the oven without spilling. Now pour the rest of the filling into the pie up to the fluted edge. Use a cup to pour the last of the filling into the pie. Gently move the pie to the center of the oven so that it can bake evenly.

    2 Let the pie bake at 425° for 10 to 12 minutes, and then reduce the oven temperature to about 360°. Continue to bake the pie for about

Fig. 10-2 Filling a soft-filled pie.

Fig. 10-3 For coconut pie, sprinkle in enough coconut to cover the bottom of the pie shell.

30 minutes. A deep pie tin contains a larger amount of filling than a shallow tin; therefore, a deep pie will take longer to bake than a shallow pie.

When done, the pie should feel slightly firm, or shimmery, if touched gently with a finger or the tip of a spoon. The edge of the custard will have risen up to, or even above, the rim of the pie and will have a golden-brown crust color. The center of the pie will be lighter in color. (Remember that the filling continues to bake or thicken after the pie is removed from the oven.) Overbaking the pie may cause the filling to separate and lose part of the liquid; this is sometimes called "weeping." Remove the pie gently from the oven and allow it to cool before serving.

3 During the first stage of baking in a hot oven, a crust forms on the top of the pie. This crust rises and acts as a cover while the pie bakes at a lower temperature. It will not crack if the oven is not too hot.

4 If you wish to sprinkle the top of the pie with nutmeg, you should sprinkle it on after the pie has been in the oven for about 5 minutes and a crust is just being formed. The soft crust will support the nutmeg pieces and keep them from settling to the bottom of the pie.

Coconut custard pie

This is made by sprinkling the bottom of the pie shell with ½ cup of unsweetened, or slightly sweetened, coconut. (Fig. 10-3.) Pour the filling over the coconut and some of the coconut will rise and be distributed throughout the pie. The coconut should be of fine shred, not of the sweetened, long-shred variety. Sweetened coconut tends to burn when exposed to the top heat of the oven during baking.

PART FOUR: VARIETY PIES

PUMPKIN PIE FILLING   Yield: *two 9-inch pies*

AIM   To learn how to prepare pumpkin pie filling.

THINGS YOU SHOULD KNOW   Pumpkin pie is a special favorite at holiday seasons such as Thanksgiving and Christmas. You can prepare your own pumpkin for the filling by steaming and straining fresh pumpkin. Straining the pumpkin removes the fibres, or strings, so that the pumpkin is smooth. Of course, it is simpler to use canned pumpkin and avoid the extra work of preparing fresh pumpkin.

THINGS TO PREPARE   Prepare the same things as you did for custard pie filling. Check the recipe for the ingredients needed. Read the special notes below about pumpkin pie in case you wish to make any changes in the basic recipe.

PUMPKIN PIE FILLING

INGREDIENTS (*measure carefully*)		HOW TO MIX
sugar	½ cup	Place all the dry ingredients into the mixing bowl and stir them together to blend well.
brown sugar	¼ cup	
salt	½ teaspoon	
cake flour (sifted)	¼ cup	
cinnamon	½ teaspoon	
nutmeg	¼ teaspoon	
ginger	¼ teaspoon	
eggs	2	Break the eggs into a cup and examine them for freshness. Add to the dry ingredients and blend in. *Do not whip the eggs.*
corn syrup or molasses	¼ cup	Add to the above mixture and stir well.
pumpkin (strained if fresh)	2 cups	
milk	2 cups	Add the milk to the custard in a steady stream, stirring while adding.

CHECK POINTS

1 The pumpkin pie filling should be allowed to stand about half an hour before using it.

2 Be sure the oven is set at 425°.

3 Are the pie shells ready? Do they have a crust?

Fill the pumpkin pies as you did the custard pies. Be sure you stir the pumpkin filling before pouring it into the shells. Bake the pumpkin pies as you did the custard pies. Remember to lower the oven temperature to 360° after the first 10 to 12 minutes of bak-

UNIT 10: SOFT-FILLED PIES AND TURNOVERS   *125*

ing at 425°. Test for proper bake as you did for the custard pie. (Pumpkin pies that have a watery top have been baked too long.)

NOTE: SPECIAL POINTS REGARDING PUMPKIN PIE FILLING

1 The corn syrup or molasses adds sweetness to the pie filling. They also soften and tenderize the filling texture and counteract the drying effect of the pumpkin on the filling.

2 Flour is used because it has a better jelling effect than cornstarch. Tapioca flour may be used in place of cake flour.

3 Since eggs have a natural thickening effect, reduce the amount of flour or other thickening used in the filling if you increase the number of eggs.

4 The combination of spices (cinnamon, nutmeg, and ginger) will flavor the pie. If molasses is used instead of corn syrup, it will produce a slightly darker color in the pie and add flavor to it.

5 Cooked squash is often mixed with the pumpkin in cans. The squash will give additional flavor and tenderness to the pies. In fact, you may use boiled and strained squash in place of pumpkin.

6 Boiled and mashed sweet potatoes or yams may be used. The amount of milk should be increased gradually if the batter is too thick.

**PREBAKED SHELLS
FILLED WITH
PRECOOKED FILLINGS**

LEMON MERINGUE PIE

AIM   To learn how to make lemon meringue pie.

THINGS YOU SHOULD KNOW   Lemon meringue pie is one of the most popular soft-filled pies. The cook can be very proud of this dessert, if it is made well. Although the pie may appear difficult to make, it is really quite simple to prepare. With the experience you have gained in making fruit-filled pies, making this pie should be easy for you. The preparation of this pie, however, is different from that of the baked custard and pumpkin pies. It is necessary to have ready a prebaked pie shell, and the filling is precooked before being poured into the shell. You may use one of the cold-process lemon fillings; all you have to do is mix it and pour it into the shell. Or you may wish to use one of the prepared lemon puddings which you cook and then put into the pie. However, many homemakers prefer to make their own cooked lemon filling, using fresh lemon juice and fresh lemon rind. The choice is yours.

How to prepare a baked pie shell

THINGS TO PREPARE Have ready the chilled pie crust dough, made from the same recipe you used for fruit-filled pies. Set the oven temperature at 425°. Grease the *back* or *outside* of the pie tin rather than the inside.

dusting flour	worktable or	French knife	table brush
rolling pin	workboard	fork	flour-dusted cloth

MAKING AND BAKING THE PIE SHELL

Refer to Fig. 10-4.

1 Place the chilled pie crust dough on a floured part of the worktable. The dough should be in roll form about 3 inches round. Cut off a piece of dough the same size that you cut for the bottom crust of the fruit pie. (Remember that a larger pie will require more dough than a smaller pie.) Round the piece of dough gently, place it upon the flour-dusted cloth, and flatten it lightly.

2 Check the bottom of the dough to see if there is enough dusting flour to keep the dough from sticking when it is rolled. Dust the top of the dough and the rolling pin as well. Roll the dough out (Fig. 10-4a) into a circle shape so that the dough is about ¼ inch thick throughout and about 1 inch larger than the top rim of the pie. Remember that the dough must also cover the sides of the pie. Use the pie tin to measure the size of the dough.

3 Turn the pie tin over so that the greased back of the tin faces up. Now fold the dough in half and lift it over the back of the pie tin so that the folded edge of the dough is in the center of the tin and half of the tin is covered with crust. Now unfold the other half of the dough to cover the entire back of the pie tin. (Fig. 10-4b.) Press the dough gently against the top and sides of the pie tin to remove any trapped air and thus prevent air pockets from forming.

4 Lift the pie tin and dough and trim the excess pie crust from around the rim of the pie. (Fig. 10-4c.) Fold the excess dough gently into a ball; this scrap dough may be used again for another pie.

5 Puncture, or *dock*, the crust with a fork. (Fig. 10-4d.) This will allow any air or steam formed during baking to escape. It also prevents the formation of blisters. Blistered pie crusts are generally very weak and tend to break in the spots where the blisters have formed.

6 Now cover the pie dough with another pie tin of the same size. (Fig. 10-4e.) Press down gently so that the dough takes on the exact shape of the tin. (You may do without the extra pie tin as a cover. If you do not use one, you may find some small bumps in the crust after the shell is baked, instead of having a smooth-surfaced shell on both sides.)

Fig. 10-4 Preparing a prebaked pie shell.

a Roll the dough evenly, as you would for a regular bottom crust.
b Place the dough over the back of the pie tin.
c Trim the excess dough from the sides with a knife.
d Dock the pie dough (make small holes in it) with a fork.
e Cover the dough with another pie tin.
f After the pie shell is baked and cooled, place it on the inside of the pie tin.

PART FOUR: VARIETY PIES

7 Bake the shell in a hot oven at 425° about 15 minutes before removing the top pie tin. Lift the top cover gently with a fork and remove it with a cloth. Bake the pie shell for 5 or 10 more minutes, until the crust is golden brown. If the oven bakes unevenly, shift the pie shell in the oven so that the pie crust is evenly baked throughout. Remember, the pie shell should be baked until crisp. It must support a hot, moist filling. If the crust is not baked through properly, it will become soggy as the pie filling cools. Allow the pie shell to cool before removing it from the back of the tin and placing it on the inside of the tin. (Fig. 10-4*f.*)

Fresh lemon pie filling   Yield: *one 9-inch pie*

AIM   To learn how to prepare lemon pie filling.

THINGS YOU SHOULD KNOW   You may use the following recipe if you wish to make your own filling instead of using a prepared filling mix. The juice of the fresh lemon contains the sour or acid part of the lemon. The yellow outside of the rind of the lemon contains the oil and flavor of the lemon. When grating a lemon, remove only the yellow part of the rind without digging into the bitter, white, pulpy part. Cover the lemon rind, when grated, with waxed paper. Left exposed to the air, it will turn brown and the pie filling will have foreign brown spots in it after you stir in the rind.

THINGS TO PREPARE   Be sure the pie shell is cooled and ready for the cooked pie filling.

| measuring spoons | saucepan | mixing bowl | whip or |
| measuring cups | grater | waxed paper | beater |

LEMON PIE FILLING

INGREDIENTS (*measure carefully*)		HOW TO PREPARE
sugar	1½ cups	Place the sugar, salt, and cornstarch in the saucepan and stir to mix them together. Stir in the boiling water in a steady stream and whip to dissolve the ingredients. Place the saucepan over a medium flame and boil until the syrup is thick and clear. Be sure to stir constantly with the whip.
salt	1 teaspoon	
cornstarch	7 tablespoons	
boiling water	2¼ cups	
eggs	3	Separate the yolks and whites, and put the whites to one side. Whip the egg yolks slightly and add about 4 tablespoons of the hot *gel* (the cornstarch mixture) to the yolks. Whip the gel and the yolks slightly and pour this mixture into the hot gel above, stirring constantly. Whip until it is smooth.
lemon juice	6 tablespoons	Add the juice, rind, and butter to the hot filling and stir it well until the butter is dissolved and the filling is smooth. Remove it from the fire.
grated lemon rind	1 teaspoon	
butter	1½ tablespoons	

UNIT 10: SOFT-FILLED PIES AND TURNOVERS   *129*

Pour the hot filling into the baked pie shell. Be careful while pouring. Shake the pie shell gently to level the filling. *Do not allow the filling to cool before pouring it into the shell,* but be sure the filling is cool before you place the meringue topping on the pie.

If the shell is too small or too shallow to hold all the filling, leftover filling may be placed in a jar and refrigerated when cool. It can be used for a filling or garnish. It may be served as a dessert with meringue topping or whipped cream.

Meringue topping   Yield: *one 9-inch pie*

AIM   To learn how to prepare meringue topping.

THINGS YOU SHOULD KNOW   Meringue is made from egg whites. You may use the three egg whites you separated and put aside when you made the lemon filling. If you used a prepared lemon filling, separate the yolks and whites of three eggs and save the yolks in a cup to use for some other dish or dessert. Cover the yolks with waxed paper to prevent a crust from forming on them. (Some prepared mixes have the pudding powder and dried egg whites, or meringue powder, in the same package.)   *Be sure to read and follow the instructions on the package when using a prepared mix.*

THINGS TO PREPARE   Check the recipe for the materials needed.

pie shell with cool filling	**measuring spoons**	**mixing bowl**
mixing machine, if available	**measuring cups**	**spatula**
hand whip		

MERINGUE TOPPING

INGREDIENTS (*measure carefully*)		HOW TO MIX
egg whites	**3**	Place the egg whites in a dry, clean mixing bowl and whip them to a froth.
sugar	**6 tablespoons**	Blend the sugar and cornstarch together. Add them gradually to the egg whites and whip until the egg whites become firm and tend to form a peak. (The cornstarch helps to absorb some of the natural water found in the egg whites. It also helps the whites to whip better and keeps the water from "weeping" out after the pie is baked.)
cornstarch	**1 tablespoon**	

APPLYING THE MERINGUE TO THE PIE

Refer to Fig. 10-5 (page 130).

Place the meringue topping on top of the cooled lemon pie filling. Use a tablespoon, a spatula, or a table knife to spread the meringue evenly over the top of the pie. You may make a design by dipping the spoon into the meringue and lifting the spoon quickly. This

Fig. 10-5 **Meringue topping.**

   a Put the meringue on top of the pie with a spatula or knife.

   b A baked meringue-topped pie.

will form peaks and the meringue topping will bake in that design. Or you may draw the edge of the spatula gently across the meringue. You can make several designs in this fashion. You may also first cover the top of the pie evenly with half the meringue; then put the rest of the meringue into a pastry bag with a tube and use the bag to make designs on the pie. The designs you make will bake on the pie.

Bake the pie in the oven at 400° until the meringue has turned light brown. Do not try to brown the meringue quickly in a very hot oven. The inside may not bake through and the protein in the egg whites may not be cooked enough to support the meringue. The meringue will tend to shrink, or fall back, when it cools if it is not properly baked. There may also be a tendency for the meringue to "weep" (lose some of its moisture) when the pie cools because the meringue has not been baked through.

It should take about 10 minutes to bake a meringue on a 9-inch pie. Smaller pies or tartlets with a smaller amount of meringue will take less time. Remember, too, that if you have a thin covering of meringue, it will take less time to bake through than a thicker meringue topping.

CHOCOLATE CREAM PIE   Yield: *one 9-inch pie*

        AIM   To learn how to make chocolate cream pie. (Meringue topping may be used.)

THINGS YOU SHOULD KNOW   Chocolate cream pie is similar to lemon cream or

UNIT 10: SOFT-FILLED PIES AND TURNOVERS   *131*

lemon meringue pie. The filling is prepared and put into a prebaked pie shell. As you may for lemon pie varieties, you may use prepared chocolate pudding mixes that need only be cooked. There are chocolate cold-process puddings as well. With any method, however, the filling must be poured into the baked pie shell as soon as it is prepared, whether cold or hot. (Follow the directions on the package when you are using a prepared mix.) You may add ½ cup of chopped walnuts to any pudding before pouring it into the pie shell. You may also use other pudding varieties such as butterscotch, vanilla, Bavarian, and Nesselrode preparations; follow the same procedure that you use for chocolate cream pie.

THINGS TO PREPARE   Check the recipe for the necessary materials. Prepare the same equipment that you did for lemon pie filling.

CHOCOLATE PIE FILLING

INGREDIENTS (*measure carefully*)		HOW TO PREPARE
sugar	¾ cup	**Place the ingredients in the saucepan and stir to blend them.**
salt	¼ teaspoon	
cocoa (sifted)	¼ cup	
cornstarch	¼ cup	
scalded milk	2¼ cups	**Add the milk in a steady stream and mix well with the whip. Place the saucepan over a medium flame and continue to stir well until the pudding thickens and starts to boil. (You may do this in a double boiler, which will keep the filling from scorching on the bottom of the pan.) Remove the pan from the flame.**
vanilla	1 tablespoon	**Add the butter and vanilla and stir the pudding until the butter is melted and the filling is smooth.**
butter	2 teaspoons	

Pour the filling into the baked pie shell. Shake the pie shell gently to level the filling. Be careful not to spill. Allow the filling or pudding to cool before finishing the pie.

NOTE: TOPPING FOR THE PIE

Refer to Fig. 10-6a and b (page 132).
You may prepare cream pies in advance and keep them in the refrigerator until you are ready to finish them with whipped cream or cream topping. If you use the cream topping which comes in pressure cans, follow the instructions on the can. You can use the tip on the can to make decorations on the pie.

For whipped cream topping, whip 1 cup of heavy cream with 4 tablespoons of sifted confectioners' sugar. Whip the cream in a chilled bowl, by hand or in a mixing machine, until the cream turns firm and soft peaks form when the beater passes through the cream.

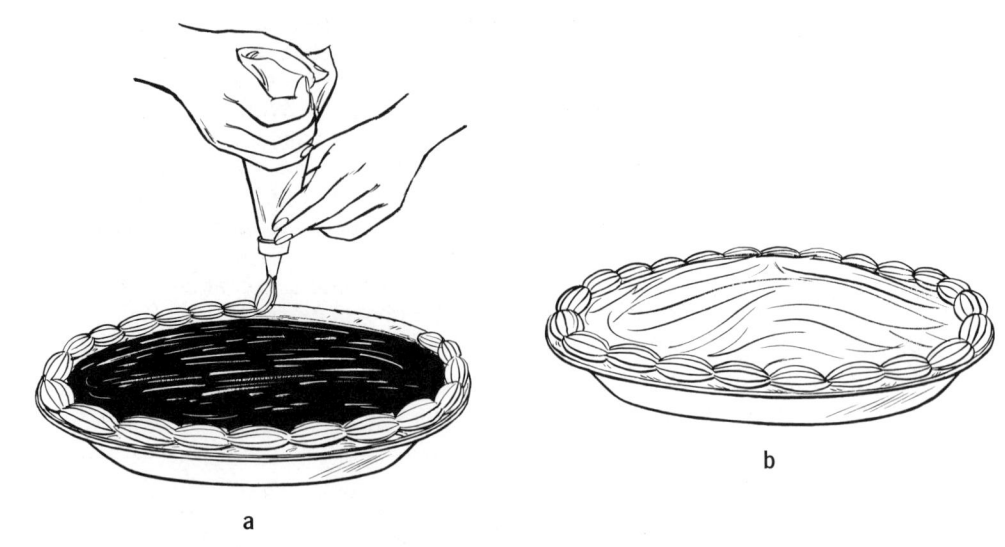

Fig. 10-6 **Whipped cream topping.**

a The whipped cream or whipped topping can be put on the cool or chilled pie with a pastry bag and tube.

b This is a sketch of a finished chocolate cream pie.

Add ½ teaspoon of vanilla to the whipped cream during the last whipping strokes. Be careful not to overwhip the cream for this will turn it to butter. (Whipped cream topping may be put on the pie as shown in Fig. 10-6.)

Chocolate cream pies must be refrigerated after they are made to keep them from spoiling. Room temperature will cause the filling and the whipped cream topping to turn sour. Spoilage or sourness is caused by an increase in the number of natural bacteria in the cream and the filling. Refrigeration retards bacteria growth.

You may also finish the chocolate pie by putting a meringue on the pie and baking it as you did the lemon meringue pie. This is often done during warm weather when whipped cream is very perishable.

PIE CRUST TURNOVERS

AIM To learn how to make pie crust turnovers.

THINGS YOU SHOULD KNOW Pie crust turnovers may be thought of as small, individual pies shaped like triangles. Turnovers are not baked in

UNIT 10: SOFT-FILLED PIES AND TURNOVERS

pie tins. The small units are placed on a larger pan and all baked at the same time. It is apparent that each turnover is made with less pie dough and contains less filling than a regular pie. However, because the turnovers are small, you can make a number of them from a pie crust dough. (The pie crust recipe for fruit-filled pies will yield about 12 turnovers cut 4 inches square before being filled and folded.) You can also use a variety of fillings to make a variety of turnovers. By making turnovers you can use up all your leftover fruit fillings. You may also have leftover pie crust dough from pies you have made, and this scrap dough can be used to make turnovers. In this way, more of the dough or filling is wasted. You will find that making turnovers can be fun, and your past experience with pies will be helpful to you.

THINGS TO PREPARE Set the oven temperature at 425°. Have ready the chilled pie crust dough. (This may be composed of scrap dough from other pies, gently kneaded into a rectangular shape.)

| fruit fillings | dusting flour | table brush | scissors | worktable |
| pastry knife or French knife | cake crumbs or bread crumbs | egg wash rolling pin | sieve for sugar simple icing | wash brush |

CHECK POINTS

1 Is the oven lighted and set at the right temperature (425°)?

2 Are all the tools and materials ready?

MAKING AND BAKING THE TURNOVERS

Refer to Fig. 10-7 (page 134).

1 Place the chilled pie crust dough on a floured part of the worktable. Flatten the dough slightly and shape into a square or rectangular shape. Check the bottom of the dough to see that there is enough flour to keep the dough from sticking when it is rolled. Dust the top of the dough and the rolling pin lightly. Roll the dough out in a rectangular shape so that it is about ⅛ inch thick. Feel the dough gently with your fingers to check the thickness. Use additional flour for dusting if the dough feels sticky. If you are going to make large-size turnovers, the dough should be about ¼ inch thick to support the larger amount of fruit filling. Small or miniature turnovers may be rolled thinner because they will contain less fruit filling.

2 Remove any excess flour from the top of the dough. For regular-size turnovers, the dough squares should be about 4 inches. You may use a ruler to measure and mark off the squares, or you may judge with your eyes where to mark off the dough. Check the marked dough to see that all the turnovers will be the same size; then cut out the squares of dough carefully with a pastry cutter (Fig. 10-7a) or French knife, following the guidelines you made.

PART FOUR: VARIETY PIES

Fig. 10-7 **Pie crust turnovers.**

    a Pastry wheel.

    b Brush the edges of rolled-out dough squares with water or egg wash; then sprinkle cake or bread crumbs in the center of each square.

    c Place the filling on the squares.

    d Fold one point of the dough square diagonally over to the opposite point and seal the edges. Slit each folded turnover with scissors or the point of a French knife.

UNIT 10: SOFT-FILLED PIES AND TURNOVERS

(You may use a large, round cookie cutter to cut out round pieces of dough. When these are filled and folded they will have a half-moon shape rather than a triangular shape. Of course, when cutting with a round cutter, you will have more scrap, or leftover, crust than you will when you cut out squares.)

3 Brush the edges of the squares of dough with water or egg wash (Fig. 10-7b) and sprinkle cake crumbs in the centers before placing the fruit filling on the dough. Be sure to place an equal amount of filling in each square. (Fig. 10-7c.) If you are using fresh or canned apples, chop the large apple slices into smaller pieces before putting them in the center of the dough squares. Sprinkle the chopped apples on each square with 1 teaspoon of cinnamon sugar to sweeten the apples.

4 Make each turnover by taking one point of the square of dough and folding it diagonally across to the other point of dough so that you form a triangle. (Fig. 10-7d.) Press the edges of the dough together to seal them, with your fingers or with the tines of a fork. The moistened edges will help to keep the dough sealed during baking.

5 Make a cut or slit in the top of each turnover, with scissors or the point of the French knife. (Fig. 10-7d.) Be careful when doing this. The cut will allow the steam which forms during baking to escape and thus prevent if from forcing the fruit filling out of the sides of the turnover. (If you prefer, you may make small holes in each turnover with a fork instead of making cuts with the scissors or knife.)

6 Place the turnovers on a lightly greased baking pan, spacing them about ½ inch apart. The turnovers may be brushed with egg wash to give them a shiny brown crust color when baked. For a dull finish, like that of the homemade variety, they may be brushed with milk or melted fat.

7 Bake the turnovers at 425° until they are golden brown. It will take about 20 to 25 minutes to bake the average-size turnover. Larger turnovers will take longer to bake than the miniature variety.

8 Remove the turnovers from the oven carefully. Check to see that they are evenly baked. The turnovers that were egg-washed before baking should be brushed with simple syrup as soon as they are taken from the oven. When cool, they may be dabbed with a little simple icing. Those turnovers that were brushed with melted fat or milk should be dusted with confectioners' sugar after they have cooled.

VOCABULARY

bacteria	foreign	puncture	rind	squash
blister	froth	(dock)	scissors	thickening
coconut	grated	prebaked	shallow	agent
custard	pudding	precooked	shell	triangle
egg white	pulpy	rectangle	shimmery	turnover
fibre	pumpkin	(review)	square	yam

Refer to *Glossary* for the explanations of words you do not know. The dictionary will be helpful for those terms not included in the *Glossary* because they are commonly used words.

PART FIVE ■■■■■□□

layer cakes & cupcakes

**INTRODUCTION:
CAKE MIXING
AND
CAKE RECIPES**

Often the most important part of the meal, or special occasion, is the layer cake or various types of cupcakes served for dessert. Most people look forward to a good dessert at the end of a meal. Often, a cupcake or slice of layer cake serves as a between-meal snack. It is natural to assume that a cook who can make good, attractive layer cakes will feel quite confident about preparing good meals in general.

There are many prepared mixes on the market which the homemaker may purchase. They contain the basic ingredients and require the addition of liquid to prepare them for baking. However, the preparation of the pans, the baking of the cakes, and the finishing of these cakes are done in almost the same way as they are for the completely homemade cake. The cook must make the same practical judgments in filling the pans, testing the cake for proper bake, and handling the cake after baking. When using prepared cake mixes, be sure to *read the directions* on the container and follow them carefully.

Many recipes for the same cake or for different types of cakes may be obtained from cookbooks, magazines, food box labels, newspapers, and other sources. Friends and neighbors share recipes. Yet one person's success in preparing a cake may be followed by another's failure even when they have both used the same recipe. *The most important part of cake making is the method of mixing or preparing the recipe.* *How* you mix the ingredients is often more important than the recipe itself. There are several basic methods of cake mixing, and it is important that you understand them before you start to make your own cakes.

Each of the basic mixing methods will be explained in this unit. Several recipes in each method of cake mixing will be presented. With experience in the use of each method of cake mixing, not only will you be able to follow any cake recipe but you will be better able to understand and use the prepared cake mixes with good results.

UNIT 11

THE CREAMING METHOD OF MIXING CAKES

AIM   To learn how to make cakes using the creaming method of mixing.

THINGS YOU SHOULD KNOW   When you are making cakes, a mixing machine is a wonderful asset. It does all the work required for combining the ingredients, not only in the creaming method, but in other mixing methods as well. Remember, however, that excellent cakes were made, and are still being made, without the help of a mixing machine. In fact, if you mix your first cakes by hand, you will develop a better sense of the timing and the stages of mixing. In this way, you will really get to know what the mixing machine can do for you. (Since these machines vary somewhat, you would do well to learn how to operate the mixer and the attachments that go with it.)

In the creaming method of mixing, sugar and shortening are the basic ingredients that are mixed in the first stage. They are first blended together to a smooth paste and then mixed further until they become soft and light. The eggs are added one at a time. Cream each egg in well before adding the next egg. The eggs, as they are creamed in, make the batter softer and lighter because of all the small air cells formed in the batter during mixing. A properly creamed batter is very soft and light. In the last stages of mixing, flour and milk are added to the creamed batter *alternately*. That is, one-third of the milk and one-third of the flour are first stirred in. Two more such additions then follow until all the flour and milk is mixed in and the batter is smooth.

A number of factors control the speed with which a batter is creamed. It is best to have the shortening and eggs at room temperature. The shortening will then be plastic and soft, making mixing easier. The shortening will blend faster with the sugar; this speeds up the absorption of air and formation of air cells. Eggs at room temperature also blend in and then cream in faster, helping the batter to develop more air cells as you mix. All these cells will expand during baking and help to leaven the cake. The cells also help to form an even grain and smooth texture. Remember, therefore, to take the shortening and eggs from the refrigerator in advance.

Adding the eggs one at a time makes it easier for the creamed sugar and shortening to absorb and hold the liquid present in the egg. (An egg is approximately 75 percent moisture.) The yolk of the egg contains a special fat which enables the batter to absorb and hold liquid, if the liquid is not added too quickly. When the amount of liquid is too great, or if the liquid is added too quickly, the fat and water separate and the batter curdles. In a curdled batter, the air cells are broken or released, and the effects of creaming are lost. The milk and flour are added alternately for this reason. The flour helps to absorb the liquid and prevents curdling or separation.

The creamed-in air cells help the baking powder or other leavening agents to raise, or leaven, the cake. Some cakes, such as old-fashioned pound cake, depend entirely on creamed-in air cells for the full leavening of the cake. The recipes that follow will show you how the creaming method of mixing is used to prepare these cakes.

YELLOW LAYER CAKE
(CREAMING METHOD)　　　Yield: *two 9-inch layers and 4 cupcakes*

This recipe may be used to prepare layer cakes, cupcakes, or other cakes baked in special pans.

THINGS TO PREPARE　Set the oven temperature at 365°. Check the recipe for the necessary ingredients. Grease and dust with flour the layer cake pans. The cupcake pans may be greased and dusted with flour or lined with paper liners. Remove the eggs and shortening from the refrigerator in advance.

UNIT 11: THE CREAMING METHOD OF MIXING CAKES

mixing bowl and spoon	measuring spoons	worktable	oven pads
rubber bowl scraper	measuring cups	flour sieve	cake rack
mixing machine			

YELLOW LAYER CAKE (CREAMING METHOD)

INGREDIENTS (*measure carefully*)		HOW TO MIX
sugar	1½ cups	Blend these ingredients together to a smooth paste. Continue to mix until soft and light. Scrape the sides of the bowl to mix all of the batter in evenly.
salt	1 teaspoon	
shortening	¾ cup	
eggs	3	Add each egg separately and cream it in well before adding the next. The batter should be soft and light.
milk	1 cup	Sift the flour and baking powder together. Add these ingredients alternately with the milk and vanilla in 3 stages, stirring gently after each addition. In the last stage, mix until the batter is smooth.
vanilla	1 teaspoon	
cake flour	2¾ cups	
baking powder	3½ teaspoons	

CHECK POINTS   Are the pans properly prepared?   Grease the pans and dust them with flour.   (Fig. 11-1*a* and *b*.)   The flour dusted in the greased layer cake pans or muffin pans provides a coating which will prevent the batter from sticking to the pan.   Excess flour should be removed by turning the pans over before filling them with batter and tapping them on the table to remove the extra flour.   Check the oven temperature.

BAKING THE CAKES

Refer to Figs. 11-1, 11-2, and 11-3 (pages 142–143) as you proceed. Fill the prepared layer cake pans or muffin pans about half full with batter.   (Fig. 11-1*c*.)   Bake the layer cakes for 25 to 30 minutes at 365°.   Smaller layer cakes and cupcakes take less time to bake. Test the cakes for proper bake or doneness after the cakes have risen and have turned a golden brown.   A gentle touch with the finger or the tip of a spoon should tell you if the cakes are done. They will spring back to a light touch.   If the mark made by the finger or spoon remains, it means that the cake is not fully baked yet.   Leave the cake in the oven until the center springs back to a gentle touch.

NOTE: THE OVEN AND BAKING   Often an oven does not have the heat equally distributed throughout.   The sides or bottom of the oven may be hotter than the center or upper shelf of the oven.   This means that baking cakes will have to be shifted from one spot in the oven to another for an even bake and crust color.   *Do not move the cakes while they are soft and shaky.   Be careful not to slam the oven door while the cakes are baking.*   Try not to place the cakes along the

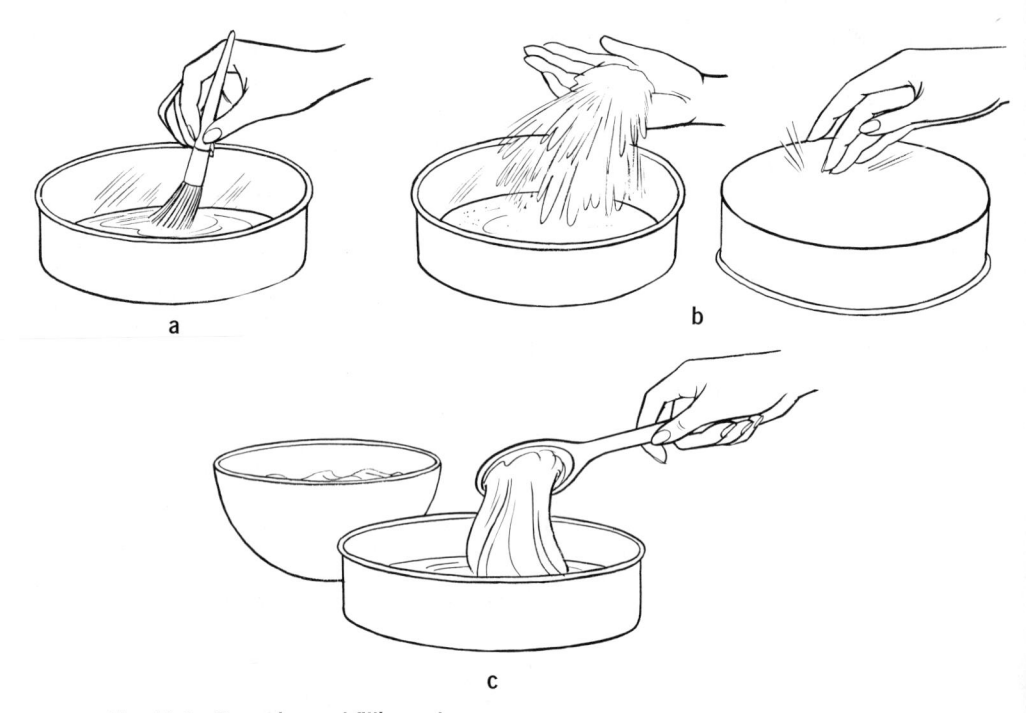

Fig. 11-1 **Preparing and filling cake pans.**

   a Grease the layer cake pan with softened shortening.

   b Dust the greased pan with all-purpose flour. Remove the excess flour by turning the pan over and tapping the pan gently against the worktable.

   c Fill the layer cake pans half full.

side walls of the oven. If the oven bottom gets very hot, set the layer pans on another baking pan before placing the cakes in the oven. (Always use oven pads when moving cakes or removing them from the oven.)

    Place the cakes taken from the oven on a rack so that air can circulate around the cake pan for faster cooling. (Fig. 11-2.) Re-

Fig. 11-2 Place the baked layers on a rack to cool.

Fig. 11-3 Cakes that stick lightly to the pan can be released by sliding a knife between the cake and the pan.

move the cakes from the pan while they are slightly warm. To remove the cake, it is best to turn the pan over on the table. When cool, the cake may be wrapped for refrigeration, placed on a plate for decoration, or left plain for use in some other preparation.

NOTE If the cake sticks to the layer cake pan, do not try to force the cake out. Return the pan to the oven to heat it slightly; then remove it from the oven and run the edge of a knife around the sides of the pan to free the cake. (Fig. 11-3.) Lift the pan and tap it gently against the table to release any part of the cake that may be sticking to the bottom of the pan. Now turn the pan over and tap the bottom again with a knife to make the cake come out of the pan. To avoid this problem of the cake sticking to the pans, be sure to grease the pan completely and evenly and then dust it with flour before adding batter. An even better method is to place a round circle of parchment or freezer paper, measured to the size of the pan, on the pan bottom after the pan has been greased. If you do this, you will not have to use dusting flour.

**CHOCOLATE
DEVIL'S FOOD
CAKE
(CREAMING METHOD)**   Yield: *two 9-inch layers*

AIM To learn how to make devil's food cake with the creaming method.

THINGS YOU SHOULD KNOW The most important ingredient in this or any other chocolate cake is the type and quality of the cocoa or chocolate

PART FIVE: LAYER CAKES & CUPCAKES

used in the recipe. The chocolate color, the taste, and the flavor of the cake all depend on the cocoa. You must understand that the cocoa needed is the pure, natural cocoa, not the kind that is used for hot chocolate or chocolate drinks in the prepared mix or package variety. These cocoa or chocolate preparations contain other ingredients, such as sugar, milk powder, and flavor, in addition to the cocoa. The same rule holds true for chocolate. Dark, natural, unsweetened chocolate should be used. Do not use milk chocolate, or chocolates that are mixed with nuts, raisins, or special flavorings. From the consumer's point of view, the natural cocoa or the unsweetened chocolate is cheaper, yet much better for the cake than the more expensive preparations.

THINGS TO PREPARE   Set the oven temperature at 365°. Prepare the pans as you did for yellow layer cake. Refer to the recipe for the necessary ingredients.

measuring spoons	flour sieve	worktable	cake rack	rubber bowl
measuring cups	mixing machine,	mixing bowl	oven pads	scraper
grease brush	if available	and spoon		

DEVIL'S FOOD CAKE (CREAMING METHOD)

INGREDIENTS (*measure carefully*)		HOW TO MIX
sugar	1¼ cups	Sift the sugar, salt, and cocoa into the mixing bowl. Add the shortening and cream it until soft and light. Scrape the bowl to be sure of complete blending and thorough mixing.
salt	1 teaspoon	
shortening	¾ cup	
cocoa (dark, natural)	⅓ cup	
baking soda	1 teaspoon	
eggs	3	Add one egg at a time; cream each egg in well before adding the next.
milk	¾ cup	Sift the flour and baking powder together. Add one-third of the flour and one-third of the milk and mix them in gently. Do this in 3 stages until all the flour and milk are mixed in; then mix until the batter is smooth and there are no lumps.
vanilla	1 teaspoon	
cake flour	2¼ cups	
baking powder	1½ teaspoons	

NOTE   If unsweetened chocolate (baking chocolate) is used in place of cocoa, melt 3 squares of chocolate in the top of a double boiler and cream the chocolate with the sugar and shortening before adding the eggs.

CHECK POINTS

1 Is the oven ready and the temperature at 365°?

2 Are the layer cake pans properly greased and dusted?

3 Are the oven pads and the cake rack ready?

Fill the layer cake pans half full. Then bake the devil's food as you did the yellow layer cake. You will have to be careful when checking

UNIT 11: THE CREAMING METHOD OF MIXING CAKES   *145*

the cake for proper bake, because chocolate cake does not show much change in crust color. It remains chocolate or brown. Wait until the cakes have been in the oven for about 25 minutes and have risen before testing them for proper bake. Smaller cakes and cupcakes take less time to bake. Use your judgment in testing. Let your eyes and your sense of touch help you.

Be careful to shift the pans in the oven if you know the oven does not bake evenly. This will not be as easily noticed with chocolate cake, but your experience with the oven will tell you whether you must move the cakes. Let the cakes cool before removing them from the pans; then place them on the cake rack to cool completely before using.

The inside or interior of a devil's food cake layer or cupcake is not quite the same as that of a chocolate layer. The devil's food has a reddish brown color instead of a deep chocolate. The grain is just a little more open than that of regular chocolate cake. These differences are due to the baking soda you used in addition to the baking powder. The soda acts upon some of the natural acid present in the cocoa and has a mild bleaching effect.

**GOLD CUPCAKES
(CREAMING METHOD)**   Yield: *15 to 18 cupcakes*

AIM   To learn how to make gold cupcakes.

THINGS YOU SHOULD KNOW   Cupcakes have many uses. They are served as regular desserts, party snacks, or special-occasion cakes, and can be made in many varieties by adding different fillings to the batter. Nuts, fruits, chocolate chips, and other special ingredients may be folded into the batter before filling the pans and baking the cupcakes. It is important to have a basic recipe for cupcakes which can be used to make many varieties. The recipe that follows is such a basic recipe.

THINGS TO PREPARE   Set the oven at 375°. Line the cupcake pans with paper liners, or grease and dust them with flour. Check the recipe for the necessary ingredients. Have ready any special additions, such as nuts and fruits, if you plan to use them. Prepare the same things as for the yellow layer cake or muffin batters.

GOLD CUPCAKES (CREAMING METHOD)

INGREDIENTS (*measure carefully*)		HOW TO MIX
sugar	¾ cup	Cream the sugar, salt, shortening, and corn
salt	1 teaspoon	syrup together until soft and light.
shortening	⅔ cup	
corn syrup	1 tablespoon	

GOLD CUPCAKES (CREAMING METHOD) (*Continued*)

INGREDIENTS (*measure carefully*)		HOW TO MIX
eggs	2	Add one egg at a time. Cream each egg in well until the batter is softer and lighter in color and texture.
egg shade (if the egg yolks are light in color)	2 drops	
cake flour (sifted)	2¼ cups	Sift the flour and baking powder together. Add the flour and milk alternately in 3 sections (one-third of each at a time), and mix the batter until it is smooth and there are no lumps.
baking powder	3 teaspoons	
milk	⅔ cup	
vanilla	1 teaspoon	

NOTE If you are going to add special fillings, such as chocolate chips, fold them in gently when the batter is almost completely mixed.

CHECK POINTS

1 Is the oven ready at the proper temperature (375°)?

2 Are the cupcake pans prepared (paper-lined or greased)?

Put the batter into the muffin (cupcake) pans in the same way as you deposited the batter for the muffins. Fill the tins half full. Try to have all the pans filled equally. Tap the muffin pan gently on the table to make the batter settle, in order to check the amount in each tin.

Bake the cupcakes at 375°. Check for proper bake, waiting until the cupcakes have risen and have developed a golden-brown crust color. Touch the center of the cupcake gently with a finger or with the end of a spoon. If the center springs back to the touch, the cupcake is considered baked. Take the cupcakes out of the oven and allow them to cool until slightly warm before removing them from the pans. Cupcakes baked in greased and dusted pans should be removed by turning the pan over on the table after the cakes are cool. Paper-lined cupcakes lift out easily. Allow the cupcakes to cool before icing or decorating them.

UNIT 12

THE BLENDING METHOD OF MIXING CAKES

AIM   To learn how to make layer cakes with the blending method of mixing.

THINGS YOU SHOULD KNOW: AN INTRODUCTION TO THE BLENDING METHOD

The blending method of mixing is one of the more recent approaches to cake mixing. It came about with the development and use of a new type of shortening called *emulsified,* or high-ratio, shortening. This is called emulsified shortening because it contains a special fat, or emulsifier, which is added to regular shortening in the final stages of manufacturing. This special cake-mixing shortening makes it possible to mix more sugar and liquid (milk) into the cake batter without causing it to curdle as it normally would in the creaming method of mixing. This special shortening also makes it possible to mix the dry ingredients (such as the flour, sugar, and salt) and the liquids (eggs and milk) together in one or two stages of mixing. The ingredients in the recipe are blended until smooth without forming as many air cells as are formed by the creaming method of mixing.

A completed batter made by the blending method has the appearance of a thick, smooth gravy, rather than the soft, plastic appearance of a creamed batter. The blending method is well

147

suited to mixing by machine. You will find that many recipes instruct you to mix for 2 or 3 minutes at special speeds. Some may advise slow speed at first, then medium speed in the final stage. You will have to use your own judgment, based upon the type of mixer you have. These recipes also blend very nicely by hand. You will have to mix longer than by machine, but the results should be as excellent as the machine-blended cakes.

Most popular shortenings are packed in 1- or 3-lb cans. The label on the can will indicate whether the shortening is the type used for the quick mixing or blending of cake batters. The label may also state that the shortening is emulsified for greater holding power of the sugar and liquids. Shortenings with these labels are the special shortenings to be used when making cakes with the blending method. You will learn to recognize the proper mixing method to use just by reading the instructions given for each cake recipe. Be careful that you select the proper shortening.

**YELLOW LAYER CAKE
(BLENDING METHOD)** Yield: *two 9-inch layers*

This recipe can be used to prepare cupcakes, square cakes in a regular baking pan, loaf cakes, and other shapes. You will note that as you first start to mix and blend the ingredients together, the paste formed will be rather thick and heavy. As you continue to mix in the eggs and milk, you will notice that the batter becomes softer because of the liquid. You will also notice that the batter takes on a lighter yellow color and becomes lighter in volume. Fill the pans only half full. They will be completely filled by the batter at the end of the baking time.

THINGS TO PREPARE Set the oven temperature at 365°. Prepare the pans you are going to use. Layer cake pans should be greased and dusted with flour, or greased and lined with parchment or freezer paper. If you are using a mixing machine, check the speeds of the machine and be sure you know how to operate it safely. Check the recipe for the necessary ingredients. Prepare the same tools and equipment you prepared for the yellow layer cake made with the creaming method of mixing.

YELLOW CAKE (BLENDING METHOD)

INGREDIENTS (*measure carefully*)		HOW TO MIX
sugar	1½ cups	Sift all the dry ingredients into the mixing bowl. Add the milk and blend well with the shortening to a smooth paste. If using a mixing machine, mix on medium speed for about 3 minutes. Scrape the sides of the bowl and blend well to remove all lumps.
salt	1 teaspoon	
special shortening	⅔ cup	
cake flour (sifted)	2¼ cups	
milk	¾ cup	

UNIT 12: THE BLENDING METHOD OF MIXING CAKES

YELLOW CAKE (BLENDING METHOD) (*Continued*)

INGREDIENTS (*measure carefully*)		HOW TO MIX
milk	¼ cup	Add the rest of the milk to the above and blend it in well until the batter is soft and smooth. If using a mixer, mix for 2 more minutes.
vanilla	1 teaspoon	
eggs	2	Add one egg at a time, blending well after each egg is added. The baking powder should be added with the second egg and blended in well. The batter should be soft and smooth, and should pour like a thick gravy.
baking powder	3 teaspoons	

CHECK POINTS

1 Is the oven ready at the proper temperature (365°)?

2 Are the pans ready for filling?

Put the batter into the pans as you did for the other layer cakes. Cupcake tins can be filled with a large spoon or soup ladle. You will note that this batter pours easily and levels off easily in the pan. You do not have to level it as you did the batter for creamed cakes.

Layer cakes will take about 25 minutes to bake. Cupcakes will take about 18 to 20 minutes to bake. Test for proper bake as you did with other cakes. The center of the cake should spring back to a gentle touch. These cakes will feel softer and springier than the creamed cakes.

NOTE: FREEZING CAKES

If the cakes are to be frozen after they are baked, allow the cakes to cool first and then wrap them well in freezer paper. You may seal the ends of the paper with tape. Label the layers with the name of the cake and the date they were baked before placing them in the freezer.

**CHOCOLATE CAKE
(BLENDING METHOD)**   Yield: *two 9-inch layers and 6 cupcakes*

AIM   To learn how to make chocolate cake with the blending method.

THINGS YOU SHOULD KNOW   If you compare this recipe with that for the devil's food made with the creaming method of mixing, you will note that special shortening is used for the blending method instead of regular shortening. You will also note that there is more leavening in this recipe than in the other. The extra leavening is needed to replace the air cells that are creamed into the batter when making the devil's food cake but are not present in the blended cake batter. Except for these two factors, there is a strong similarity between the recipes, aside from their mixing methods.

THINGS TO PREPARE   Set the oven at 365°. Prepare the same things as for the yellow layer cake.

CHOCOLATE CAKE (BLENDING METHOD)

INGREDIENTS (*measure carefully*)		HOW TO MIX
sugar	1¾ cups	Sift all the dry ingredients into the mixing bowl. Add the shortening and milk and blend well to a smooth, soft paste. Mix for 3 minutes with a mixing machine. Scrape the sides of the bowl to blend in any lumps.
salt	1 teaspoon	
cake flour (sifted)	3 cups	
cocoa (sifted)	⅓ cup	
special shortening	¾ cup	
milk	1 cup	
milk	½ cup	Add the milk and baking soda and blend to a smooth consistency. Mix for 2 minutes with a mixer.
baking soda	1 teaspoon	
eggs	3	Add the eggs, one at a time, blending each egg in well. Add the baking powder with the last egg and blend it in well. The batter should be smooth.
vanilla	1½ teaspoons	
baking powder	2½ teaspoons	

Pour the batter into the prepared pans. Fill the pans half full, as you did for the yellow layer cake made with the blending method. Bake the cakes carefully, remembering that chocolate cake remains chocolate in color and does not develop a light brown crust like the yellow layer cake. When the cakes have risen and have been in the oven for the right amount of time (use the same time as you did with the yellow cake batter), test them for proper bake. Allow the cakes to cool until slightly warm before removing them from the pans. (These cakes may be prepared for the freezer in the same way as you would the yellow layers.)

WHITE CAKE (BLENDING METHOD)

Yield: *two 9-inch layers*

AIM   To learn how to make white layer cake with the blending method.

THINGS YOU SHOULD KNOW   The recipe for this cake calls for egg whites. (The efficient homemaker will use up here any egg whites that were left over when the egg yolks were used in preparing other foods.) If you have no leftover egg whites, separate the yolks and whites from fresh eggs. Avoid getting specks of yolk in the whites as you are separating them. The egg yolks should be placed in a glass dish or cup and

UNIT 12: THE BLENDING METHOD OF MIXING CAKES

covered with waxed paper to prevent a crust from forming on the yolks. They should be refrigerated if they will not be used immediately.

THINGS TO PREPARE Set the oven at 365°. Prepare the pans as you did for the yellow or chocolate layers. Check the recipe for the necessary ingredients. Prepare the same tools and equipment as you did for the yellow layer cake.

NOTE: DIFFERENT FLAVORS If you do not have almond flavor, you may substitute orange or lemon flavor. Blend either of these flavors with the vanilla flavoring.

WHITE CAKE (BLENDING METHOD)

INGREDIENTS (*measure carefully*)		HOW TO MIX
sugar	1½ cups	Sift the dry ingredients into the mixing bowl. Add the shortening and milk and blend well to a smooth paste. Mix for 3 minutes by machine. Scrape the sides of the bowl to remove lumps.
salt	1 teaspoon	
cake flour (sifted)	2½ cups	
special shortening	¾ cup	
milk	½ cup	
milk	½ cup	Add the milk and flavors and blend well until the batter is soft and smooth. Mix for 2 minutes by machine. Scrape the sides of the bowl to blend in any lumps.
vanilla	1 teaspoon	
almond flavor	½ teaspoon	
egg whites	1 cup	Use the separated whites of about 6 eggs. (It will take about 8 small eggs to make 1 cup of whites.) Add the egg whites in 3 stages and blend in well after each addition. Add the baking powder with the last of the egg whites. Be sure the batter is blended well and that there are no lumps. Use the rubber scraper to scrape the sides of the bowl to remove and blend in any possible lumps.
baking powder	3 teaspoons	

CHECK POINTS

1 Is the oven ready and at the proper temperature (365°)?

2 Are the pans properly greased or lined with paper?

Fill the pans about half full. Pour the batter in carefully. Use a large mixing spoon or soup ladle to fill the cupcake pans with the batter.

White cakes bake with a light brown crust color. Check for proper bake after the batter has risen and the cakes have been in the oven for the proper length of time.

VOCABULARY

approach	helpful	separation	*Review*	
asset	liquid	shortening	alternately	curdle
content	mass	texture	consistency	grain
emulsified	plastic	unsweetened	creaming	shapes

Refer to *Glossary* for the explanations of words you do not know. The dictionary will be helpful for those terms not included in the *Glossary*.

UNIT 13

THE WHIPPING METHOD OF MIXING CAKES

AIM   To understand the principles of the whipping method of cake mixing.

THINGS YOU SHOULD KNOW: AN INTRODUCTION TO THE WHIPPING METHOD
The term *whipping* refers to the whipping of eggs. The eggs may be fresh or frozen; they may be in the form of whole eggs, egg yolks, or egg whites. By whipping the eggs, we incorporate air into them and the eggs become light and fluffy. The air cells formed in the batter this way expand during baking and give the cake a sponge-like appearance. Also, the eggs themselves naturally expand during baking and help to raise, or leaven, the cake batter. A sponge cake made with enough eggs and properly whipped will completely leaven itself without the use of baking powder. However, a sponge or whipped type of cake made with a large percentage of eggs can be quite expensive. Most whipped cakes, particularly those made with whole eggs, have some water or milk in the recipe to help dissolve the sugar and moisten the flour. To leaven this extra liquid, baking powder is added to the recipe. All of these things together (the eggs, the baking powder, and the whipping method) cause these cakes to be light and spongy. These cakes are different from those made by the creaming or blending methods of mixing.

SPECIAL THINGS YOU SHOULD KNOW ABOUT CAKES MADE BY THE WHIPPING METHOD

1. Fresh, whole eggs whip better and faster when they are at room temperature, or slightly warmer. Therefore, eggs should be taken from the refrigerator in advance if you plan to make a cake with the whipped method. On the other hand, egg whites whip better when they are cool, even chilled.

2. If you should use frozen eggs, allow the eggs to defrost at room temperature before you whip them. You may defrost them faster by placing the frozen eggs in a cool water bath. The cool water will circulate around the frozen eggs and help defrost them faster. *Do not defrost frozen eggs by placing them in hot water.*

3. The mixing bowl and whip must be free from grease. Greasy or fatty substances cut through the air cells after the eggs have been whipped, or partially whipped, and cause the entire structure to fall back. Double-check the mixing bowl and the whip to make sure they are clean. It is best to rinse them in hot water to dissolve any greasy particles.

4. Although a mixing machine is best for whipped cake batters, mixing or whipping by hand is equally effective. It may be advisable to heat the eggs and sugar until they are slightly warmer than body temperature. This should be done in a double boiler, not over a direct flame. Stirring the mixture over the hot water bath will dissolve the sugar faster and soften the egg yolks, making it easier to whip the batter by hand. This is especially effective for sponge cakes.

5. The flour is sifted and then carefully folded into the cake batter in several stages. Use an overhand motion so that you fold the flour in without forcing air cells out of the batter.

6. Pans for whipped cake batters should be prepared as directed in the recipe. A layer cake pan for a sponge cake is usually prepared by greasing the pan and then dusting it with flour. The excess flour is removed by tapping the pan against the table. Some pans, such as loaf pans for sponge cake loaves, are usually lined with parchment paper as you did when you made loaf-type quick breads. Still other pans are rinsed with cool water after they have been cleaned and are allowed to remain moist. Pans for angel cake are prepared in this manner.

7. Whipped cake batters should be put into the prepared pans as soon as the batter is ready. After the pans have been filled, they should be placed into the oven to be baked immediately. If the batter is allowed to stand, the air cells in the batter tend to break down, there is a loss of volume, and the cakes will be a bit heavy.

8. One of the most important factors in whipping egg batters is to know when the batter has been whipped enough. The eggs, sugar, salt—

UNIT 13: THE WHIPPING METHOD OF MIXING CAKES 155

and perhaps syrup—are whipped until the wire whip of the mixing machine or the hand whip leaves marks through the batter that look like creases. These creases show and then gradually blend into the batter again. At this point, the batter is quite thick and foamy.

Egg whites are whipped until they form a wet peak. That is, the beater will lift the beaten whites and the peaks formed will tend to fold over slightly. The batter will also have a shine, or lustre. This is called beating to a wet peak. When you made the meringue, you whipped the egg whites a little longer to a stiff, almost dry, peak.

9 After whipped cakes are baked, they should be turned over on a sugar-dusted cloth to cool. You may turn them onto a regular wire rack or roasting rack; however, the wires will leave marks in the crust of the cake. Turning them onto a cloth will allow the cake to settle evenly, and any peaks on the cake will flatten out. If the cake tends to stick to the pan, tap it lightly against the table and pull the edges gently away from the sides of the pan with a knife. Angel cakes should be turned over as soon as they are removed from the oven. Angel cake pans have a higher center tube and will rest on the tube rather than on the cloth. When the angel cakes are cool, tap the pan firmly against the table and the cakes will come out of the pan, leaving a light crust on the inside of the pan. (Angel cake pans should be soaked in water as soon as the cakes are removed to make the final washing of the pans easy.)

SPONGE CAKE BATTER (WHIPPING METHOD)

Yield: *four 8-inch layers or two 8- by 12-inch flat pans for jelly rolls*

AIM   To learn how to make sponge cake batter for layers and jelly roll.

THINGS YOU SHOULD KNOW   Refer to *Introduction to the Whipping Method* for information regarding sponge cake batters. You will be told about any special things as you proceed with the mixing and baking of the cakes.

THINGS TO PREPARE

mixing machine, if available	hand whip	measuring cups	sugared cloth	cake rack
mixing bowl	worktable	measuring spoons	parchment paper	flour sieve
	spatula			

Set the oven temperature at 365° to 370° for sponge cake layers. Set it at 400° for jelly rolls. Be sure the oven is heated before you complete the mixing. Layer cake pans and pans for jelly rolls may be greased and dusted with flour, or they may be greased and lined with parchment paper. Check the recipe for the necessary ingredients. Remove the eggs from the refrigerator in advance.

SPONGE CAKE

INGREDIENTS (*measure carefully*)		HOW TO MIX
sugar	1 cup	Whip the eggs to a froth in the mixing machine. Add the sugar, salt, and syrup and beat to a thick, foamy batter in which the creases made by the whip will show. If whipping by hand, warm the eggs and sugar first in a double boiler.
salt	½ teaspoon	
eggs	5	
corn syrup	1 tablespoon	
hot water	4 tablespoons	Add the water and rind to the above batter and stir in gently. Let the machine run at medium speed at this point.
lemon rind	1 teaspoon	
cake flour (sifted)	2 cups	Sift the flour and baking powder together. Add in 3 stages, folding it in gently with an overhand motion. *Be sure all the flour is folded in and there are no lumps.*
baking powder	1 teaspoon	

CHECK POINTS

1 Is the oven heated to the proper temperature?

2 Are the pans prepared for the batter?

3 Has the batter been whipped properly?

Put the batter into the prepared pans. Fill the layer cake pans half full. Tap them gently on the table to level the batter and to remove any large air pockets. Place the layers in the oven and bake them at 365° to 370° until the cakes have risen and the crust has turned light golden brown. Touch the center of the layer cake gently with a finger or the tip of a fork. If the cake springs back to the touch, it is baked. Remove the pans from the oven, allow the cakes to cool slightly, and turn them upside down on a cloth or cake rack to remove the cakes from the pan.

For sponge cake loaves, line the pans with parchment paper liners. (Refer to Fig. 3-2.) Bake the loaves at 355° to 360°. Loaf cakes take longer to bake. The average sponge cake layer takes about 25 minutes to bake, and the loaf cake takes 35 to 40 minutes. Test the loaf cake for proper bake as you did the layer cake. If the oven has too much heat at the bottom, the cake pans may be placed on a flat pan and then put into the oven. The double pan will prevent the bottom of the cake from burning or browning too much.

JELLY ROLL

To make jelly roll from the sponge cake batter, add 3 extra tablespoons of hot water to the batter with the lemon rind. This will make the batter softer and easier to spread in the baking pans.

UNIT 13: THE WHIPPING METHOD OF MIXING CAKES   157

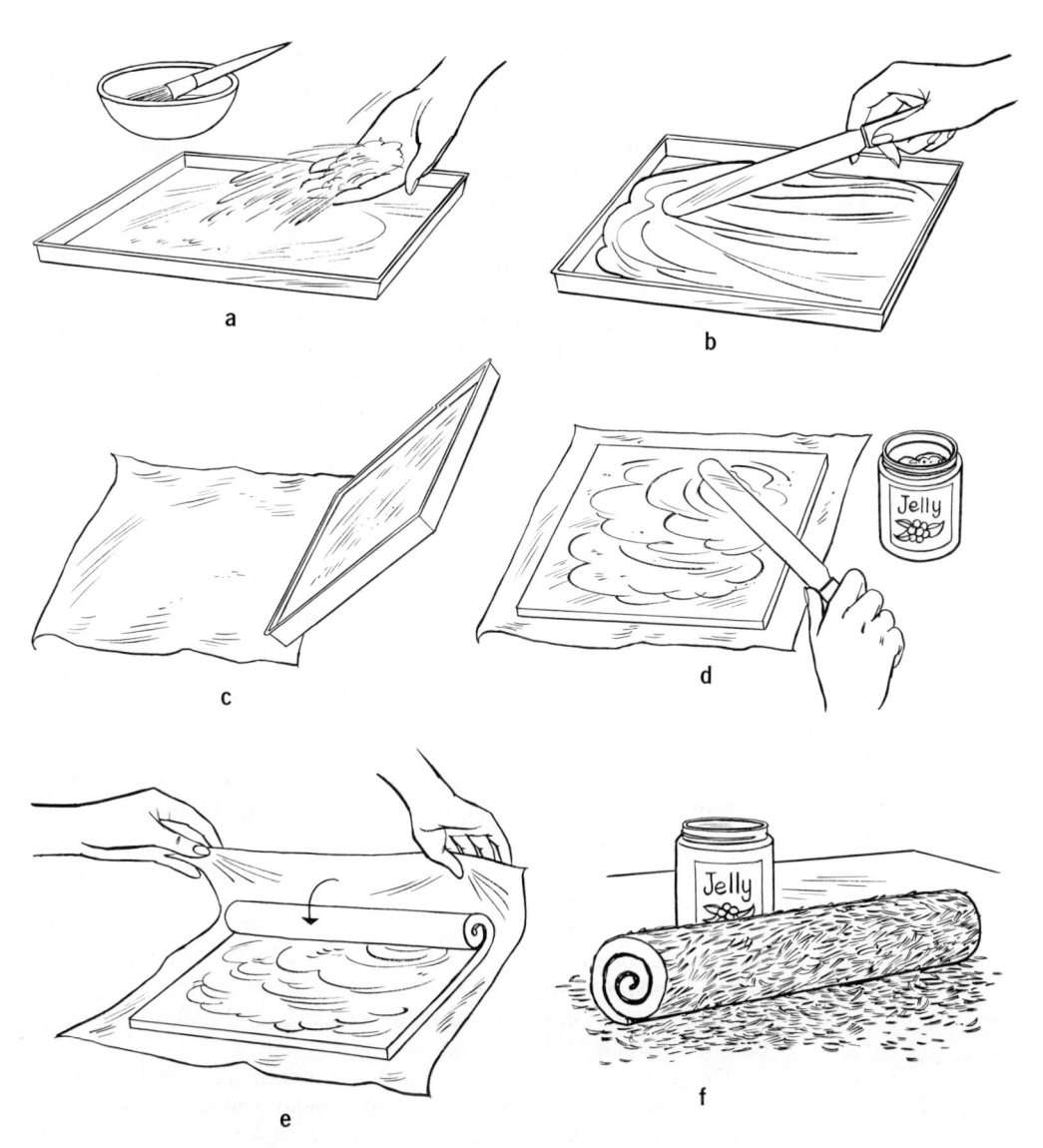

Fig. 13-1 **Jelly roll.**

    a Grease the baking pan for the jelly roll with soft shortening and then dust it with flour.

    b Spread the sponge batter evenly in the pan.

    c Turn the baked jelly roll cake onto a flour-dusted cloth while the cake is still quite warm.   Roll up loosely in the cloth.

    d After cooling, unroll and spread a thin coating of jelly over the sheet cake.

    e Roll the jelly-coated sheet cake up in the floured cloth to form a tight roll.

    f Cover the top of the jelly roll with jelly and roll it in coconut.

The flat baking pans (8 by 12 inches) should be greased and then dusted with flour. (Fig. 13-1*a*.) Remove the excess flour by tapping the pan on the table. (The pans may be greased and lined with parchment paper.) Put the batter into the pans and spread it out evenly with a spatula or knife. (Fig. 13-1*b*.) Be sure the batter is of even thickness. Very thin spots will overbake or burn while the thicker parts remain unbaked or raw. Try to spread the batter with as few strokes as possible, however, to avoid toughening the batter.

Jelly rolls are baked at a higher oven temperature (400°) than the sponge cake. The thin sponge sheet should bake quickly without drying out. It should take about 10 minutes; if overbaked, it will dry. This will cause the cake to crack when it is rolled. Remove the cake from the oven at the just-done stage (when it has a light brown crust and springs back to the touch). Carefully turn the pan over onto a floured cloth (Fig. 13-1*c*) or sheet of parchment paper. The flour will absorb moisture as the cake cools and keep it from sticking to the cloth or paper. If the cake is allowed to cool slightly before turning, sugar may be dusted on the cloth (or parchment paper) in place of the flour. After turning it over, keep the pan on top of the sheet cake for about 10 minutes, and then tap the pan lightly to be sure the cake is free of the pan. Remove the pan and gently roll the cake up loosely in the cloth or paper. Allow the sheet cake that has been rolled up to cool completely before unrolling it again.

FINISHING THE JELLY ROLL   While the jelly roll is cooling, choose the jelly or jam filling you will use and put it into a soup bowl. Mix it until the jelly is smooth and there are no lumps. Unroll the sheet cake gently and spread the jelly or jam over the entire surface of the cake. (Fig. 13-1*d*.) Be sure to spread the jelly evenly. A thin layer of jam or jelly is all that is necessary; excess jelly will run after the cake is cut and may make the cake too sweet. Roll the jelly roll up (Fig. 13-1*e*) just as you rolled up the dough when you made the cinnamon buns. The roll should be tight. Use the cloth or paper to help you roll the cake. Wrap the cake in the paper or cloth, and chill the jelly roll before finishing or decorating it.

The jelly roll may be dusted with confectioners' sugar. The roll may be spread on top with a thin covering of the same jelly or jam that was used for the filling, then rolled in a flat pan containing sweetened, shredded coconut. (Fig. 13-1*f*.) The roll may be sprinkled with other toppings such as chocolate sprinkles or chopped nuts. Slice the jelly roll and serve.

**ANGEL CAKE
(WHIPPING METHOD)**   Yield: *one 9-inch tube pan*

AIM   To learn how to make angel cake.

THINGS YOU SHOULD KNOW   The basic foundation of angel cake is egg whites. In

UNIT 13: THE WHIPPING METHOD OF MIXING CAKES

Introduction to the Whipping Method you were told that egg whites whip best when they are cool. It is advisable to separate the whites from eggs that have just been removed from the refrigerator. This will not only give you egg whites that are cool but also separating the eggs is much easier when the eggs are chilled. Of course, if you have egg whites set aside because you used the yolks for other dishes, use those whites.

Cream of tartar acts upon the egg whites to soften, or condition, the protein and alkaline content, and helps the whites whip to a softer consistency. Cream of tartar also has a whitening or bleaching effect that gives the interior of the cake a whiter appearance.

The angel cake pan is round with a metal tube in the center which is higher than the sides of the pan. The pan is rinsed out and left damp before the batter is poured into it. This makes the cake batter stick to the sides after the cake has risen, and the cake is thus supported until its structure is set. After the cake is baked, the pan is turned over. It rests on the tube and the surface of the cake does not touch anything while the cake is inverted.

THINGS TO PREPARE Set the oven temperature at 360°. Prepare the pan by washing it, rinsing it, and leaving it moist. The droplets of water will help the cake stick to the sides of the pan. Check the recipe for the necessary ingredients.

| measuring spoons | mixing machine | hand beater | worktable |
| measuring cups | mixing bowl | sieve | cake rack |

ANGEL CAKE

INGREDIENTS (*measure carefully*)		HOW TO MIX
egg whites	1 cup	Be sure the mixing bowl is free from grease. Whip the egg whites to a light froth.
sugar	¾ cup	Blend the sugar, salt, and cream of tartar together. Add to the egg whites in 3 stages, whipping well after each stage. Whip the whites to a wet peak.
salt	¼ teaspoon	
cream of tartar	¼ teaspoon	
vanilla	½ teaspoon	Stir the flavors gently into the whipped egg whites.
almond flavor	¼ teaspoon	
cake flour (sifted)	¾ cup	Sift the sugar and flour together twice to blend them well. Add them to the whipped batter in 3 stages, folding them in gently. Be sure there are no lumps of beaten egg whites or flour.
sugar	1 cup	

CHECK POINTS

1 Is the oven ready at the proper temperature?

2 Are the pans ready and still moist? If not, rinse them again, leaving drops of water on the sides.

3 Is the batter whipped to a wet peak?

Put the batter into the prepared pan, filling it about three-quarters full. Spread the batter in the pan evenly, and tap the pan gently on the table to remove any large air pockets. A table knife may be run through the batter after it is in the pan to break any large air pockets without breaking the smaller air cells which were whipped into the batter during mixing. If large air pockets remain, they will cause large holes in the baked cake.

Place the cake into the oven and bake it for about 30 minutes until the crust is golden brown and the cake feels spongy to a gentle touch. Remove the cake from the oven and turn it upside down so that the cake is balanced on the center tube. Allow the cake to cool completely; then tap the pan against the table. The cake will fall out, leaving a crust in the pan.

The angel cake may be finished, or garnished, by dusting it with confectioners' sugar before cutting and serving it. The cake may be chilled, then covered with a thin film of jelly or jam. Next, cover the jam or jelly with a thin coating of simple icing, which will run over the top and sides. Place the cake on a rack so that the icing can drain. Allow the icing to dry before cutting the cake.

OLD-FASHIONED POUND CAKE (CREAMING AND WHIPPING METHOD) Yield: *2 loaf cakes*

This cake is made by combining the creaming and whipping methods.

AIM To learn how to make old-fashioned pound cake.

THINGS YOU SHOULD KNOW As you read the recipe, you will note that the shortening and other fats are *creamed* and the eggs and sugar are *whipped*. The two are then combined to complete the cake batter. You will also note that there is no leavening or baking powder in this recipe. The leavening is supplied by the air cells that are creamed into the batter and those that are whipped into the batter.

THINGS TO PREPARE Set the oven temperature at 345°. Prepare the pans with paper pan liners. (Refer to Fig. 3-2.) If you are going to make a marbled type of cake, melt the chocolate (3 squares of sweet chocolate) in advance so it is ready to be folded into the batter. Prepare the tools and equipment that you would for creamed and whipped cakes. Check the recipe for the necessary materials.

UNIT 13: THE WHIPPING METHOD OF MIXING CAKES   *161*

OLD-FASHIONED POUND CAKE

INGREDIENTS (*measure carefully*)		HOW TO MIX
shortening	¾ cup	Blend the butter and shortening together until they are plastic and no lumps of fat remain.
butter or margarine	¾ cup	
all-purpose flour (sifted)	1¼ cups	Sift the flours together. Add to the fat, and cream together until soft and light.
cake flour (sifted)	1¾ cups	
sugar	1½ cups	Whip the eggs, sugar, and salt, as you did for sponge cake. Fold the vanilla in. Add the whipped eggs to the creamed flour and fat and fold them in gently until the batter is smooth.
salt	1 teaspoon	
eggs	6	
vanilla	1½ teaspoons	

Fill the paper-lined loaf pans half full with the batter. (Melted chocolate may be striped through the batter while it is in the pans, or the chocolate may be mixed into part of the batter and then marbled through the rest of the cake.) It takes about 45 to 50 minutes to bake the cake.

VOCABULARY

air pockets	enable	invert	spatula	whipping
alkaline	fatty	lustre	spread	
bleaching	foam	marbled	substance	*Review*
completely	formation	procedure	supplement	expand
crease	immediately	rinsed	wet peak	particles

Refer to *Glossary* for an explanation of any words you do not know. The dictionary will be helpful for those terms not included in the *Glossary* because the term is a frequently used word.

UNIT **14**

VARIETY FROSTINGS

AIM To learn how to make a variety of frostings or icings, and to learn how to decorate cupcakes and layer cakes with the prepared frostings.

THINGS YOU SHOULD KNOW When you think of a cupcake or layer cake, you usually have a picture in your mind of a cake covered with frosting, or icing. You may also be thinking of garnishes, such as nuts, fruits, sprinkles, and other decorations, which make the frosted cake look attractive. In addition to the basic frostings used to decorate cakes, there are many colors and flavors which may be added to vary them. You will soon be able to acquire the skill and understanding which will enable you to combine appropriate frostings with the cakes you make or the desserts you prepare.

There are three basic types of frostings or icings: (1) the flat or simple type of frosting; (2) the fluffy or creamed type of frosting; and (3) combination icings, for which several mixing methods and sets of preparations may be used.

Flat or simple frostings are those which are made by mixing sifted confectioners' sugar with water, syrup, and flavor. Colors and

UNIT 14: VARIETY FROSTINGS

flavors may be added to the basic icing as desired. You will find the recipe for this frosting listed with the other frosting recipes; it includes instructions for the storage and use of leftover frosting of this type.

Creamed or fudge-type frostings combine confectioners' sugar and shortening as basic ingredients; they are either blended or creamed, depending upon the specific frosting and its use. For example, a fudge icing requires the blending method of mixing. The fluffy, or creamed, type requires the creaming method of mixing; that is, the sugar and shortening are first blended, then creamed with the other ingredients in the recipe. Recipes for these frostings are listed with the other frosting recipes, and the instructions tell you how they may be used to best advantage.

Combination frostings are made by mixing a simple or flat-type icing with a creamed-type frosting. For example, a flat icing may be mixed with buttercream. This will increase the frosting's sweetening effect. Whipped egg whites and sugar are combined with a boiled syrup to form an icing that tastes like marshmallows. In some special preparations, the creamed shortening and part of the sugar are blended with whipped egg whites and sugar for a French type of fluffy buttercream.

After the basic type of frosting has been prepared, you may color it with an approved food coloring. Flavors of your choice may be added to improve the icing. For example, you may make a lemon frosting by adding a few drops of yellow color and lemon flavor to the basic frosting. This same method may be adapted for preparing orange and other fruit-type frostings. Chopped fruits may be added to this frosting before spreading it on the cake; the pieces of fruit will show in the frosting and add a natural, homemade look to the cake.

Frostings are often used as fillings for cakes. Layer cakes may be filled with the same frosting that is used for the top and sides of the cake, or the frosting may be combined with jelly or jam to make a special combination filling. Thus the frosting not only helps to hold layer cakes together but also adds flavor and greater variety to them.

FLAT OR SIMPLE FROSTING

Yield: *enough for two 9-inch layers or 18 to 24 cupcakes*

THINGS TO PREPARE Check the recipe for the necessary ingredients.

| measuring cups | double boiler | worktable | measuring spoons | cakes to be iced |
| sieve | mixing spoon | saucepan | cake pan or rack | or frosted |

FLAT OR SIMPLE FROSTING

INGREDIENTS (*measure carefully*)		HOW TO PREPARE
confectioner's sugar (sifted)	3½ cups (a 1-lb box)	Place the sugar, syrup, vanilla, and hot water in the saucepan and blend to a smooth, thick paste. Place this in the top of a double boiler and warm to about 110° (slightly warmer than body temperature).
hot water	⅓ cup (variable)	
corn syrup or pancake syrup	1 tablespoon	
vanilla	1 teaspoon	

SPECIAL NOTES ABOUT FLAT OR SIMPLE FROSTING   If the icing is too soft and runny, add a small amount of sifted confectioners' sugar to thicken it. Add about 3 or 4 tablespoons, and more if needed. (Use your judgment when adding the sugar.)   This should be done before the frosting is warmed in the double boiler.

If the frosting is too thick, add 1 tablespoon of hot water to soften it, stirring the water in well.   Check the thickness or consistency of the frosting, adding more water if necessary.   Remember that the icing will be further softened when it is warmed in the double boiler.

If you wish to add fruit colors or other certified colors, add them after the frosting has been warmed and is ready for use.   Add the color carefully, one drop at a time, because simple frosting colors very easily and quickly.

If the icing must stand a while before it can be used, keep it warm in the double boiler over a very low heat.   *Do not permit the frosting to become hot or heat the icing over a direct flame.*   This frosting, when overheated, loses its gloss or shine after it is put on the cake and the icing cools.   Frosting which has been overheated tends to dry very quickly when spread on the cake, often becoming flaky. The flakiness will cause the icing to peel off the cake surface.

Leftover simple frosting should be kept in a cup or jar and covered with a teaspoon of water to prevent a crust from forming on the surface.   The frosting may then be stored in the refrigerator for use at some later time.

WHITE FUDGE FROSTING   Yield: *enough for two 9-inch layer cakes or 16 to 20 cupcakes*

THINGS TO PREPARE   Check the recipe for necessary ingredients.   Prepare the same things as for the simple frosting.

THINGS YOU SHOULD KNOW   The shortening used for this frosting should be the special, or emulsified, type of shortening such as that used for cakes made with the blending method of mixing.   This shortening will

UNIT 14: VARIETY FROSTINGS *165*

hold the water in the frosting and will allow the frosting to dry and form a thin crust on top.

WHITE FUDGE FROSTING

INGREDIENTS (*measure carefully*)		HOW TO PREPARE
confectioners' sugar (sifted)	4 cups (approximately 1 box)	Blend the sugar, salt, and shortening together to a smooth paste. Be sure there are no lumps.
salt	pinch	
special shortening	½ cup	
hot water	⅓ cup	Add the water and vanilla and blend the frosting smooth. At this point, it is ready to use. If the icing must stand for a while, keep it in a double boiler over a very low flame to prevent the icing from overheating.
vanilla	1 teaspoon	

SPECIAL NOTES ABOUT WHITE FUDGE FROSTING   If the fudge frosting is too soft, add a few tablespoons of sifted confectioners' sugar to thicken it. Do this before you warm it. This icing should be put on the cake while it is still warm. When the icing cools, it will form a light crust on the surface and be tender and moist inside. Food coloring and flavoring may be added to the white fudge frosting for variety or to meet a need for some special type of cake you are making and decorating. Leftover frosting should be placed in a cup or jar and covered with a teaspoon of water to prevent a crust formation. Store the leftover frosting in the refrigerator.

CHOCOLATE FUDGE FROSTING

Yield: *enough for two 9-inch layers or 15 to 18 cupcakes*

THINGS TO PREPARE   Check the recipe for the necessary ingredients. Have the cakes ready to be frosted. Prepare the same equipment as you did for the simple or flat type of frosting.

CHOCOLATE FUDGE FROSTING

INGREDIENTS (*measure carefully*)		HOW TO PREPARE
confectioners' sugar (sifted)	3 cups	Place all the ingredients in the saucepan and mix to a smooth paste.
salt	pinch	
corn syrup	1 tablespoon	
cocoa (dark, natural) (3 chocolate squares, melted, may replace the cocoa)	¼ cup	
hot water	¼ cup	

CHOCOLATE FUDGE FROSTING (*Continued*)

INGREDIENTS (*measure carefully*)		HOW TO MIX
melted shortening	3 tablespoons	Add the melted shortening and vanilla to the above paste and blend smooth. Put the frosting into the double boiler and heat until the frosting is warm (about 110°). You will note that the frosting develops a shine or gloss as it is warmed. The fudge should be applied to the cake while it is still warm. As the frosting cools, it will become thick, making it hard to spread the fudge when cool. This frosting will form a light crust when it cools and remain tender inside.
vanilla	1 teaspoon	

BUTTERCREAM FROSTING

Yield: *enough to cover or decorate two 9-inch layers*

THINGS YOU SHOULD KNOW This frosting is a basic buttercream. It may be colored with approved fruit or certified colorings. Additional flavors may be added to it. Melted chocolate may be used in it for a chocolate buttercream frosting. Jams, jellies, and fruit pieces may be mixed with it for even greater variety. This is the frosting which is most often used as the basic icing for layer cakes which are to be decorated for special occasions. You will note that the recipe asks you to use both regular shortening and the special shortening for cakes made with the blending method. The combination of shortenings helps to cream the frosting as well as to hold the water or egg whites without letting the frosting curdle. You may use *sweet* butter to replace some of the regular shortening.

BUTTERCREAM FROSTING

INGREDIENTS (*measure carefully*)		HOW TO PREPARE
confectioners' sugar (sifted)	3 cups	Blend all the ingredients together to make a smooth paste.
salt	pinch	
hot water	¼ cup	
regular shortening	¾ cup	Blend the shortening well into the above paste. Continue to mix and cream until it is soft and light.
special shortening	¾ cup	

BUTTERCREAM FROSTING (*Continued*)

INGREDIENTS (*measure carefully*)		HOW TO MIX
egg white, or	1	Add the egg white or the water to the above mixture and cream in well. Add the vanilla and blend. Additional colors and flavors may be added at this time.
hot water	2 tablespoons	
vanilla	1 teaspoon	

Store the buttercream in a large jar or bowl. Cover the frosting with a light plastic wrap to prevent a crust from forming on it. In hot weather, store the frosting in the refrigerator.

UNIT 15

FINISHING AND DECORATING CUPCAKES

INTRODUCTION

Now that you have prepared the cakes you plan to serve, you are going to use the icing or frosting you have made to decorate them. *Before you do so, read the information in this unit.* (Look at Figs. 15 and 16 while you are working. Doing so will be very helpful to you.) Various cakes will be discussed in terms of the different ways they can be finished or decorated. You should know the following basic rules when decorating cakes:

1 Cakes should be cool before you apply the icing. This is especially important when you are decorating with whipped cream or other frostings made with butter or milk. A warm cake may cause the butter to melt or turn rancid. The milk in the frosting may turn sour. Frostings made with perishable ingredients should be kept cool before and after they are put on a cake.

2 When you are cutting cakes to fill them or to apply toppings, cut the cakes evenly. It is best to use a saw knife or a knife with a serrated edge. Cut the cake with a sawing motion. Be careful and observe safety practices when using a knife.

UNIT 15: FINISHING AND DECORATING CUPCAKES   *169*

3 It is good practice to have the cakes ready so that the frosting may be applied without delay when it is done. As we mentioned in explaining the preparation of frostings, most frostings should be applied while they are still warm. Whipped cream should be applied almost immediately after it is ready.

4 Use enough frosting to decorate or ice the cake properly so that the finished cake looks inviting. The cake should appeal to the eye. Not enough icing will give the cake a skimpy appearance; too much icing will make it look heavy and overly sweet. It is good practice to refrigerate leftover icing rather than pile it on the cake.

5 Work cleanly and neatly. The finished, decorated cake will reflect how well you have worked.

AIM   To learn how to decorate variety cupcakes.

THINGS YOU SHOULD KNOW   Cupcakes can be made from many different recipes. You know that cupcakes can be baked in muffin pans that are lined with special cupcake liners and can also be baked in muffin pans which have been greased and dusted with flour. The important thing to remember is that the shape of the muffin pan gives the cupcake its basic form, and you decorate around the form. The method you use to decorate the cupcake often gives the cupcake its name.

**FROSTING
PAPER-LINED
CUPCAKES
WITH SIMPLE FROSTING**

Be sure the cupcakes are cool and the simple frosting is ready. (Refer to the recipe and procedure for making the frosting.) Stir the icing with a mixing spoon to remove any possible skin which may have formed on the surface. Grasp the cupcake at its base and dip the top of the cake into the warm frosting just enough to make the frosting stick to the top surface of the cupcake. (Fig. 15-1*a*.) Lift the cupcake to see that the icing covers the entire surface. If it does not, dip the cake gently again. Do not permit the paper liner to go into the frosting. Lift the cupcake so that the excess icing drips off; then quickly wipe any excess icing from the sides with one finger or a table knife. (Fig. 15-1*b*.) Return excess icing to the pan. (The icing may also be spread across the top of the cupcake with a teaspoon or table knife.) If the icing should become thick and hard to use, warm it again in the double boiler. If necessary, add a teaspoon of syrup or hot water to soften the icing. Scrape any droplets of frosting from the pan and return them to the saucepan.

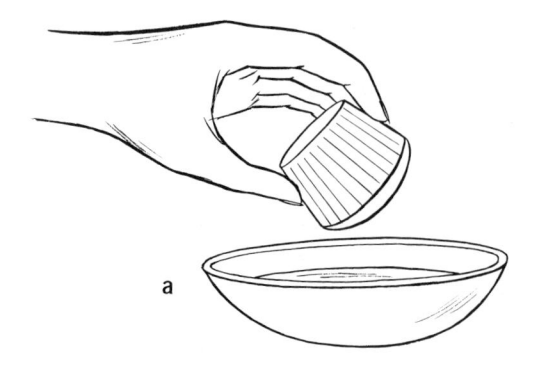

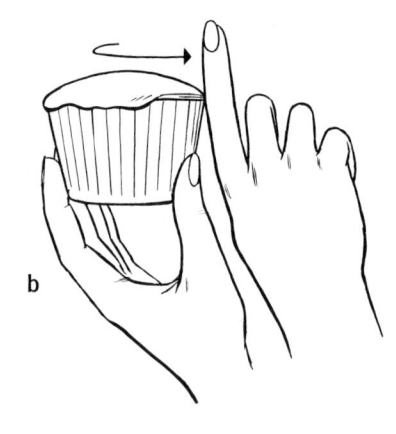

Fig. 15-1 **Icing cupcakes.**

   a Dip the top of the cupcake into the warm icing.

   b The extra icing can be removed by running the forefinger or a knife around the edge of the cupcake.

FROSTING CUPCAKES WITH FUDGE-TYPE ICING, BUTTERCREAM ICING, OR WHIPPED TOPPINGS

Fudge-type icings are usually applied with a spatula or table knife. Dip the spatula into the fudge and lift some of the icing on the tip of the knife. Spread the fudge on the cupcake so that you form a center peak. When you have enough icing on the cake, gently dip the tip of the spatula or knife into the center of the fudge and give the cupcake a half turn. This will cause a ridge to appear which will give the cupcake a simple, but attractive, decoration. (Fig. 15-2*a*.) This method is quick and ices the most cakes.

   The fudge or buttercream icing may be placed into a pastry bag or cookie press with a fancy decorating tube or stencil at the end. (Fig. 15-2*b*.) The icing is then squeezed through the tube onto the cupcake. (Fig. 15.2*c*.) The design you make will be entirely up to you. Be careful that you do not let the pointed edge of the tube touch the surface of the cupcake. This may cause the crust of the cake to tear and crumble. Be sure to press gently at first to control the speed with which the fudge or buttercream is forced out of the pastry bag. With practice, you will be able to regulate the speed and improve the appearance of the design.

   Whipped toppings may be applied to the surface of the cupcake right from the can. You may spiral the cream on the cupcake as you do for a sundae. After the cupcakes have been frosted, they may be garnished with nuts, sprinkles, or other toppings for greater variety and to improve their appearance.

UNIT 15: FINISHING AND DECORATING CUPCAKES   *171*

Fig. 15-2 **Fudge-iced or buttercream-iced cupcakes.**

    a Spread icing on the cupcakes so that a center peak is formed. Make the design by turning a spatula or table knife in the icing, or by giving the cupcake a half turn.

    b Pastry bag.

    c A possible pastry-bag icing design.

FINISHING OR DECORATING MINIATURE CUPCAKES BAKED WITHOUT PAPER LINERS

Cupcakes are often baked in small muffin pans. These miniature cupcakes may be decorated by dipping the entire cake into warmed simple frosting. Be sure the icing is warm and stirred before you dip the cakes. Insert a fork into the widest part of the cupcake (this was the top of the cake while the cake was still in the muffin tin) and dip the cupcake into the icing. Turn the cupcake gently in the icing so that the top (formerly the narrower bottom of the cupcake) and the sides of the cake are covered with icing. Remove the cupcake and place it on a grate or rack so that the excess icing can drip onto the table or the pan. Allow the icing to dry before lifting the cupcake gently from the rack to a clean pan. Scrape the icing drippings back into the saucepan to reheat for other cupcakes. The iced cupcakes may then be decorated with a glacé cherry or a pecan. Other designs may be made when the top of the cake has dried.

**FINISHING
OR DECORATING
METROPOLITANS**

Metropolitans are made from cupcakes baked in greased and flour-dusted muffin tins.

Refer to Fig. 15-3 as you work.

1 Place some jelly or jam into a bowl and stir it well until the lumps are gone and the jelly is smooth. If you use jam and it is a bit too thick, add a teaspoon of syrup to it to thin it. The jelly or jam should be thin enough to spread easily on the cakes without causing them to crumble.

2 Fill a flat pan or dish with shredded coconut. If there are lumps in the coconut, rub it together in the palms of your hands. Ground nuts or chocolate sprinkles may be used in place of the coconut.

3 With experience, you may be able to pick up and hold the cupcakes two at a time. Place the narrow parts of the cakes together (see Fig. 15-3*a*), and spread the jelly or jam around the sides of the cupcakes. However, you should begin with one cupcake at a time, holding the top and bottom of the cupcake with your middle finger and thumb. Apply the smooth jelly or jam with a butter knife or table knife like a thin spread. Make sure the sides of the cupcake are covered all around.

4 Next, roll the sides of the cupcake in the coconut or other topping so that the sides are completely covered. (Fig. 15-3*b*.) Place the cupcake on a pan with the small side up and the larger side (formerly the top) down.

5 Fill a pastry bag or cookie press with white or colored buttercream. Using an even pressure, draw a circle around the edge of the cupcake. (Fig. 15-3*c*.) Check to see that all the cupcakes have even borders of buttercream frosting. Go over them if they do not.

6 With a teaspoon or a paper cone filled with jelly, fill the center of each circle of buttercream with jelly. (Fig. 15-3*d*.) Be sure the entire center is filled and an equal amount is placed into the center of each cupcake. You may sprinkle some green-colored coconut on the top of the center as a garnish. Be neat and clean as you work. It will be reflected in the appearance of the decorated cupcakes.

UNIT 15: FINISHING AND DECORATING CUPCAKES   *173*

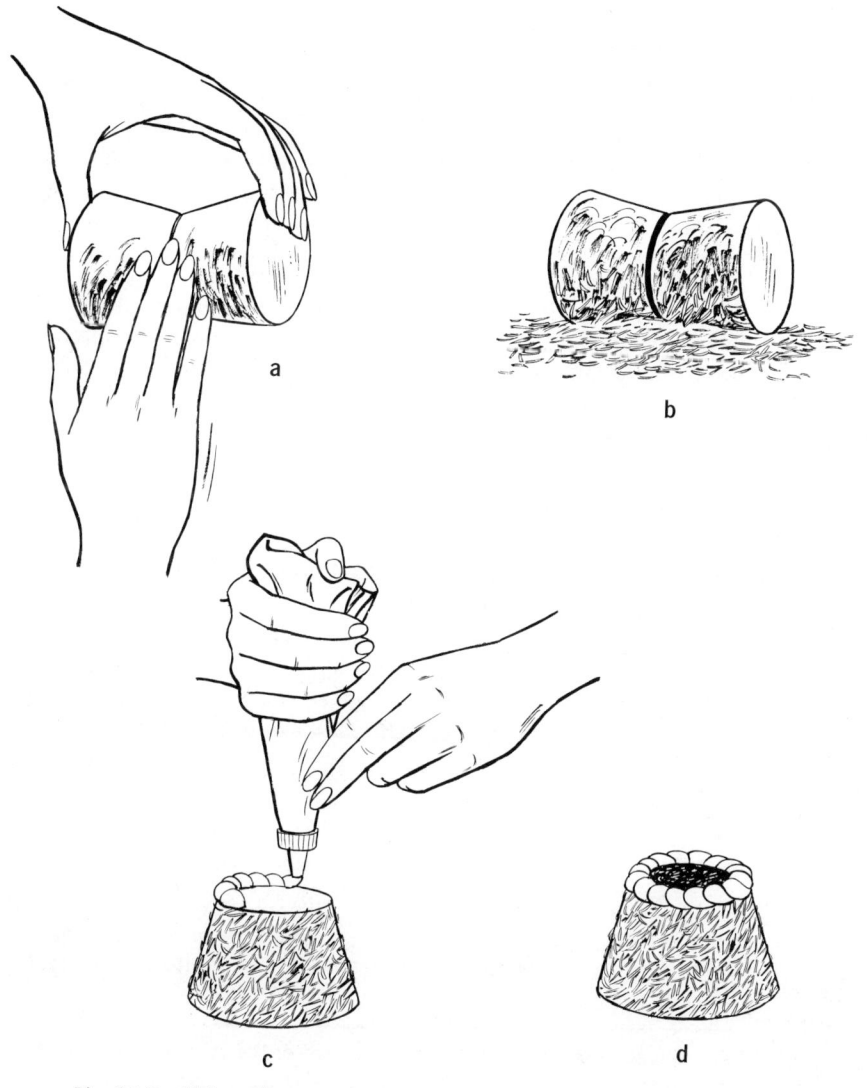

Fig. 15-3 **Metropolitans.**

    a Apply smooth jelly to the sides of the baked cupcakes. You may hold the cupcakes with tops together as shown. Jelly may be applied with a knife or with the fingers.

    b Roll the jelly-spread sides of the cupcake in coconut, covering the sides completely.

    c Place the cupcake on a pan with the small side on top. Fill the pastry bag with buttercream and draw a circle around the rim of the cupcake.

    d Fill the center of the buttercream circle with jelly. (You may use a teaspoon or a paper cone.) A finished metropolitan is shown here.

DECORATING OR FINISHING DROP CAKES

If you use the basic recipe for gold cupcakes and spoon the batter onto a baking pan greased and dusted with flour, the batter will spread because the sides of the muffin pan are not there to hold it in shape. Drop cakes are made in this way, and they are quite popular.

To make drop cakes, add ¼ cup of cake flour to the gold cupcake batter to thicken it slightly. Spoon the batter out onto greased and flour-dusted pans, about 1½ inches apart to allow for spreading. Bake at 390° until they are golden brown. The drop cakes will have a flat bottom surface which will be the side that you ice, after the cakes have been allowed to cool and are turned over.

Refer to Fig. 15-4.

1 Turn the cooled drop cakes over so that the smooth sides of the bottoms will be the sides that are iced.

2 Prepare the simple frosting, leaving it white. Be sure the frosting is warm and can be spread evenly.

3 Use a spatula or table knife to apply the frosting. Hold the cake in one hand and apply the white frosting over half of the flat cake. Try to do this in one or two gentle strokes to avoid crumbling the cake's surface. Return the half-iced cake to the pan.

4 Add some sifted cocoa or melted chocolate squares to the white frosting, coloring it chocolate. The cocoa or chocolate will thicken the frosting, so warm it a bit and add 1 tablespoon of syrup to soften it. Make additional frosting if you do not have enough.

5 Pick up the half-iced cakes again, one at a time, and cover the uniced half with chocolate frosting. Be careful not to smear the white frosting. Try to have the amounts of white and chocolate icing equal.

NOTE Run the edge of the knife around that half of the cake you are icing to remove any drippings. This will save icing, as well as giving the finished cake a neater appearance.

DECORATING OR FINISHING BUTTERFLY CUPCAKES

If you plan to make butterfly cupcakes, make the cupcakes slightly higher by filling the muffin pans with a little more cake batter. Fill

UNIT 15: FINISHING AND DECORATING CUPCAKES *175*

Fig. 15-4 **Icing drop cakes.**

   a The baked drop cake as it appears on the pan.

   b Turn the drop cake over to get a smooth surface for icing.

   c Apply white frosting to one half of the drop cake.

   d A drop cake with one half white-frosted.

   e A drop cake with both halves covered—half white and half chocolate.

PART FIVE: LAYER CAKES & CUPCAKES

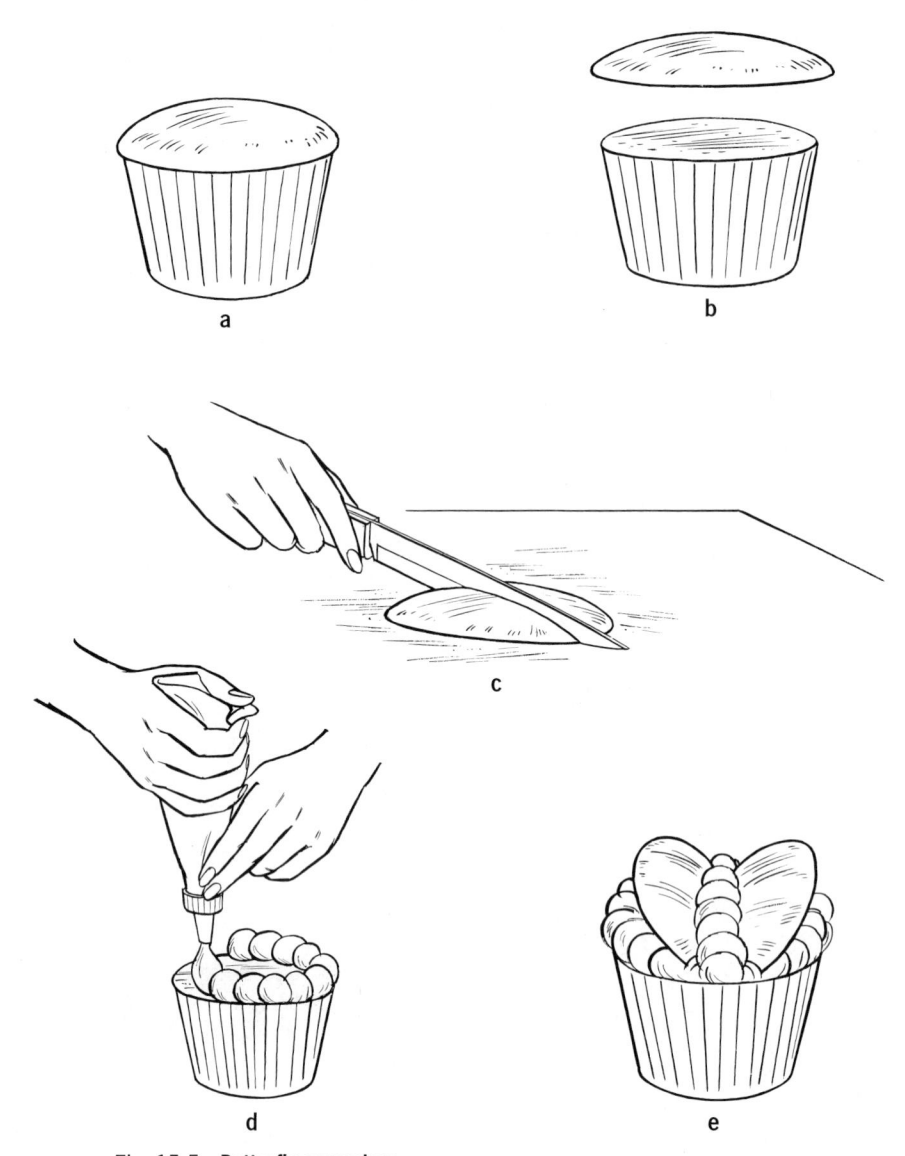

Fig. 15-5 **Butterfly cupcakes.**

    a A baked cupcake.

    b The top of the cupcake is cut off even with the edge of the paper cupcake liner.

    c Cut the removed top part of the cupcake in half.

    d Whipped cream or buttercream frosting is bagged out on top of the cupcake.

    e The two halves of the removed top of the cupcake are inserted into the cream as wings.

UNIT 15: FINISHING AND DECORATING CUPCAKES

the pans a little more than half full so that the baked cupcakes will be higher than the rim of the paper cupcake liner. (Be sure to bake the cupcakes a little longer because of the extra batter. Test for proper bake as usual.) Use the following procedure to decorate the butterfly cupcakes.

Refer to Fig. 15-5.

1. After the cupcakes are baked and cooled (Fig. 15-5*a*), cut off the tops of the cupcakes at the point where the paper liner meets the top of the cupcake (Fig. 15-5*b*). Slice the tops off carefully with a sawing motion. Be careful while you are cutting.

2. Place the tops in straight lines next to each other on the table or pan. Cut through the center of each top, dividing each into two equal halves (Fig. 15-5*c*). Dust the halves lightly with confectioners' sugar.

3. Take a pastry bag with a star tube, or a cookie press, and fill it with white or colored buttercream. You may use whipped cream instead of buttercream frosting. Make a ring of frosting or cream around the edge of the cupcake (Fig. 15-5*d*). The frosting or cream should be about ½ inch high and at least ½ inch thick. This will enable the frosting to support the cut halves of the top of the cupcake.

4. Place the two halves of the cut top into the frosting or cream so that the round edges stick out like wings (Fig. 15-5*e*). Be sure to tilt the halves slightly like wings. The confectioners' sugar should be facing up, so the whiteness of the sugar will serve as background for the finishing decorations.

5. With the same pastry bag and tube, or cookie press, make a spiral design in the center, between the two wings. This will connect the two wings at their base in the center of the cupcake. The center of the butterfly may be garnished with a glazed cherry, chopped nutmeats, colored coconut, or even a drop of jam or jelly. The color contrast with the whiteness of the wings will make the butterfly more attractive.

NOTE If you use whipped cream or whipped topping to decorate the butterfly, be sure to refrigerate the butterflies until you are ready to serve them.

UNIT **16**

DECORATING
LAYER CAKES

AIM   To learn how to decorate layer cakes.

THINGS YOU SHOULD KNOW   Layer cakes will vary according to the recipes they are made from. For example, a sponge cake layer will be lighter and of finer texture than a layer made from a creamed or blended batter. The sponge cake layer will therefore need a more delicate filling and frosting than other types of layer cakes. To be even more specific, the sponge cake layer would generally have a whipped cream or whipped topping frosting. The other types of layers could take almost any kind of frosting. Thus, the type of cake often determines the frosting to be used.

You may have several layers in the freezer. You might wish to combine a yellow layer with a chocolate layer. A combination of cake layers will make you think about the filling and frosting you should use. You might decide upon a chocolate buttercream frosting as filling and a similar type of frosting for the outside of the cake. The cake arrangement will have an effect on the frosting you use.

Special-occasion cakes or holiday cakes often tell you exactly what kind of frosting to use and even the colors to use. For ex-

UNIT 16: DECORATING LAYER CAKES   *179*

ample, birthday cakes require different color combinations for boys and girls. The kind of cake will also help determine the frosting to be used. Special cakes, such as Hallowe'en cakes, will indicate special colors, such as orange and chocolate, for the frosting and cake decorations. The personal taste of individuals should be considered. You know what preferences you have, and if the cake is to be made for others, you should inquire about the preferences of those who will eat it. You should understand certain basic rules and procedures that apply to the decorating of layer cakes in general. These are as follows:

PREPARING LAYER CAKES FOR ICING

1 Most layer cakes, when baked, have a slight mound or raised center. Since the layer cake is generally turned over for decorating, the rounded top will cause the cake to rock when it is frosted. Thus it is best to slice the mound from the center of the cake so that it rests on a flat surface which will not rock. The cut-off piece of cake can be used for cake crumbs to garnish the sides of the layers.

2 If the layer cake is high enough, it may be sliced crosswise into 3 equal sections. The average layer section is about ½ to ¾ inch thick. If the layer cake is not high, cut it into 2 equal sections. (Fig. 16-1*a*.) (Remember that the three-layer cake will need two fillings and the two-layer cake will have only one.) When slicing a layer cake, it is best to place the palm of one hand on the top of the layer and press down gently as you saw, or slice, the cake with the knife in your other hand. Be careful when cutting; try to slice the

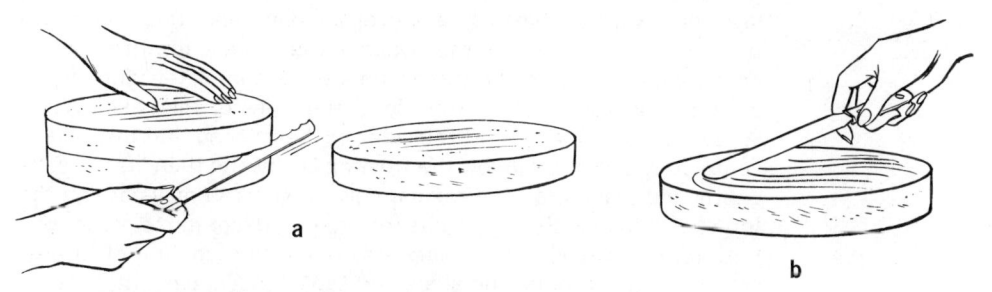

Fig. 16-1 **Cutting and filling cake layers.**

    a Cut the cake layers evenly. Higher layers should be cut into 3 equal sections.

    b Spread the filling evenly over the layer.

layers so that each layer is of even thickness. Cakes that are very delicate should be chilled in the refrigerator to make slicing them easier and neater.

3 Separate the layer sections and set them on the table the same way you removed them from the layer. This will enable you to replace them in the same order. Remember, however, that the bottom layer should become the top because the layer cake pan has made the bottom flat and even.

4 Place an equal amount of filling on each of the layers to be covered. (Fig. 16-1*b*.) Spread the filling evenly with the spatula so that the layer cake will remain even. This is especially important when you have added jam, jelly, or fruit to the filling. Place the first layer on a flat plate to support the layer steadily. After it has been decorated, the cake may be transferred to a regular cake dish lined with a doily.

5 Return each layer section to the plate in the same order that you removed it. Press each layer down gently after placing it on the filled layer. If the cake appears uneven (higher on one side than the other), insert a small slice of the cake you cut from the top layer when you started. If this is gone, add a little more filling to build up the low side. *Do not try to press the high side down to meet the level of the low side.* This will only force the cake filling out and spoil the delicate structure of the cake.

**APPLYING THE FROSTING
AND DECORATING
THE LAYER CAKE**

Refer to Fig. 16-2 while you work.
1 If a simple or flat frosting is to be used to ice the layer cake, set the layer on a wire or roasting rack over a clean pan. Pour the warm frosting over the center of the layer and then spread it with a spatula or table knife so that the top of the layer is completely and evenly covered and the frosting runs down the sides of the cake. Then spread the frosting around the sides of the layer so that the cake is completely covered. Allow the frosting to dry and then lift the cake gently and place it on the regular cake dish. You may garnish the top of the cake with nuts, fruits, or frosting decorations made with buttercream. It is good practice to put a thin coating of buttercream frosting around the sides and top of a layer cake that will be frosted with simple icing or fondant icing. Chill the cake to firm the buttercream coating before pouring the icing on the cake. This method gives the cake a smooth, even finish.

2 For fudge or buttercream types of frosting, the cake is placed on a plate (Fig. 16-2*a*) and frosting is applied with a spatula. These

UNIT 16: DECORATING LAYER CAKES   181

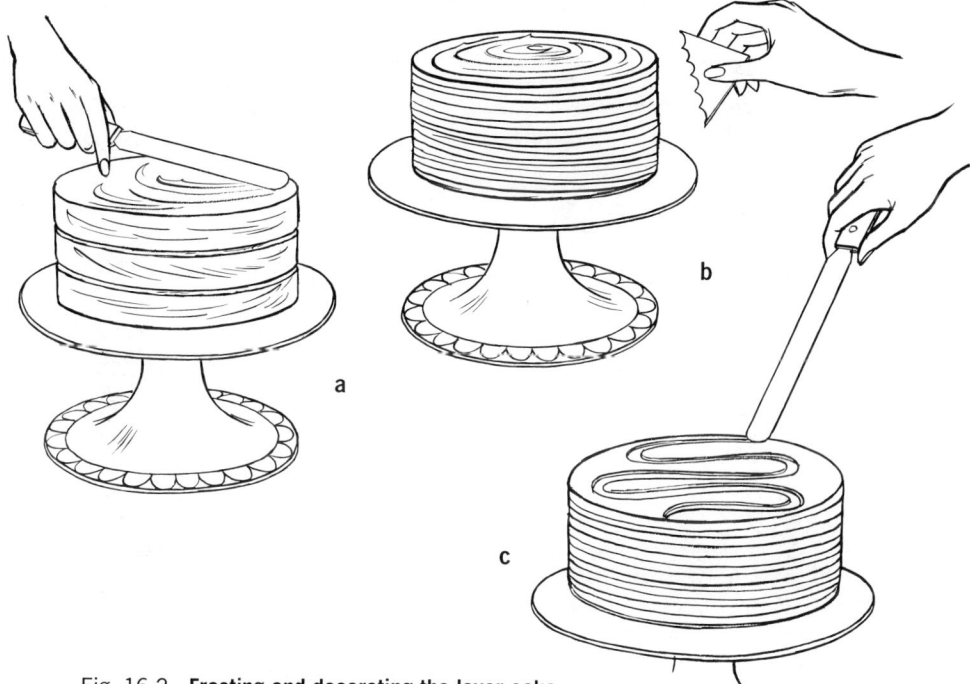

Fig. 16-2 **Frosting and decorating the layer cake.**

    a Place the cake on a plate or cake stand. Apply the frosting with a spatula or table knife.

    b The sides of the cake may be ridged with a comb cut from cardboard.

    c A layer cake finished by making swirls in the frosting with a knife.

icings spread easily if they have been properly prepared. It is very important that you spread the frosting evenly over the top and sides of the cake. A wedge, or slice, of cake looks much better when the frosting is even. To decorate the sides of the cake, take a piece of cardboard and cut a straight, even edge. Then cut small teeth, like those of a comb, in this edge. Pull the cardboard comb around the sides of the layer cake. (Fig. 16-2*b*.) This will make ridges in the frosting that will appear as added decoration. The sides of the cake may also be garnished with chopped nuts, sprinkles, or cake crumbs. Garnish or decorate the top as you wish or as the special purpose requires. A swirl pattern may be made in the top icing with a knife. (Fig. 16-2*c*.)

3 With marshmallow icing, light buttercream frosting, whipped cream, or similar soft frostings, a pastry bag with a tube is often used to decorate the top of the cake. You should make simple designs at first, but with practice, you will become quite good, even expert, at decorating layer cakes. (See Fig. 16-3, page 182.)

Fig. 16-3 **Decorating with marshmallow icing.**

    a Cut the layer into equal thirds.

    b Fill the layers evenly with marshmallow.

    c Ice the cake with marshmallow frosting and make a design on top by swirling the knife. You may use chocolate cake crumbs for the sides of the cake.

    d Sweetened, long-shred coconut can be used for the top and sides of the layer.

    e The cake may be striped with melted sweet chocolate after being covered with frosting.

UNIT 16: DECORATING LAYER CAKES

VOCABULARY

additional	fudge	picture	swirl	attractive
appropriate	glace	reflect	variable	combination
decorate	level	sandwich		determine
delicate	multiplies	serrated	*Review*	skimpy
direct	overheat	sundae	applying	topping

Refer to *Glossary* for an explanation of those words you do not know. The dictionary will be helpful for words not included in the *Glossary*.

PART SIX ■■■■■■□□

puff pastry products . . . eclairs & cream puffs

UNIT 17

**PUFF
PASTRY
DOUGH**

**INTRODUCTION:
BASIC FACTS ABOUT
PUFF PASTRY DOUGH**

The term *puff pastry,* as applied to dough, means exactly what the term *puff* would indicate. It refers to something very light and airy; and a puff pastry dough, when properly made, will result in baked products that are light and flaky, with a large volume.

You have made fruit-filled turnovers from the same pie crust dough you used to make fruit pies. You may have also used the same pie crust dough to make other products, such as chicken and beef pot pies. You can now use that experience as you start to prepare puff pastry dough and products made from it.

Think for a moment of turnovers you may have eaten that were made from a puff pastry dough. You will probably remember that they were much lighter and flakier than turnovers made from pie crust dough; they even looked completely different. Now think of other dishes which you may have eaten, such as those using patty shells to hold special fillings. Perhaps you have eaten miniature frankfurters wrapped in a flaky dough and served hot. Surely you

UNIT 17: PUFF PASTRY DOUGH   *187*

must have had a napoleon or other flaky cream dessert. It is almost certain that all these dishes and desserts were made with a puff pastry dough. Puff pastry dough is indeed a very useful dough for the cook who takes pride in food preparation.

Many people have been led to believe that puff pastry dough and the products made from the dough are difficult to make. On the contrary, it is no more difficult to make puff pastry than it is to make pie crust or any other dough. Puff pastry dough is handled differently, but with your past experience in making other baked products, you are quite capable of making puff pastry products with good results.

THINGS YOU SHOULD KNOW

1 The recipe for puff pastry dough calls for the use of all-purpose flour. This flour is stronger than cake or pastry flour, and if you have a strong bread flour, it would be even better to use that. Puff pastry dough is very rich in fat content and requires a strong flour to support the fat. The dough must be rolled several times to form layers of fat and dough. A strong flour will enable you to roll the dough without breaking down the layers and causing the fat to run out. It is also especially important when the product is being baked. Thus you see that a strong flour is necessary to support the fat, keep the fat in during rolling, and hold up the many layers of dough and fat that make the pastry flaky.

2 As mentioned above, the dough is rich in fat content. You will note that the recipe calls for almost equal weights of flour and fat (butter and margarine). The fat, when rolled into the dough, adds tenderness and flakiness. The instructions will tell you how to prepare the fat for use, place the fat over the dough, and then roll the dough to form layers of fat surrounded by layers of dough. Stress is placed upon the need for a firm, plastic fat instead of a hard, brittle type.

3 Cold or iced water is required to make the dough. A cold dough will keep the fat from becoming soft and sticky while the dough is being rolled. The temperature of the room also tends to warm the dough while you are rolling it. You will therefore be directed to refrigerate the dough between rollings.

4 Acid-type ingredients are added to the dough. The recipe calls for cream of tartar, which is a mild acid. In place of the cream of tartar, lemon juice or table vinegar (2 tablespoons of either, but not both) may be used. The acids have a softening effect on the dough and the gluten (remember the gluten in yeast doughs?) and the dough relaxes much faster after it has been rolled out. This makes it possible to roll the dough out again soon without having to wait too long.

5 You will be advised to roll the dough and then place it in the refrigerator. This will keep the fat firm and make rolling easier. The

dough is generally kept in the refrigerator 15 to 30 minutes between rollings. You will also be directed to prepare the puff pastry dough the day before you plan to make it up so that the dough may be aged, or conditioned, in the refrigerator for 24 hours or longer. The conditioning of the dough permits greater expansion of the layers and thus more volume during baking.

6 Special stress is laid on making small holes in the dough with a fork. This is often called *stippling*. This permits the dough to become flaky without the formation of large blisters or holes. Large holes or blisters form weak spots, and the product tends to break easily at these points.

7 There is no baking powder or yeast in puff pastry dough to leaven it or make it rise. Puff pastry is leavened by the layers of fat and dough and the moisture that is trapped within these layers. The water in the dough and small amounts of water in the butter and margarine provide the moisture. It is this moisture which, when changed to steam during baking, causes the leavening effect. The steam tries to force its way out of the dough through the small holes made with the fork. Only a small amount of the steam can get out while the remainder is trapped within the layers. Thus, the layers and the flakiness are created as the dough is blown up into a flaky product. The small holes avoid trapping the steam in large pockets or blisters. This description should make clear the importance of careful rolling of the dough, as well as the other factors which contribute to the making of a good puff pastry product.

PUFF PASTRY DOUGH   Yield: *approximately 20 to 24 turnovers*

AIM   To learn how to make puff pastry dough.

NOTE   If you should use a strong bread flour with a high gluten content, you may have to add 2 or 3 extra tablespoons of water, because this type of flour can absorb and hold more water than weaker types of flour.

THINGS TO PREPARE   Check the recipe for the necessary ingredients.

mixing bowl and spoon	brush and oil	rolling pin	measuring spoons
cloth or dish towel	pastry blender	worktable	measuring cups
refrigerator space	flat baking pan	flour sieve	dusting flour

UNIT 17: PUFF PASTRY DOUGH   *189*

PUFF PASTRY DOUGH

INGREDIENTS (*measure carefully*)		HOW TO MIX
all-purpose flour or bread flour	4 cups	Sift the flour and cream of tartar together. If lemon juice or vinegar is used instead, add it with the water. Cut the shortening into the flour to make small lumps.
cream of tartar or	1 tablespoon	
lemon juice or vinegar (*not both*)	2 tablespoons	
salt	1 teaspoon	
shortening	2 tablespoons	
egg	1	Blend the egg with the water. Add to the flour mixture and mix very well to a smooth dough. Place the dough on a floured portion of the table and fold it over into a rectangular shape. Cover the dough with a cloth to prevent a crust formation while the dough is relaxing.
cold water	1 cup plus 3 tablespoons	
butter	½ lb	Sprinkle the butter and margarine with 2 tablespoons of flour. Chop them into small pieces. Now blend the butter and margarine together to a smooth, plastic paste. The flour will absorb any of the moisture that may be lost when the fats are chopped and blended. Should the fatty paste become soft, place it in the refrigerator to firm it.
margarine	½ lb	

CHECK POINTS

    1 Is there enough flour on the table and under the dough?

    2 Is the dough relaxed enough to be rolled?

ROLLING IN PUFF PASTRY DOUGH

    See Fig. 17-1 (page 190).

    1 Sprinkle the top of the dough and the rolling pin with flour. Roll the dough out into a rectangular shape about ¼ inch thick. Be sure the dough is of even thickness all over.

    2 Brush the excess flour from the surface of the dough. Now dot the firm, plastic butter and margarine over two-thirds of the dough. Space equal dots of fat, about the size of an almond, ½ to 1 inch apart over the dough.

    3 Lift that third of the dough without the fat and fold it over one-third of the dough with the fat. You now have a sandwich of fat and dough, with one-third of the dotted dough still open. Now fold this dotted portion over the sandwiched dough and you will have a

PART SIX: PUFF PASTRY PRODUCTS . . . ECLAIRS & CREAM PUFFS

Fig. 17-1 **Rolling in puff pastry dough.**

    a Roll the dough out to a rectangular shape.

    b Dot two-thirds of the rectangle with the fat to be rolled into the dough.

    c Fold the third of the dough without fat over one-third of the dough with the fat.

    d Fold the remaining third of the dough with fat over the top so that three layers of dough and two layers of fat are formed.

    e Turn the dough sideways on the floured table and begin the rolling-in process.

double-decker sandwich of three layers of dough and two layers of fat.

4 Spread some of the leftover flour on the table using some fresh flour if necessary. Sprinkle the top of the dough lightly with flour. Now roll the dough again into a rectangular shape about ¼ inch thick. Check to see that there is enough flour on the table to prevent the dough from sticking. When you have rolled the dough out properly, remove any excess flour, and fold the dough into thirds again. Fold the dough the same way as you did when you folded the fat and dough together. Remove excess flour from the folds. This is called the first roll. Place the dough into the refrigerator to chill the fat; this will take about 15 to 20 minutes. Roll the dough three more times to complete the rolling-in process. You have now formed 243 layers of fat and dough. (You formed 3 layers when you folded the fat and dough. After each roll, multiply each of the layers formed by 3: $3 \times 3 = 9$; $9 \times 3 = 27$; $27 \times 3 = 81$; $81 \times 3 = 243$.)

5 After the fourth roll, brush the top of the dough with a little vegetable or salad oil to prevent the formation of a crust on the top of the dough. Place the dough in the refrigerator to condition it; it will be ready for use the following day. Or the dough may be wrapped in freezer paper and frozen for use at some later time; this is a regular practice with many cooks.

It is advisable to keep a cloth over the dough, even after it has been oiled, to ensure the prevention of a crust. If a crust is permitted to form and is quite a heavy crust, it will make strips of toughness on the inside of the product.

UNIT 18

PUFF
PASTRY
VARIETIES

FRUIT-FILLED　　　　　　　Yield: *about 20 to 24 turnovers*
TURNOVERS　　　　　　　　　*made from 4-inch dough squares*

AIM　To learn how to make fruit-filled turnovers.

THINGS YOU SHOULD KNOW　Turnovers made properly from puff pastry dough are light and flaky and make a delicious dessert. The variety of turnovers you can make depends upon the kinds of fruit filling used and how the baked turnovers are decorated. You may have noticed that some turnovers have the fruit filling almost completely exposed. These turnovers are made by folding and baking the dough and then opening the turnover. The opened turnover is filled with a cooked fruit filling. These turnovers are finished by dusting them with confectioners' sugar. Some more popular varieties are made by baking the turnovers with the fruit filling in them. These turnovers are egg-washed before baking and finished later with a simple icing.

　　You must bear in mind that a turnover crust of well-made puff pastry dough will rise and become very flaky, unlike the turnovers made from pie crust dough. (The turnovers are alike only because

UNIT 18: PUFF PASTRY VARIETIES

both are triangular in shape and contain fruit fillings.) You must remember to roll this turnover dough thinner than the pie crust dough.

THINGS TO PREPARE Have the baking pans lightly greased or lined with parchment paper. Set the oven temperature to 400°.

French knife or pastry wheel	table brush	wash brush	dusting flour
spoon for filling	water brush	egg wash	worktable

MAKING THE TURNOVERS

Refer to the instructions and illustrations for making pie crust turnovers (Fig. 10-7).

1 Roll the puff pastry dough to about ⅛ inch thickness. (This is thinner than the dough rolled for pie crust turnovers.) Check the dough and the table to see that there is enough flour to keep the dough from sticking. Use your fingers to check the dough for even thickness throughout.

2 Allow the dough to relax on the table for about 5 minutes before you cut the squares of dough. While it is resting, you may mark off the exact sizes of the squares as a guide for cutting. Cut the squares out evenly and then brush their edges with water or egg wash.

3 Use a tablespoon or serving spoon to place the fruit filling in the center of the squares. An equal amount of filling should be placed in each turnover.

NOTE Fruit filling should be slightly thicker than that used for pies. Thin fruit filling will run even before the turnovers are folded and the edges sealed, and it will also run during baking. You can add some cake crumbs or unseasoned bread crumbs to thicken the filling. Do not use chocolate crumbs.

4 Fold the edges over and seal each turnover well. The tines of a fork do well to seal the edges. Place the turnovers on a prepared baking pan and then puncture, or stipple, each of the turnovers with the fork. Wash the tops of the turnovers with egg wash. Let them rest at least 15 to 20 minutes before baking them. This allows the dough to relax so that the gluten in the dough can expand as the turnovers rise in the oven. This prevents shrinkage and helps keep the filling in the turnover.

5 Bake the turnovers at 400° until they are golden brown on top. This will take about 25 minutes, although large turnovers will take longer. Frost the tops of the turnovers with simple icing.

PART SIX: PUFF PASTRY PRODUCTS ... ECLAIRS & CREAM PUFFS

**FRUIT-FILLED
BASKETS**
Yield: *20 to 24 baskets*

AIM   To learn how to make variety fruit-filled baskets.

THINGS TO PREPARE   Prepare the same things as for puff pastry turnovers.

MAKING THE FRUIT-FILLED BASKETS

See Fig. 18-1.

1 Roll the dough a little thicker than you did for the turnovers. The dough squares will not be folded as they were for turnovers and should be almost twice as thick as the dough for the turnovers.

2 The squares should be a little smaller than those for the turnovers, about 3 to 3½ inches square. Allow the dough to rest for a few minutes after rolling it out and then cut it into equal squares.

3 Use the back of a spoon to make depressions (press down into the dough) in the center of each square of dough. *Be careful not to make holes in the dough or make the dough too thin.* The depressions or hollowed centers will hold the filling.

4 Wash the edges of each square with a little egg wash or water. Fill each of the hollowed centers with fruit filling as you did for the turnovers. Be sure you have an equal amount in each fruit square.

5 Roll out a small piece of the puff pastry dough (you may use the edges of the dough which you have cut away), and cut it into strips about 4½ inches wide. Cut these strips of dough into thin strips about ½ inch wide. Now brush these thin strips with egg wash. Place 2 strips across each square diagonally so that they cross in the center. Press the strip ends into the edge of the dough square. (Refer to Fig. 18-1*b*.) Place the squares on a baking pan which has been prepared as for turnovers.

6 Allow the squares to rest for half an hour before baking them at 400°. You will note that the dough squares were not punctured with a fork. This causes the dough to rise higher because the steam is trapped in the dough. The center will not rise as high as the rest of the dough square because the fruit keeps the dough from rising as much, and thus the edges will be higher than the center. Bake the baskets at 400° for about 20 to 25 minutes until the squares are golden brown and feel crisp. A gentle touch will tell you that the squares are crisp because they will flake slightly. If the basket is not fully baked, the dough will feel soft and tend to settle back as the units cool. Underbaking will result in a gummy, raw product.

7 Brush the fruit baskets with warm simple syrup as soon as they are removed from the oven. This will give the basket handles and the fruit filling a shine or lustre. Allow the baskets to cool until they

UNIT 18: PUFF PASTRY VARIETIES   *195*

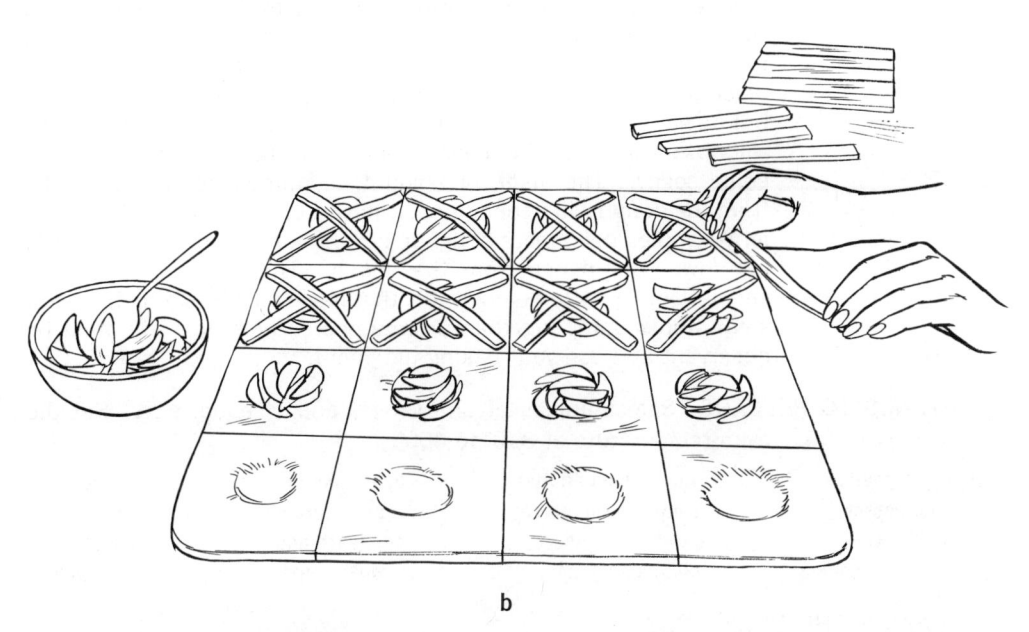

a

b

Fig. 18-1 **Fruit baskets.**

    a For fruit baskets, roll the dough a little thicker than for turnovers and cut it into 3- or 3½-inch squares.

    b Press the center of each dough square down slightly. Place the filling in the depressed center. Place two strips of dough diagonally across the fruit square.

are slightly warm; then frost the tops of the baskets with warm simple icing.

NOTE The baskets or fruit squares may be made without the crossed strips. Then additional fruit filling can be put into the centers after the squares are baked. This will make the squares look richer and more attractive.

APPLE DUMPLINGS

Yield: *16 to 24 dumplings, depending on the size of the apples*

AIM To learn how to make apple dumplings.

THINGS YOU SHOULD KNOW Refer to the procedure you followed when you made apple turnovers or other fruit-filled turnovers. The apple dumpling differs because you will use a whole peeled and cored apple as filling. When you made fresh apple pie, you learned that hard or firm apples should be used. Soft and sugary apples will shrink and lose their shape when baked.

Peeled apples will turn brown if exposed to the air for some time, so if the peeled apples must wait until you are ready with the dough, place them in a bowl and cover them with a wet cloth. You may place them in a solution of lemon juice or pineapple juice and water, but do not allow them to remain in water too long because the apples will absorb some of the moisture and even the hard apples will become soggy. The *yield*, or amount, of dumplings you can make from the dough will depend upon the size of the apples. Naturally, larger apples need more dough to cover them. This means you will get fewer dumplings from the dough. The opposite is true of smaller apples. Remember, too, that it will take less time to bake a small apple dumpling than a large one. Therefore, you must be observant and use your baking judgment.

THINGS TO PREPARE Select apples of one variety and of equal size. Set the oven temperature at 390° to 400°.

apple peeler	small cookie cutter	light cake or	simple icing
apple corer	simple syrup glaze	bread crumbs	or frosting
pastry wheel or	bowl for apples	egg wash and	rolling pin
French knife	cinnamon sugar	wash brush	saucepan

MAKING THE DUMPLINGS

Refer to Fig. 18-2.

1 Wash the apples before you use them. Peel the apples, making sure all the skin is removed. You may remove any dark spots or bruise blemishes if you wish. Put the apples into a bowl and cover them with a cool, wet cloth to keep the air from turning them brown (oxidizing them).

UNIT 18: PUFF PASTRY VARIETIES 197

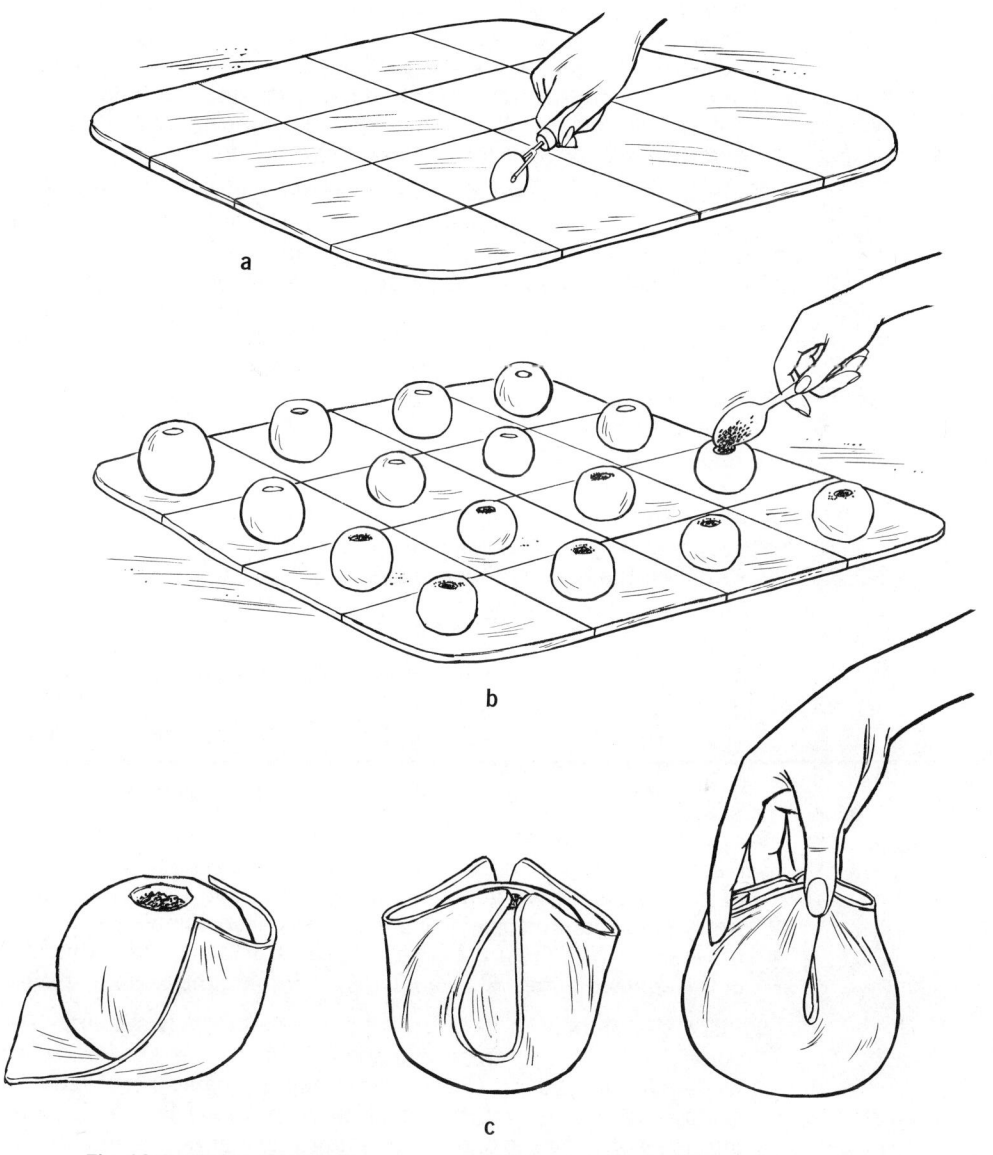

Fig. 18-2 **Apple dumplings.**

    a For apple dumplings, divide the rolled-out dough into 4-inch squares. Large apples will require larger squares of dough to cover them.

    b Place a peeled and cored apple in the center of each square. Fill the center of the apple with cinnamon sugar.

    c Bring the points of the square of dough over the center of the apple and pinch the points together. Place a small disc of dough on top of each dumpling and press it down gently.

2 Roll the dough out as thin as you did for turnovers (⅛ inch thick). Place one of the apples at the corner of the rolled-out dough and estimate how large the square of dough should be in order to cover the entire apple. It is better to have a little too much dough than not to have enough to cover the apple. Now measure the dough and mark off the squares before you cut the dough.

3 Cut the dough into equal squares. If the apples are in a fruit juice solution, be sure to drain them well before using. Brush the edges of the dough squares with egg wash or water. Place one tablespoon of light cake crumbs or unseasoned bread crumbs in the center of each square. The cake crumbs will absorb any juices or syrup which forms, and prevent the bottom of the dumpling from becoming soggy and sticking to the pan. Set one apple on the crumbs. Be sure it is in the center of the dough.

Fill the center or empty core space of the apple with cinnamon sugar, using a teaspoon. Larger apples will need more sugar. The cinnamon sugar may be made stronger by increasing the amount of cinnamon mixed with the sugar. If the apples are very tart or sour, you may even sprinkle the top of the apples with sugar before wrapping the dough around them.

4 Lift each corner of the square of dough and bring it to the top center of the apple over the open core space. Place one corner of dough over the other so that all four corners overlap each other. Press the points together gently so that they stick. Roll out a piece of dough about ⅛ inch thick. (This may be from the edges you cut off when you rolled out the dough.) Use a small round cookie cutter (about 1 inch in diameter) and cut small discs from the rolled-out dough.

5 Brush the tops of the dumplings with egg wash and set one dough disc on the top of the dumplings where the dough points meet. Press the disc down gently. The disc will keep the dough points from opening during baking and make the baked dumpling look more attractive. Now press the edges, or seams, of the dough at the sides of the apple together with your fingers. Be sure they are well sealed.

6 Place the dumplings on a baking pan about 2 inches apart. The pan should be lightly greased or lined with parchment paper. Bake the apples at 390° to 400°. Larger apples should be baked at a slightly lower temperature. Bake until the crust is golden brown and feels crisp to the touch. Use your judgment. An underbaked dumpling will have a soggy dough that will collapse when the dumpling cools. An overbaked dumpling will have an apple that falls apart or shrinks badly.

7 When they are baked, wash the dumplings with warm syrup wash to give them a shine or lustre. Allow them to cool until slightly warm, and then brush the tops of the dumplings with simple icing or frosting. Serve the dumplings while they are slightly warm. If they are baked ahead of time to be served later, you may refrigerate the

UNIT 18: PUFF PASTRY VARIETIES   *199*

dumplings and then warm them for a few minutes in a preheated oven. Frost them after they have been heated again and then serve them while they are still warm.

NAPOLEONS   Yield: *three 8- by 12-inch sheets of dough*

AIM   To learn how to make napoleons.

THINGS YOU SHOULD KNOW   You may have seen the pastries known as napoleons and perhaps even eaten them without knowing their real names. The name is said to have been derived from a specialty pastry made by a French chef for Emperor Napoleon. Briefly and simply, napoleons are made from baked sheets of puff pastry dough that are sandwiched together with custard-type filling. The tops of the pastries are then finished or decorated in various different ways. With some experience, you will become quite adept in making a variety of napoleons and you may use your judgment to develop new ideas and approaches to decorating them. They are really interesting and fun to make. You have only to follow the instructions by *reading carefully* and let the sketches and your past experience guide you.

THINGS TO PREPARE   Set the oven temperature at 375° to 380°.

chilled custard of any variety you choose	three 8- by 12-inch baking pans	prepared puff pastry dough	serrated knife or saw knife
fork	French knife or pastry wheel	sieve for confectioners' sugar	simple icing or frosting

MAKING THE NAPOLEONS

Refer to Fig. 18-3 (page 200).

1 Divide the puff pastry dough into 3 equal pieces. You will use 1 piece for each pan. Roll the dough out in a rectangular shape so that it is about ½ to 1 inch larger than the pan on all sides. (Fig. 18-3*a*.) (Place the pan over the rolled-out dough to measure it.) Be sure the dough is of even thickness all over. Thin and thick spots will cause the sheet to bake unevenly. Parts may burn while other parts will be raw or gummy. Moisten the edges of the pan with a little water. Lift the rolled-out dough and place it in the pan. (Fig. 18-3*b*.) Be sure the pan is entirely covered with the dough. Avoid stretching the dough so that the thickness becomes uneven. Press the edges of the dough against the moistened pan edges. This will cause the dough to stick slightly and help keep the dough from shrinking.

2 With the fork, puncture the dough (make small holes) at ½-inch spaces so that the sheet of dough is punctured all over. (Fig. 18-3*c*.) This is very important because large blisters or air pockets will form where the dough is not punctured. These blisters will

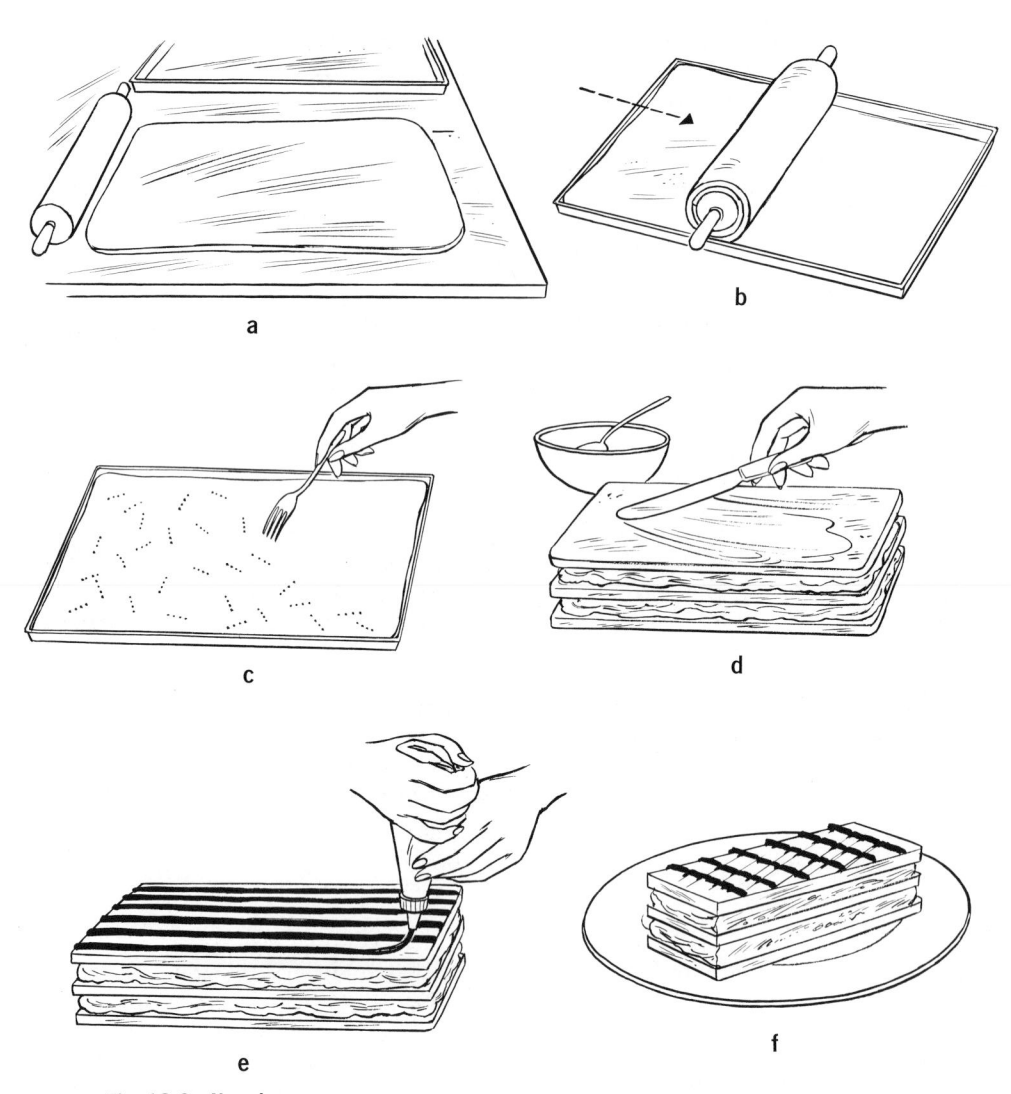

Fig. 18-3 **Napoleons.**

- **a** Roll the dough ½ to 1 inch larger than the pan to be used for the napoleon sheet.
- **b** Roll the dough up on the rolling pin, then unroll it into the prepared pan.
- **c** Make small holes in the dough (stipple it) with a fork.
- **d** Use three baked puff pastry sheets or one sheet that has been cut into 3 equal parts. Put the sheets together with two layers of custard filling. Frost the top layer with simple frosting or another frosting or topping.
- **e** The finished napoleon sheet with the layers of custard and with frosting on top.
- **f** A napoleon that has been cut from the full sheet.

UNIT 18: PUFF PASTRY VARIETIES

become weak spots and the sheet of baked puff pastry may break at those points when you lift it to sandwich the sheets together.

3 If you have only one pan, you will have to bake one sheet at a time. While it is baking, you may roll out the other pieces of dough. Also, you could use only the one baked puff pastry sheet and make fewer napoleons, cutting the baked sheet into 3 equal strips and putting them together. Or you may bake all three sheets at once and wrap two of them for later use.

4 Allow the dough to relax in the pan for at least ½ hour so that it does not shrink during baking. There will be a little shrinkage but this is normal because part of the moisture in the dough evaporates during baking. Bake the sheet of puff pastry until it is golden brown and the dough feels crisp and flaky when touched gently. Remove it from the oven and allow the sheet to cool. Shake the pan gently to free the baked sheet from the pan. If the sheet should stick slightly, return it to the oven for a minute and then loosen the baked sheet.

FILLING AND CUTTING THE BAKED SHEETS

1 Remove the chilled custard you have selected from the refrigerator and stir it smooth with a spoon. It may be placed into the mixing machine and worked smooth. You may add 1 or more cups of soft buttercream frosting to the custard to make it lighter. This blend of custard and buttercream is called a French custard. You may also beat 1 or 2 cups of heavy cream until stiff and gently fold the whipped cream into the smooth custard. This is called a Bavarian type of cream. Thus, you note the variations which may be made in the filling used to sandwich together the baked puff pastry sheets.

2 Place one of the baked sheets on a cutting board or pan with the smooth side down and the bumpy side up. The bumpy side is the top of the baked sheet. Spread the prepared custard filling evenly over the top of the sheet, working gently and carefully with a spatula. Place the second baked sheet or strip over the first, this time placing the bumpy side down into the custard filling. Press the sheet down gently by placing the pan over it and applying a little pressure. This will cause the sheets to stick together and level the filling. Fill the top of the second sheet with custard as before. Place the third sheet on top of the second with the bumpy side down into the custard and the smooth side facing up. Once again, press the sheets together with the pan. (Fig. 18-3*d*.)

3 With a saw or serrated knife, trim the sides of the sheets to make them even. Save the cut edges. You may wish to use them as a garnish or topping. Place the filled sheets in the refrigerator to chill.

METHODS OF FINISHING OR DECORATING THE NAPOLEONS The top of the napoleon sheet may be covered with white, simple icing or frosting evenly spread over the top. After the icing dries, it may be striped with lines of chocolate icing. A knife edge drawn lightly through the chocolate lines will create a marbled effect. (Fig. 18-3e.)

The edges cut from the sides may be chopped finely. Spread the top of the napoleon with more custard filling and sprinkle the chopped edges over the custard. Sprinkle or dust these with confectioners' sugar.

The tops of the napoleons may also be decorated with a soft fudge icing in a homemade design made with the edge of the spatula or table knife.

You may use whipped cream or whipped topping from the compressed cans to decorate the tops. The toppings may be further garnished with glacé cherries, nuts, or sprinkles.

Napoleons are usually cut into rectangular shape. (Fig. 18-3f.) An average-size serving would be 2½ to 3 inches long by 1½ inches wide. Smaller and daintier pieces may be cut. For ease in cutting them, be sure the napoleon sheets are chilled. Dip the saw or serrated knife into hot water and cut with a gentle sawing motion. Dip the knife into the hot water frequently to keep the pastry from dragging and smearing the custard filling and icing top. Napoleons should be kept refrigerated until they are served. The custard filling and cream toppings are perishable and subject to spoilage if left at room temperature for a lengthy period.

PATTY SHELLS Yield: *about 24, depending on the size of the cutter used*

AIM To learn how to make patty shells.

THINGS YOU SHOULD KNOW Patty shells made from puff pastry look like high, flaky cookies that have a hollow center. They have many uses in many dishes. As one example, the centers of cold baked patty shells may be filled with a variety of fruit fillings and custard. These may then be covered with a whipped cream or topping and garnished in different ways. They are also used to hold hot, creamed fillings such as chicken à la king, sautéed meats, or Newburg specialties. The good cook and efficient homemaker will find many uses for patty shells. Patty shells are often made in advance and stored in a cool, dry place for future use. They may also be frozen.

THINGS TO PREPARE Set the oven temperature at 390°.

prepared puff pastry dough	worktable	fork	cookie cutters
dusting flour	wash brush	egg wash	(large and small)
	baking pans		

MAKING THE PATTY SHELLS

Refer to Fig. 18-4.

1 Roll out the puff pastry dough to about ⅛-inch thickness. Be sure

UNIT 18: PUFF PASTRY VARIETIES   203

the thickness is even throughout. Cut out circles of dough with a cookie cutter about 2 to 2½ inches in diameter. (Fig. 18-4a.) Cut the circles close together to avoid a lot of scrap dough. Place the circles on a lightly greased baking pan; then puncture them with a fork.

2 Fold the scrap dough together and form into a square or rectangular shape. Place this dough to one side to relax. Roll out more dough for the tops of the patty shells if you do not have enough left on the table. Cut out circles once again with the same size cookie cutter

a

b

c

d

Fig. 18-4 **Patty shells.**

    a For patty shells, roll out the dough evenly, about ⅛ inch thick. Cut out the bottoms and the tops for the patty shells.

    b The bottoms are whole round circles of dough.

    c The tops are circles of dough with the centers cut out like doughnuts. The tops are placed on the egg-washed bottoms and baked.

    d Baked patty shells.

you used before. Be sure you cut the same number of circles as those you have on the pans.

3 Take the small cutter (1 inch in diameter) and cut the center out of each of the circles of dough on the table, (Fig. 18-4b)—*not those on the pan.* Brush the circles of dough on the pan (Fig. 18-4c) lightly with egg wash and then cover them with the circles that have their centers cut out. Be sure one circle fits evenly on top of the other.

4 Allow the patty shells to relax for at least ½ hour; then bake them at 390° until they are golden brown and crisp. Check the shells while they are baking. Should any of the shells rise higher on one side than the other, press the high side down gently with the back of a spoon. If the dough was evenly rolled out, this will not happen. You will note that the top circles were not punctured with a fork. This allows these circles to rise higher than the bottom circles. The finished shells are shown in Fig. 18-4d.

VOCABULARY

				Review
adept	capable	expansion	overlap	acids
blemishes	depression	exposed	surrounded	airy
brittle	dish towel	observant	vegetable	flakiness
bruised	double-decker	opposite	vinegar	support

Refer to *Glossary* for an explanation of any terms you do not know. The dictionary will be helpful for words not included in the *Glossary.*

UNIT **19**

**CREAM PUFFS
AND ECLAIRS**

AIM   To learn how to make eclairs and cream puffs.

THINGS YOU SHOULD KNOW   Cream puffs and eclairs are made by filling pre-baked shells with custards and whipped cream, and here the shell is the most important factor. It is made from a special batter that is prepared differently from any other batter you have made. You may find this same batter listed under the French name, "choux paste." "Choux" is pronounced like "shoe." This paste or basic batter has many other uses in addition to that of making cream puff and eclair shells. Bakers fry circles of the batter in hot fat like doughnuts. These are called "French crullers." The same batter may be dropped onto a pan in tiny mounds and baked into small hollow balls which are used in clear soups. They are often called "soup nuts." Many cooks prepare cream puff shells and use them in place of patty shells. They cut the shells in half and fill them with hot meat and other fillings. They then replace the covers and serve the filled shells. Thus, the recipe for, and preparation of, the basic paste may be put to many varied uses. Your past experience should make the preparation of the choux paste much like the preparation of other doughs and batters you have made. *Read carefully and follow instructions exactly.*

PASTE FOR CREAM PUFF AND ECLAIR SHELLS

Yield: *20 to 24 puffs or shells*

THINGS TO PREPARE   Set the oven temperature at 415°. Clear one burner space on the top of the cooking range or stove. Refer to the recipe for ingredients.

measuring spoons	saucepan	mixing bowl or	pastry bag and
measuring cups	baking pans	mixing machine	plain tube
tablespoons	oven pads		

CREAM PUFF PASTE

INGREDIENTS (*measure carefully*)		HOW TO MIX
water	1 cup	Place the water, salt, and oil in a saucepan at least one quart in size and bring them to a boil.
salt	¼ teaspoon	
vegetable oil	½ cup	
all-purpose flour (sifted)	1¼ cups	Add the flour to the liquid, stirring constantly with a wooden mixing spoon. Stir until it forms a thick, smooth paste, very much like a thick cereal, which tends to pull away from the sides of the saucepan as it is stirred. Be sure there are no lumps of flour showing. The paste will have a grayish appearance. Remove the pan from the stove.
eggs	1 cup (4 or 5)	Place the hot paste into the mixing bowl or the mixing machine bowl and allow the paste to cool until it is warm. Add one egg at a time and blend in well after each egg is added. Add the baking powder and milk together and blend the mixture until smooth. The batter should be medium soft and should keep its shape when spooned out. If the batter is too thick, add one or two eggs to thin it. You may add extra milk, but if you do, add ½ teaspoon of baking powder for each ¼ cup of milk added. Test the consistency of the batter by dropping a teaspoon of batter on a pan. The spooned batter should be soft, yet hold its shape on the pan. It will flatten slightly. With experience, you will be able to judge the right consistency, or thickness.
milk	¼ cup (approximately)	
baking powder	½ teaspoon	

CHECK POINTS

1. Are the pans ready for the batter to be spooned out?
2. Is the oven temperature correct and ready?
3. Is the batter of proper consistency?
4. Do you have the necessary spoons or pastry bag and tube?

UNIT 19: CREAM PUFFS AND ECLAIRS

MAKING AND BAKING CREAM PUFF AND ECLAIR SHELLS

Refer to Fig. 19-1 (page 208).

1 To make the *cream puff shells,* place the batter with a spoon onto dry baking pans. It is advisable to line the pans with parchment paper if you have it. If the pans have been washed often, brush them very lightly with a film of melted fat; then wipe the fat off. This will fill the pores of the metal with an oily film and keep the shells from sticking.

The size of the cream puff shell will depend upon the amount of batter you spoon onto the pan. Try to keep all the shells the same size. It is important because small ones will bake faster than the larger ones, creating problems for you. The best way to deposit the batter is to put it in a pastry bag with a medium-size plain tube. Hold the tube over the pan and squeeze the pastry bag with the palm of the hand to force the batter through the tube. (Fig. 19-1*a* and *b.*) Practice will make this quite simple for you to do as you gain experience. *Space the shells about 1 inch apart on the pan.* To make a round shape, dip the spoon in milk and run it around the drops of batter on the pan to shape them.

2 To make the *eclair shells,* you must have a pastry bag and plain tube in order to make the long, even shape of the eclair. (Fig. 19-1*c.*) Fill the pastry bag as you did for the cream puffs. Now apply pressure, at the same time moving the end of the tube in a straight line for about 3 inches. Keep the pressure steady so that the batter coming out is of even thickness. If the first few eclairs are uneven, scrape the batter together with a spoon, return the batter to the pastry bag, and start again. Space the eclair shells about 1 inch apart to allow for expansion during baking. Do not place too much batter into the pastry bag at one time. Twist the pastry bag to force the batter down after you bag out every three or four shells on the pan.

3 The shell batter should be baked as soon after it is deposited on the pans as possible. Letting the batter stand will make a crust form on the shells which will cause excessive cracking when the shells are baked. Place the pans in the oven at 415°. The shells will rise rather quickly in the oven during the first 10 to 15 minutes of baking. This is caused by the expansion of the eggs you blended into the batter. Heat has the same effect on eggs in a batter as heat has upon eggs poured into a hot skillet when you make an omelette. Baking powder also causes the batter to rise rapidly.

All this rapid action creates the hollow effect in the shell. The hollowness is due to the fact that you have precooked the flour and the structure in the shell is formed by the gluten or protein in the flour and the protein supplied by the eggs. (Albumen or egg white contains most of the protein present in eggs.)

When the shells have started to turn golden brown, lower the temperature to 375° and bake the shells for 5 to 10 more minutes

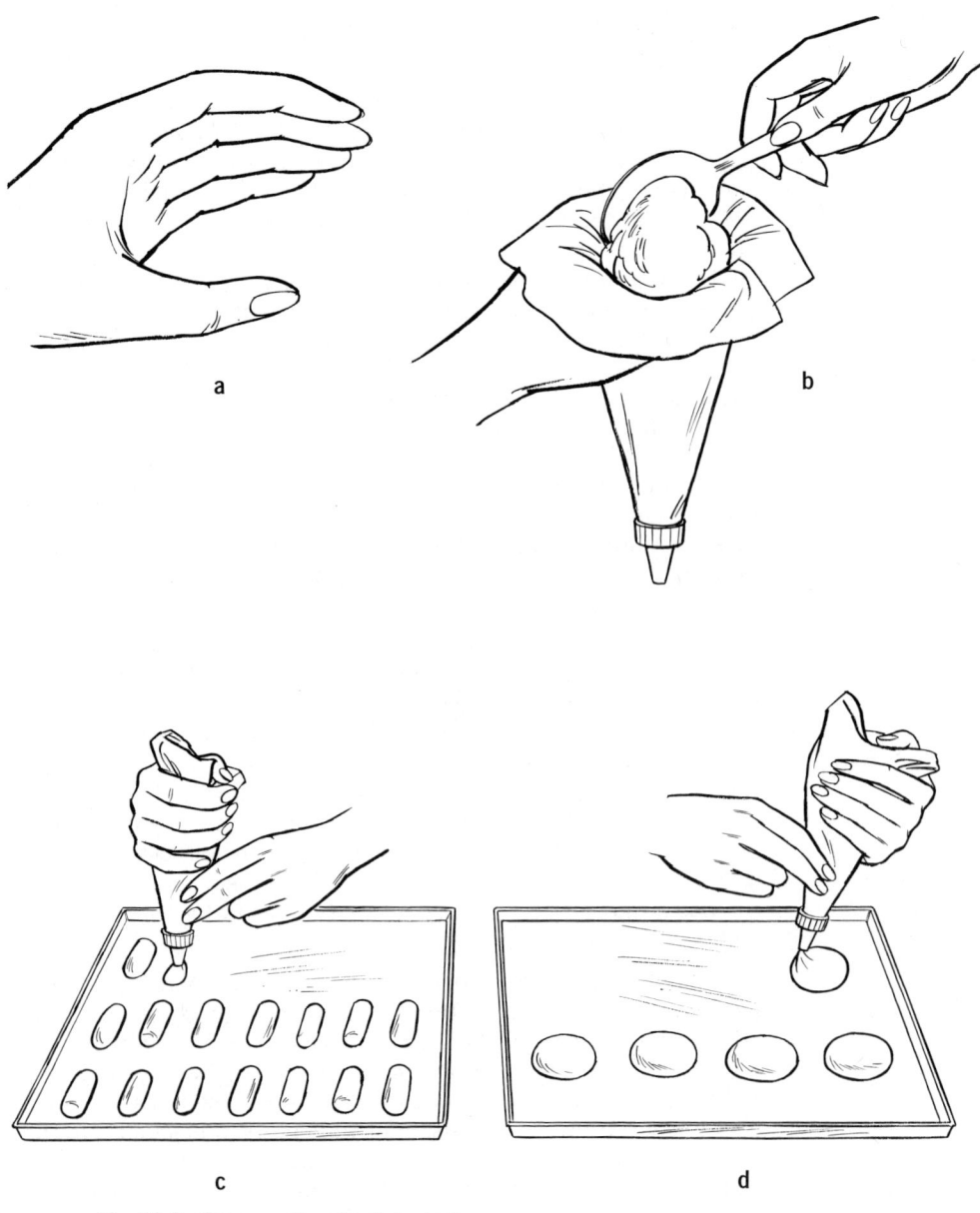

PART SIX: PUFF PASTRY PRODUCTS ... ECLAIRS & CREAM PUFFS

Fig. 19-1 **Cream puff and eclair shells.**

    a If you are using a pastry bag, hold your hand in this position as a support while you are filling the bag.

    b Keep the pastry bag spread open with your fingers while you fill the bag with batter.

    c Bag the eclairs out evenly and space them about 1 inch apart.

    d Bagging out cream puffs.

UNIT 19: CREAM PUFFS AND ECLAIRS

to be sure they are dry and well baked on the inside. If you touch the shells at this point, they will feel dry, crisp, and hollow. If the shells are brown on the outside and still moist on the inside, it means that their structure is not fully set. This will cause the shells to collapse or shrink while they cool. Since the shells are generally filled with moist fillings such as custards, creams, or even hot foods, they must be dry and well baked in order to support the fillings without becoming soggy.

BASIC CUSTARD FILLING

Yield: *enough for 20 to 24 cream puff or eclair shells*

AIM To learn how to prepare basic custard filling.

THINGS YOU SHOULD KNOW In the unit on napoleons you were told to use whatever filling you liked for the sandwiched layers. You may do the same when filling cream puffs or eclairs. If you wish, you may use any of the prepared custard-type puddings for the filling. However, there is a basic custard that you can make yourself. This custard may be converted to many other varieties by adding buttercream, whipped cream, chocolate, and other color and flavor combinations to it. This was mentioned in the unit on napoleons, in describing the French custard and the Bavarian-type custard.

THINGS TO PREPARE Have space ready in the refrigerator for storing the custard. Check the recipe for the necessary ingredients.

| saucepan or double boiler | measuring spoons | mixing bowl |
| pan for the cooked custard | measuring cups | hand whip |

CUSTARD FILLING

INGREDIENTS (*measure carefully*)		HOW TO MIX
milk (scalded)	1½ cups	Dissolve the sugar and salt in the milk. Put the mixture into a pan over hot water or in a double boiler and allow it to simmer.
sugar	⅔ cup	
salt	pinch	
eggs	2	Place the eggs into a cereal or soup bowl and whip slightly.
cool water	½ cup	Dissolve the starch in the water. Add the starch solution to the eggs and stir in well. Add about ⅓ cup of the hot milk to the egg and starch solution and blend it in well. Add the egg and starch mixture to the simmering milk and sugar in a slow, steady stream, stirring constantly with the whip or beater. Continue to stir until the custard thickens and starts to boil, or until puffs of steam rise through the center of the custard.
cornstarch	⅓ cup	

CUSTARD FILLING (Continued)

INGREDIENTS (*measure carefully*)
butter   3 tablespoons
vanilla   2 teaspoons

HOW TO MIX

Add the butter and vanilla to the thickened custard and stir in well until the butter is melted and the custard is smooth. Pour the custard into a clean bowl or baking pan that has been rinsed with cold water and left moist. The droplets of water will act as a lubricant and make removal of the custard easy after it has cooled. Sprinkle the top of the hot custard with about 1 tablespoon of granulated sugar. The sugar will melt and form a syrupy cover on the custard, which will prevent the formation of a crust on the custard. Allow the custard to cool and then place it in the refrigerator to chill.

FINISHING CREAM PUFFS AND ECLAIRS

Refer to Fig. 19-2.

1 Prepare the custard that has been chilled by stirring it well to make it smooth. At this point, you may add buttercream to make French custard, whipped cream for Bavarian cream, melted chocolate for a chocolate custard, or make any other changes you wish.

2 The cream puff or eclair shells may be cut open and the custard, or other filling, spooned into the center. (Fig. 19-2*a*.) The tops are then replaced and pressed down so that they stick to the custard. The filled shells are sprinkled with confectioners' sugar and they are ready to be served. (Fig. 19-2*b*.) If you plan to serve the cream puffs or eclairs at a later time, refrigerate them after they are filled and dust them with confectioners' sugar just before serving them. The moisture of the refrigerator will dissolve any confectioners' sugar which may have been dusted on them before refrigeration.

3 The cream puff and eclair shells may be filled without cutting the tops off. Put the custard into a pastry bag with a small plain tube. (You may make a parchment paper pastry bag for the same use. If you make a parchment paper bag, cut a small hole in the end with scissors.) Insert the tube into the cream puff shell about ½ to 1 inch and squeeze the custard into the shell. When filling an eclair shell, insert the tube or tip at each end of the eclair and squeeze the custard into the shell. (Fig. 19-2*c*.) This is much the same way in which you filled the jelly doughnuts. The tops of the shells may then be dipped into warm chocolate frosting or another frosting

UNIT 19: CREAM PUFFS AND ECLAIRS
211

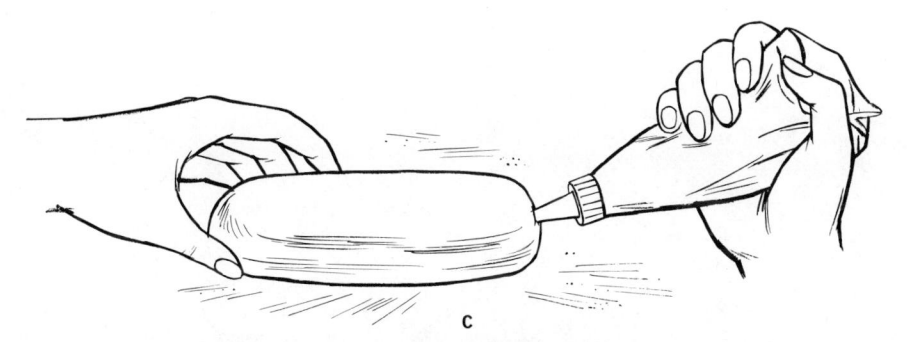

Fig. 19-2 **Filling and finishing cream puffs and eclairs.**

    a Cut the cream puff shells in half, fill the bottom half with whipped cream or other filling, and then replace the top.

    b A finished cream puff.

    c The pastry bag is used to fill the eclairs with custard filling. The same method may also be used for cream puffs.

made from simple icing. The shells may also be covered with fudge icing or simply dusted with confectioners' sugar.

4 You may also use whipped cream to fill the cut-open shells. The cut tops of the shells are often dipped into frosting, then allowed to dry. These tops are then placed on the whipped cream. *Custard- and cream-filled desserts must always be refrigerated until they are served.*

VOCABULARY

			Review
action	consume	rapid	basic
approximately	lubricant	replace	consistency
collapse	pronounce	visible	shells

Refer to *Glossary* for an explanation of any words you do not know. The dictionary will be helpful for terms not included in the *Glossary.*

PART SEVEN ■■■■■■□

variety cookies

INTRODUCTION:
RULES FOR COOKIES

AIM To understand the general rules and practices of cookie making. Cookies are often called a "universal" or "all-purpose" dessert. Think of the many different ways cookies are served. You have probably seen them served as a quick snack, served with ice cream, accompanying hot chocolate, displayed in an assortment on a cookie platter, packed with lunches, and used in many other ways.

There are many types of cookies. Some have elaborate or foreign names. Others, such as sugar cookies, have rather simple names. Still others are named after holidays or special occasions, such as Christmas cookies and bridge cookies. Many cookies can be kept for long periods of time without spoiling or becoming stale. You will find many varieties of cookies in this section, with a recipe for each variety. The recipes will give good results if you follow instructions and understand the basic facts about making cookies.

Cookies fall mainly into two basic types: (1) the soft drop type (spooned or bagged out); and (2) the firmer, dough-type variety. The soft variety may be spooned out onto a prepared baking pan or properly bagged out through a pastry bag and tube or a special cookie press. Naturally, many more varieties and shapes may be made with a pastry bag or cookie press than with a spoon only. As you can see, this is why it is important to develop some skill in the use of a pastry bag and tube. By this time, you may have had some experience using a pastry bag to decorate layer cakes, cupcakes, pies, and other desserts.

The firmer cookies made from dough can be varied in a great many ways. The variations will depend upon the number of different cookie shapes and cookie cutters you use. Variety in cookies also comes from different methods of garnishing and finishing the cookies. Variety in cookie making is the result of your good judgment and ability to create new ways of finishing the cookies. You should know and understand the following basic rules about each of the major cookie varieties.

RULES FOR CUTOUT OR SHORTBREAD VARIETY COOKIES

1 Be sure the flour is sifted carefully to remove lumps. The flour should be folded in gently in the final stages of mixing.

2 It is best to chill the cookie dough before rolling it. This will reduce the chances of the dough sticking to the table or the cloth, and therefore reduce the amount of dusting flour needed.

3 A flour-dusted cloth will make rolling the dough much easier and will help keep the dough from sticking to the worktable.

4 Scrap or leftover dough that remains after the first cookies are cut

INTRODUCTION

out should be worked gently in with fresh cookie dough and rolled out again.   If no fresh dough remains, knead the scrap dough gently and roll it out again, using as little flour as possible to avoid toughness.

5 Be sure to see that the cookie dough is rolled out evenly so that all the cookies are of the same thickness.   This will make possible an even crust color when baking the cookies, avoiding the raw, or pale, crust color and the burned, or dark, crust color which result when cookies of uneven thickness are baked on the same pan.

RULES FOR SPOONED OR BAGGED-OUT VARIETY COOKIES

1 It is especially important that you mix in the flour gently in the last stage.   Mix just enough to incorporate the flour, as overmixing will make the batter tough.   It will also make it difficult to bag the batter through the pastry bag and tube.

2 Prepare the sheet pans for the cookies carefully.   If the pan is to be lightly greased, be sure you cover the entire surface with an even coating of fat.   Ungreased spaces will cause the cookies to stick.

3 Spoon or bag out the cookies so that they are all the same size and shape.

4 Space the cookies evenly, with enough space between them for the cookies to spread during baking without running into each other. Cookies such as wafers need more room to spread than other cookies.

5 Cookies that are to be garnished with nutmeats, sprinkles, jam, or jelly should be garnished before they are baked.   Large pieces like nuts and glacé fruits should be pressed into the cookies so that they do not fall out after the cookies are baked.

6 Cookies to be garnished or decorated with frostings or chocolate should be baked first, allowed to cool, and then garnished with your choice of frosting.

7 Cookies to be garnished before baking should not be allowed to stand too long.   A crust formed on the cookie will prevent the garnish from sticking to the cookie.

GENERAL RULES FOR ALL VARIETIES OF COOKIES

1 Cookies should be baked until they are just done.   Most cookies continue to bake for a few minutes after they are removed from the oven, because the heat of the oven causes the cookie to continue to dry while it is still on the hot pan.   A cookie that is well baked or slightly overbaked will be very dry, even crumbly, when it cools.

2 Wafer-type or thin cookies should be baked until they are almost done and then removed from the oven.   They will complete their baking on the pan because they are thin.

3 Cookies that have been colored with food or vegetable coloring should be baked in a moderate oven (365° to 380°). The color should be clear and distinct after the cookies are baked. Too hot an oven will cause a dark crust color to form which will cover the color of the cookie. You can tell when the cookie is baked in a moderate oven by checking the bottom crust. If it is light or golden brown, the cookie may be considered as done.

4 Vegetable or food coloring should be used carefully. Pastel or light colors are more attractive than dark, sharp, or very bright colored cookies. Christmas cookies, or cookies used for special occasions requiring bright colors, may be made a little darker or sharper in shade.

5 Cookies should be allowed to cool before they are decorated or garnished with frostings. Cookies should be stored in dry containers and in dry places. *Do not store cookies in damp places.*

NOTE The following cookie recipes will illustrate for you the basic varieties that can be made, both from the firm cookie doughs and the softer cookie batters that are spooned or bagged out. *Refer to Figs. 20 through 22 for guidance as you make the cookies. Follow the instructions for mixing carefully.*

UNIT **20**

DOUGH-TYPE OR CUTOUT COOKIES

SUGAR COOKIE DOUGH   Yield: *about fifty 2-inch cookies*

AIM   To learn how to make sugar cookies.

THINGS YOU SHOULD KNOW   Refer to the rules for making cutout or shortbread cookies.

THINGS TO PREPARE   Refer to the recipe for the necessary ingredients. Set the oven temperature at 385°.

mixing bowl	worktable	cookie cutters	baking pans
mixing spoon	floured cloth	egg wash or milk	flour sieve
measuring cups	rolling pin	wash brush	garnishes
measuring spoons	dusting flour	table brush	oven pads

SUGAR COOKIES

INGREDIENTS (*measure carefully*)		HOW TO MIX
sugar	1 cup	Blend all the ingredients to a smooth, soft paste.
salt	1 teaspoon	
shortening	¾ cup	
corn syrup	2 tablespoons	

PART SEVEN: VARIETY COOKIES

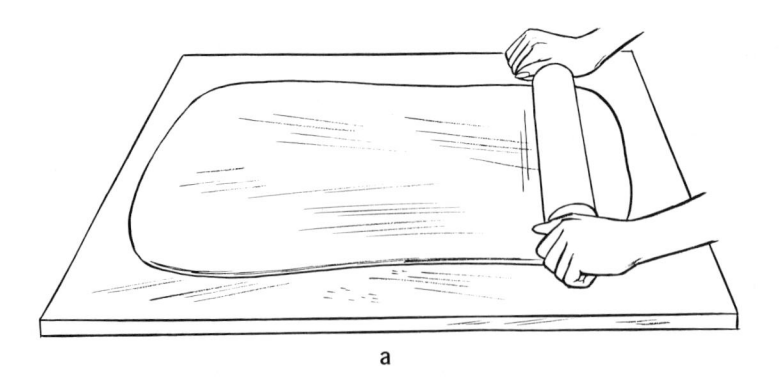

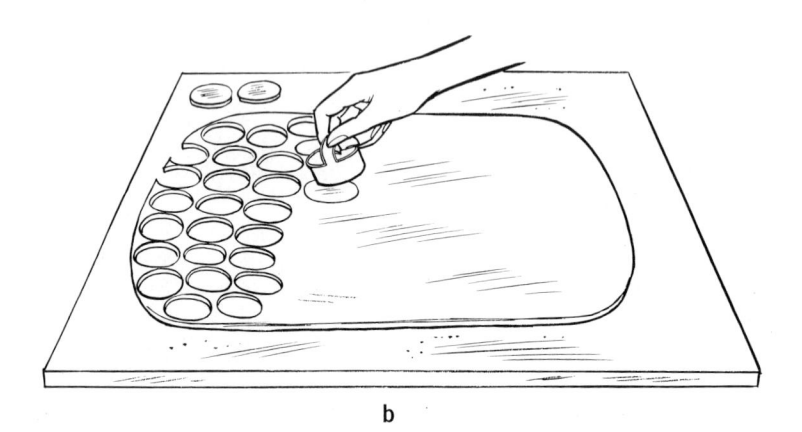

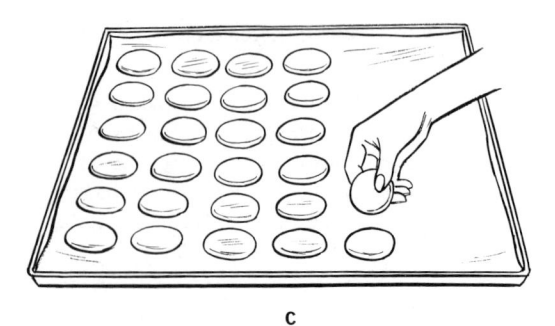

Fig. 20-1 **Preparing cookies for baking.**

    a Roll the dough out evenly about ⅛ inch thick.

    b Cut out the cookies as close to each other as possible to avoid excessive scrap dough.

    c Place the cookies on a sheet pan lined with parchment or freezer paper. Space the cookies evenly apart.

UNIT 20: DOUGH-TYPE OR CUTOUT COOKIES

SUGAR COOKIES (*Continued*)

INGREDIENTS (*measure carefully*)		HOW TO MIX
eggs	2	Add one egg at a time and blend each egg in well.
milk	⅓ cup	Add the milk and the vanilla to the batter above and stir in gently.
vanilla	1 teaspoon	
cake flour (sifted)	4 cups	Sift the flour and baking powder together. Add to the above mixture and fold it in gently until all the flour is absorbed. *Do not overmix.* The dough should be medium firm and a bit sticky. Refrigerate the dough before using.
baking powder	1¼ tablespoons	

CHECK POINTS

    1 Is the oven set at the proper temperature (385°)?

    2 Are the worktable and equipment ready?

    3 Are the garnishes ready?

MAKING, BAKING, AND FINISHING THE COOKIES

Refer to Fig. 20-1.

1. Place a dish towel or thick, plain cloth on the worktable and dust it with flour.

2. Take about half of the chilled sugar cookie dough and knead it very gently into a rectangular shape. Dust the top of the dough and the rolling pin lightly with flour.

3. With an even pressure on the rolling pin, roll the dough until it is about ⅛ inch thick, or a bit thicker. (Fig. 20-1*a*.) Check to see that the dough is of even thickness all over. Remove any excess flour from the surface of the dough.

4. At this point, you may wash the surface of the dough with egg wash or milk and then sprinkle the dough with sugar, ground nuts, chocolate sprinkles, or other toppings before cutting out the cookies. If the cookies are to be garnished after they are baked, leave the dough plain.

5. Select the cookie cutters you plan to use. Cut the cookies out as close to each other as you can to avoid too much scrap dough. (Fig. 20-1*b*.)

6. The baking pans should be lightly greased or lined with parchment paper. Lift the cookies gently with a spatula or knife and place them evenly on the pan. Space them about ½ inch apart to allow for mild spreading during baking. (Fig. 20-1*c*.)

7. Bake the cookies at 385° until they are golden brown. You may have to shift or turn the pans during baking if the oven does not bake evenly. Be careful when doing so. *Do not overbake.*

8 Allow the cookies to cool before frosting them with icing or dipping them into melted chocolate.

NOTE Chocolate to be used for dipping cookies or garnishing the cookie tops should be melted in a double boiler. Do not permit the chocolate to get very warm. Allow the dipped cookies to dry at a cool temperature, but not in the refrigerator. Frostings such as simple icing or fudge should be mildly warm when applied to the cookies.

SHORTBREAD CUTOUT COOKIES

Yield: *approximately 100 small cookies*

AIM To learn how to make a variety of shortbread cutout cookies.

THINGS YOU SHOULD KNOW Refer to the rules concerning shortbread cookies.

THINGS TO PREPARE Prepare the same things as for sugar cookies.

SHORTBREAD COOKIES

INGREDIENTS (*measure carefully*)		HOW TO MIX
sugar	1¼ cups	Blend all the ingredients in this stage to a soft, smooth paste.
salt	1 teaspoon	
shortening	2 cups	
corn syrup	2 tablespoons	
eggs	2	Add one egg at a time and blend each egg in well. Add the vanilla with the second egg and blend in well.
vanilla	2 teaspoons	
all-purpose flour (sifted)	3 cups	Sift the flours together and add to the above mixture. Fold the flour over gently and mix until it is absorbed into the batter. The dough should look a bit lumpy and feel sticky. Refrigerate the dough until firm before using it.
cake flour (sifted)	3 cups	

CHECK POINTS Check the same things you did for the sugar cookie dough.

MAKING, BAKING, AND FINISHING THE SHORTBREAD COOKIES

Refer to Fig. 20-1.

1 Prepare the worktable and the cloth as you did for sugar cookies. Be sure the cookie dough is chilled and firm.

2 Roll the dough out to about ¼ inch in thickness. Be sure the dough is of even thickness throughout. Use your fingers to check. The

UNIT 20: DOUGH-TYPE OR CUTOUT COOKIES

dough is rolled thicker than sugar cookie dough because it may be rolled again to impress a garnish into the dough before cutting out the cookies.

3 The cookies may be cut out at this time with a variety of cookie cutters. For example, bridge cookies may be cut out with heart shapes, diamond shapes, or other cookie cutter shapes. The cookies may also be cut with a pastry wheel or French knife into small squares or rectangles. Mark off measured guidelines before you cut the cookies with the pastry wheel. Cut slowly and carefully to be sure the cookies are even in size and shape. Various animal or other types of cutters may be used. You may also cut large cookies of varying shapes from this dough. However, large cookies may be difficult to handle because this dough is rich and the cookies are delicate.

4 If the cookies are to be garnished with chopped nutmeats, sugar, sprinkles, or other fine toppings, brush the top of the rolled-out dough with egg wash and then sprinkle the surface of the dough with the topping. Next, roll the rolling pin very gently over the topping to be sure the topping will stick. *Do not press firmly.* You may brush the dough with the yolk of an egg and then draw lines through the yolk wash with the tines of a fork. This will produce an attractive crisscross effect when the cookies are baked. Make the lines before the yolk wash dries. Cookies to be dipped and garnished after baking should be cut out plain.

5 Cut out the cookies as close together as possible to avoid excess scrap dough. This is especially important when the dough has been garnished before cutting out the cookies. Work the scrap dough very gently and roll it out again. Cut the scrap dough into squares or rectangles. This will enable you to use up all the dough without having any left over.

6 Place the cookies on dry pans or parchment paper–lined pans. Since these cookies are rich (that is, they contain a large percentage of shortening), the pans do not have to be greased. Space the cookies about ¼ to ½ inch apart. Small cookies need little space since these cookies do not spread much.

7 Bake the cookies at 385° until they are golden brown. Shift or turn the pans if the oven does not bake evenly. Check the bottoms of the cookies to see if the cookies are baked. Do not wait until the cookies show a deep brown crust color on top. In fact, cookies that are plain and to be garnished after baking should have only a very light gold color in the center. The contrast of this crust color with the frosting or chocolate will make the cookie even more attractive.

8 *See Fig. 20-2 (page 222) for ways of finishing or decorating the cookies.* Let the cookies cool before dipping or decorating them. When dipping the cookies in fudge, frosting, or chocolate, dip only the

outer surface and avoid getting the back of the cookie dipped. You will note in the illustrations that some cookies have a small star design made with fudge frosting and a pecan is placed in the center of the star before the fudge dries or develops a crust. You may also place half of a glazed cherry in the center of the chocolate fudge. *Neatness and cleanliness are very important. The cookies should look attractive and reflect the care with which you prepared them.*

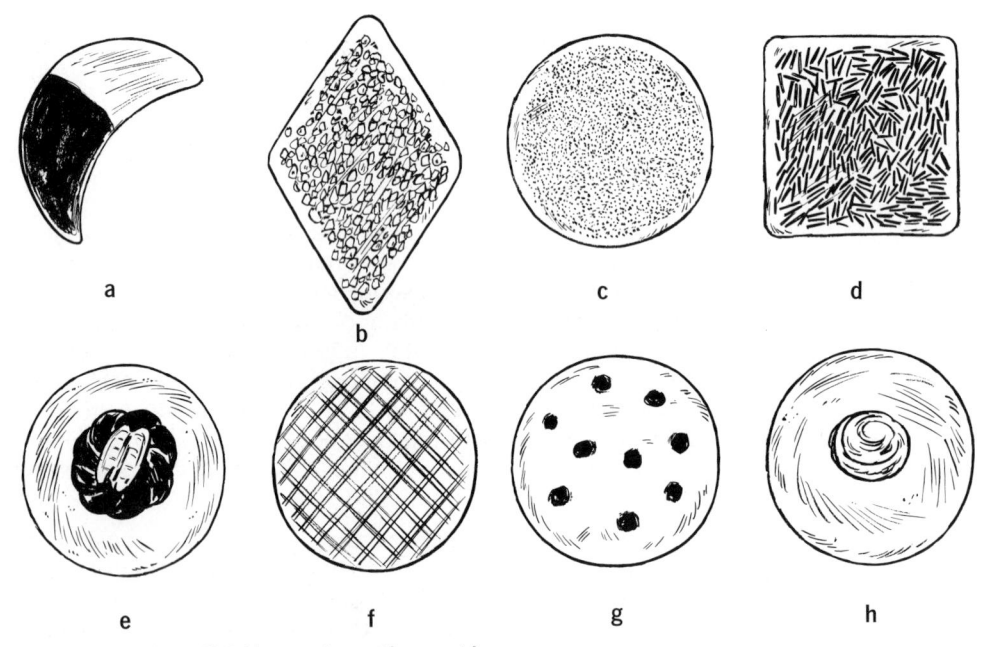

Fig. 20-2 **Finishing or decorating cookies.**

    a A crescent-shaped cookie that has been baked, cooled, and then dipped in melted chocolate.

    b A diamond-shaped cookie that was brushed with egg wash or milk and then sprinkled with toasted ground nuts before baking.

    c A round cookie that was brushed with egg wash or milk and then dipped in sugar before baking.

    d This square cookie was cut from a dough that was brushed with egg wash or milk and sprinkled with chocolate sprinkles.

    e This round-shaped cookie was baked before the center of fudge frosting was placed on it. A pecan was placed in the fudge before the fudge dried.

    f This cookie was brushed twice with egg wash; then lines were made in the egg wash with a fork before baking. Egg yolk may be used for brushing.

    g This cookie was sprinkled with chocolate chips before it was cut out and baked.

    h This round cookie had a dot of jam put in the center before it was baked.

UNIT 21

BAGGED-OUT OR SPOONED COOKIE VARIETIES

AIM To learn how to make bagged-out or spoon-dropped cookies.

THINGS YOU SHOULD KNOW As mentioned previously, the spooned or bagged-out variety cookies are made from a softer batter. You can easily see that it would be very difficult to bag out a firm or stiff batter. It is important to know that the greatest variety of cookies may be made from this type of batter. The large jumble type, the French variety, sandwich types, wafer types—these are but a few of the many recipes you will find. The success of these cookies depends upon your skill in placing them on the pan in varying shapes but with the same size and same appearance. Thus you see the value of learning to use a pastry bag and tube or a cookie press skillfully. The greater the variety of tube designs you use, the greater the number of cookie shapes you can make. Practice with the pastry bag will make you expert at making bagged-out cookie varieties.

Bagged cookies may vary not only in shape but also in the way they are finished. For example, the larger jumble-type cookies differ because of their shapes and the way in which two colors may be combined in one cookie. Smaller French cookies can vary in their many shapes, as well as in the colors of the cookies. These cookies are often sandwiched together with a filling and then dipped. Others may be garnished and baked. Different nuts or fruits will give the cookie different appearances. The variety of bagged or spooned cookies you can make, like the firmer cutout cookies, will depend upon your creative ideas and imagination.

JUMBLE COOKIES

Yield: *about 36 cookies*

THINGS TO PREPARE The oven is generally set at 385° to 390°. Check the recipe for the necessary ingredients. Pans for these cookies are usually lightly greased. Parchment paper–lined pans prevent sticking. (Note that wafer-type cookies which are bagged or spooned are deposited on lightly greased pans.)

variety garnishes	measuring spoons	measuring cups	cookie press
mixing spoon or mixing machine	spoon for dropping the batter	spatula or large spoon	pastry bag and tube
flour sieve	worktable	oven pads	

JUMBLE COOKIES

INGREDIENTS (*measure carefully*)		HOW TO MIX
sugar	¾ cup	Blend the ingredients together and mix to a smooth, soft paste.
salt	½ teaspoon	
shortening	¾ cup	
corn syrup	1 tablespoon	
eggs	2	Add the eggs one at a time and *cream* well after each egg is added.
milk	⅓ cup	Add the milk and vanilla and stir lightly.
vanilla	1 teaspoon	
cake flour (sifted)	3 cups	Sift the flour and baking powder together into the bowl. Mix lightly until the flour is absorbed. Do not overmix. The batter should be sticky and medium soft.
baking powder	1 tablespoon	

CHECK POINTS

1 Is the cookie batter ready to be placed into the pastry bag? Check the bag and the tube.

2 Is the oven set at the proper temperature?

3 Are the garnishes ready for use?

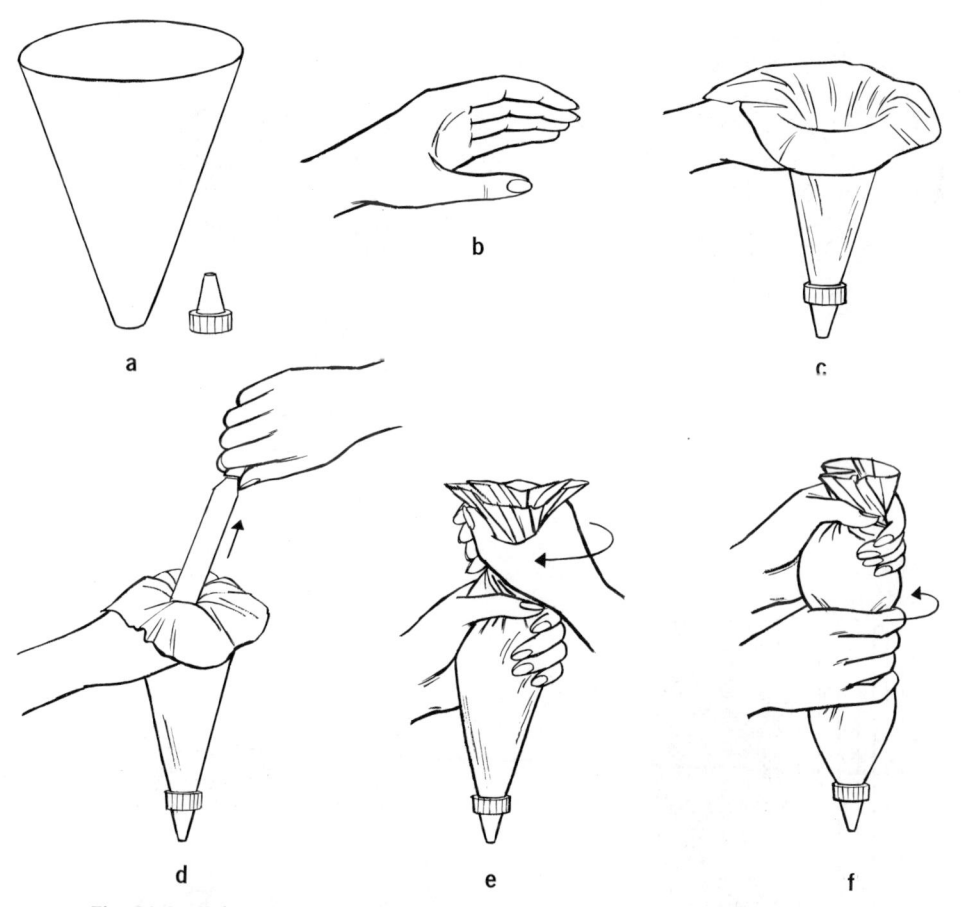

UNIT 21: BAGGED-OUT OR SPOONED COOKIE VARIETIES   225

Fig. 21-1 **Using the pastry bag.**

    a A pastry bag and a plain tube.

    b This is the position of your hand when you are holding the pastry bag underneath the fold.

    c To fill the bag, the edge of the pastry bag is folded over your hand. Put the bag in your hand and turn the edge down 6 inches.

    d The pastry bag is filled with batter by using a knife, spatula, or spoon. Insert the batter with the knife or spoon. Close your hand over the knife or spoon above the batter and then withdraw the knife or spoon. The batter will remain in the pastry bag.

    e Twist the top of the pastry bag to keep the batter in and also to force the batter down to the tube end.

    f The pastry bag can be held at the top twist and then twisted once again in the center. This divides the batter in half and makes it easier to press the batter out of the tube.

PART SEVEN: VARIETY COOKIES

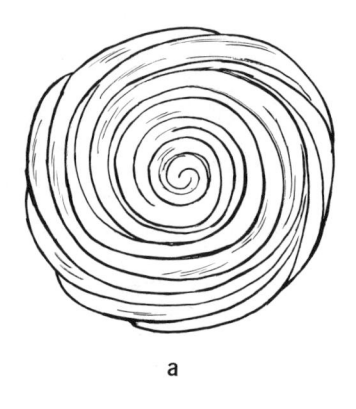

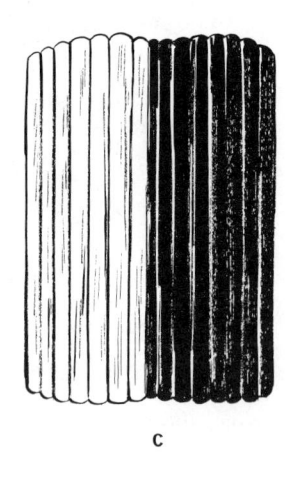

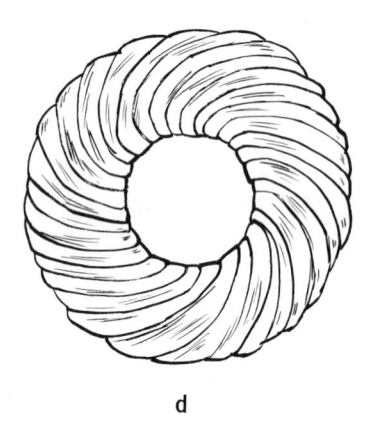

Fig. 21-2 **Shapes for jumble cookies.**

    a A rosette jumble cookie.

    b An S-shaped jumble cookie.

    c This jumble cookie is made by bagging out a single line of yellow cookie batter and bagging out a line of chocolate cookie batter alongside it. The two batters join by spreading into each other during baking.

    d A ring-shaped jumble cookie.

UNIT 21: BAGGED-OUT OR SPOONED COOKIE VARIETIES

BAGGING OUT, SPOONING, GARNISHING, AND BAKING THE JUMBLE COOKIES

NOTE If you are using a pastry bag, see Fig. 21-1 to learn how to fill the pastry bag with cookie batter, and see Fig. 21-2 for the variety of cookie shapes you can bag out.

1. The cookie pans should be lined with parchment paper or lightly greased with melted shortening.

2. If the batter is spooned out, be sure you drop it in equal amounts and shape the drops round with the back of the spoon. You may dip the spoon in some milk to keep the batter from sticking to the spoon. Space the cookies about 1 inch apart to allow for spreading.

3. You may add melted chocolate to part of the batter and bag the chocolate batter alongside the yellow batter for a two-color effect. You may make a chocolate dot on top of the yellow batter for variety. You may make an all-chocolate cookie out of the batter. You may use additional food colors for other varieties.

4. The cookies may be garnished with nuts, glazed fruits, sprinkles, jam, jelly, or other suitable toppings before baking them.

5. Bake the cookies at 385° until they are golden brown. Do not overbake. Remember that cookies continue to bake and dry after they are removed from the oven.

6. Allow plain cookies to cool before you stripe or dip them with frosting or chocolate.

NOTE The pastry bag and tube should be washed well inside and out as soon as you are through. Hang the bag up to dry.

FRENCH COOKIES Yield: *approximately 100 cookies*

AIM To learn how to make French cookies (plain or sandwiched).

THINGS YOU SHOULD KNOW These cookies are best suited for bagging out with a pastry bag and tube. A star tube or French tube can be used to make a complete variety of shapes and designs. These cookies will not spread too much so the designs made will be seen. You may use a plain tube to make small button-type cookies or small finger-shaped cookies which can be sandwiched after they have been baked and cooled. (You can use a teaspoon to drop these cookies out but it is quite difficult to get the cookies the same size.) A cookie press may be used very nicely with this cookie batter.

228   PART SEVEN: VARIETY COOKIES

THINGS TO PREPARE   Prepare the same things as you did for jumble cookies. The pans for French cookies need not be greased because the batter is rich in fat content. Parchment paper is useful in baking these cookies. Check the recipe for the necessary ingredients.

FRENCH COOKIES

INGREDIENTS (*measure carefully*)		HOW TO MIX
sugar	1 cup	Blend the ingredients together to a smooth paste.
salt	½ teaspoon	Scrape the sides of the bowl and continue to
shortening	1½ cups	*cream* until the batter is soft and light.
vanilla	1 teaspoon	
eggs	1 cup (4 average)	Add one egg at a time and cream well after each addition. The batter should be soft and light like buttercream.
cake flour (sifted)	1 cup	Sift the flours together. Add them to the batter
all-purpose flour (sifted)	3 cups	and fold in very lightly until all the flour is absorbed. The cookie batter should be slightly lumpy and medium thick.

CHECK POINTS   These are the same as for jumble cookies.

Fig. 21-3   **Sandwich-type cookies—round button shape.**

   a A baked round button cookie. It is bagged out with a plain tube.

   b The cookie is turned over when cool and filled with a small center of jam or fudge frosting.

   c Another cookie of the same type and shape is placed over the filled cookie, making a sandwich.

   d This sandwiched cookie has been dipped halfway into melted sweet chocolate or fudge frosting.

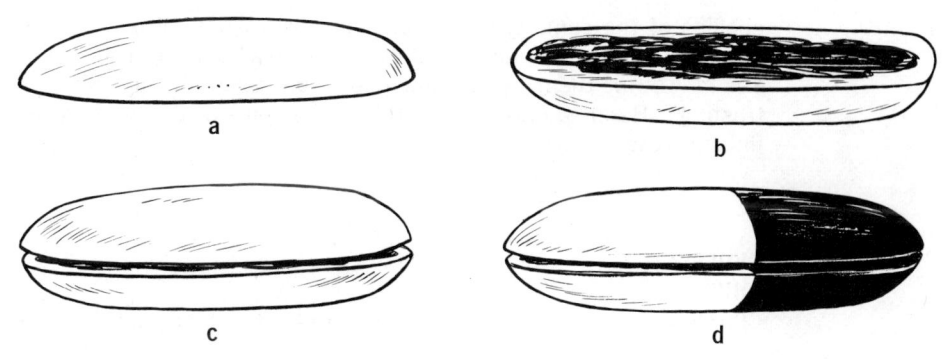

Fig. 21-4 **Sandwich-type cookies—finger shape.**

    a The short, finger-shaped cookie.

    b The cookie is baked and cooled, then turned over and filled with a strip of jam or fudge frosting.

    c Another finger cookie of the same type is then sandwiched to the filled cookie.

    d The sandwiched, finger-shaped cookie is then dipped into melted sweet chocolate or fudge frosting.

BAGGING OUT, SPOONING OUT, BAKING, AND FINISHING THE COOKIES

See Figs. 21-3 and 21-4 for finishing the sandwich-type cookies.

1 The pans for these cookies should be clean and dry. A parchment paper liner is helpful but not necessary.

2 Bag out the cookies into *equal sizes and shapes.* If you are using a pastry bag with a star or French tube, you make make star shapes, small finger shapes, round shapes, pear shapes, horseshoe shapes, and many others. Space these cookies about ½ inch apart to allow for spreading. (If the cookies are larger than 1 inch, allow a little more space between cookies on the pan.)

3 Cookies to be garnished with nuts, fruits, sprinkles, or similar garnishes should be garnished as soon as the cookies are bagged or spooned out.

4 Bake the cookies at 385° until they are light brown. Do not overbake. Allow the cookies to cool before decorating and finishing them.

5 When you are finishing sandwich type cookies, count the number of similar cookies you have. If you have fifty round button types and fifty long finger types, turn only twenty-five cookies of each variety over. Prepare a paper cone or pastry tube and fill it with smooth jelly or jam, or fudge frosting. Place a few drops of the jelly or frosting on the turned-over cookie. Now sandwich the twenty-five cookies of the same type to these cookies. When all the cookies are sandwiched, you may dip them in sweet chocolate or frosting. You may stripe them, using a fine paper cone filled with chocolate or frosting. Refer to Figs. 21-3 and 21-4 for some of the methods of finishing them.

CHOCOLATE CHIP COOKIES

Yield: *approximately 36 medium-size cookies*

AIM To learn how to make chocolate chip cookies.

THINGS YOU SHOULD KNOW Chocolate chip cookies are often called Toll House cookies. They may be called sprinkle cookies or by some other name. You will recognize these cookies from their appearance and taste. They are rather flat and crisp after baking. They may be spooned out onto a greased pan or they may be bagged out with a pastry bag without the use of a tube. (The chocolate chips tend to clog the tube, making it difficult for you to force the batter through.) Be sure to allow enough space between cookies on the pan since these cookies spread considerably during baking. If chocolate chips are not available, you may use chocolate sprinkles instead.

THINGS TO PREPARE Set the oven temperature at 375°. Check the recipe for the necessary ingredients. Baking pans should be greased lightly but evenly.

| measuring spoons | oven pads | table brush | mixing spoon |
| pastry bag or spoon | worktable | mixing bowl | measuring cups |

CHOCOLATE CHIP COOKIES

INGREDIENTS (*measure carefully*)		HOW TO MIX
brown sugar	¼ cup	Blend these ingredients together to a smooth paste.
granulated sugar	½ cup	
corn syrup	1 tablespoon	
shortening	⅔ cup	
eggs	2	Add the eggs one at a time and cream well after each egg is added. Add the vanilla and stir it in.
vanilla	1 teaspoon	
all-purpose flour (sifted)	1¼ cups	Add the sifted flour and blend the batter until smooth. Add the chips and fold in until the chips are evenly distributed throughout the batter.
chocolate chips	¾ cup	

CHECK POINTS

1 Is the oven set at the proper temperature?

2 Are the pastry bag and spoons ready?

3 Check the pans for proper greasing.

MAKING AND BAKING CHOCOLATE CHIP COOKIES

1 Fill the pastry bag with the batter. Place the tip end of the bag over the greased pan and drop the cookies out by squeezing the pastry bag from the top. Try to make all the cookies the same size. If you use a spoon to spoon the cookies onto the pan, use one spoon to lift the batter from the bowl and another spoon to push the batter from spoon to pan. Space the cookies about 1 inch apart to allow room for spreading during baking.

2 Bake the cookies at 375°. The cookies will first spread and then start to turn brown. Allow the cookies to turn a medium brown. Shift or turn the pans in the oven if the oven does not bake evenly. The cookies should feel a little soft in the center when you remove them. They will finish baking on the pan after they are taken out of the oven.

3 Remove the cookies from the pan after they are cooled. Chocolate chip cookies will bend while they are still warm. These cookies are usually left undecorated and served plain. If you wish to decorate or finish them, you may dip one edge of each cookie into chocolate fudge frosting or melted chocolate and then dip that edge into chocolate sprinkles.

UNIT 22

**ICEBOX
COOKIE
VARIETIES**

AIM   To learn how to make a variety of icebox cookies.

THINGS YOU SHOULD KNOW   Icebox cookies are very popular. Their popularity may be due to their colorful appearance, the ways they are served, the desserts with which they may be served, and the ways they may be prepared for special occasions. An added advantage in making icebox cookies is that the dough can be mixed in advance and kept in the freezer or refrigerator, to be removed, sliced, and baked as the cookies are needed. In addition to making the varieties shown in this unit, you will learn to create a number of your own colorful cookie designs.

**ICEBOX
COOKIE
DOUGH**   Yield: *about 100 small cookies*

THINGS TO PREPARE   Be sure you have refrigerator or freezer space to store the cookie dough or the unbaked cookies. Check the recipe for the

UNIT 22: ICEBOX COOKIE VARIETIES

necessary ingredients. If the cookies are to be baked as soon as they are mixed, set the oven temperature at 375°. Prepare the same things as you did for sugar cookies or shortbread cookies.

ICEBOX COOKIE DOUGH

INGREDIENTS (*measure carefully*)		HOW TO MIX
confectioners' sugar (sifted)	1¼ cups	Add the sugar to the other ingredients and blend well to a smooth paste.
salt	1 teaspoon	
shortening	1½ cups	
corn syrup	1 tablespoon	
eggs	2	Add one egg at a time and blend in well.
vanilla	2 teaspoons	Add the vanilla with the second egg and blend in well.
all-purpose flour (sifted)	4½ cups	Add the flour and mix to a smooth dough.

PREPARATION AND COLORING OF THE DOUGH

1 The dough may be left plain or you may add chopped nuts to it. Place the dough in a shallow pan, flatten it to about 1 inch high, and then freeze it. This dough may be sliced later into small rectangular shapes and baked as nut cookies.

2 You may divide the dough into 2 or more pieces and color each piece of dough separately. Remove the entire dough from the mixing bowl to a lightly floured part of the worktable. Divide the dough into sections and then color each section separately in the mixing bowl.

3 Be careful when adding the color. Do not make the colors too dark. Blend them in well so that there are no streaks of color showing unevenly through the dough. When using chocolate, be sure the chocolate is completely melted before adding it. This will make blending the chocolate in much easier and smoother. If you add cocoa, you should also add 1 or 2 teaspoons of milk to the batter because the cocoa will stiffen the batter too much without the use of milk. Be sure to color the dough sections before you chill or freeze the cookie dough.

4 Chilling the dough in the refrigerator makes the dough easier to handle and means that you will need less flour when rolling out a piece of the dough. Chilling or freezing the made-up dough makes it much easier to slice the individual cookies without smearing their patterns. (The colors in soft doughs will smear when cut.) The cookies will also keep their shape.

PART SEVEN: VARIETY COOKIES

ICEBOX COOKIE VARIETIES

AIM To learn how to make an assortment of icebox cookies.

THINGS YOU SHOULD KNOW The assortment presented in this unit includes only the most popular varieties of icebox cookies. You can make many other varieties just by thinking and planning. Look at cookie displays in bakeries for ideas. Note special varieties served in different places and at social meetings. Once you have learned how to prepare the basic dough, chill it, color it, and assemble it into units ready for slicing, you can make almost any colorful variety you see. Review *Preparation and Coloring of the Dough* to remind yourself of the things you should know. Remember, for example, that colors should not be too strong or dark. Doughs should be chilled so that they can be handled more easily. Cookies should be sliced only when the dough is very cold, almost in a frozen state, so the cookies will cut cleanly and not smear. You must think of what you are doing and do it carefully.

THINGS TO PREPARE Set the oven temperature at 380°, if you plan to bake the cookies soon after you have made them up. Be sure to chill the dough before slicing the cookies.

refrigerator or freezer space	egg wash or egg white wash	French knife floured cloth	worktable pans
small rolling pin	dusting flour	wash brush	

PINWHEEL ICEBOX COOKIES

Refer to Fig. 22-1.

1 The pinwheel may be made from 2 or 3 differently colored pieces of cookie dough. Decide how many colored doughs you want and then divide the dough you have made into 2 or 3 equal parts. Color each part thoroughly and then chill the doughs. You can chill them in a few minutes by placing the colored doughs in the freezer.

Fig. 22-1 A rolled-up pinwheel cookie roll. Two or three different-colored layers of cookie dough are sandwiched together with egg wash or egg whites and then rolled up.

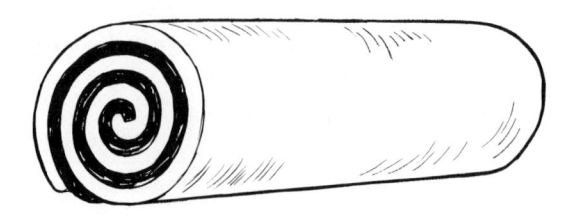

UNIT 22: ICEBOX COOKIE VARIETIES

2 Remove the chilled doughs and knead them slightly to make them plastic. Flatten each piece of dough on the flour-dusted cloth. (Use just enough flour to keep the dough from sticking to the cloth.) Sprinkle the top of the dough and a thin rolling pin with a little flour. Now roll the piece of dough into a rectangular shape about ¼ inch thick, trying to keep the thickness even all over.

3 Gently lift the rolled-out dough and set it to one side. Roll out the next piece of colored dough in the same way. Now brush the top of the first piece with egg wash or slightly beaten egg whites. Place the second piece of dough on top of the first and even out the sides. Use your fingers or the side of a knife to push the dough together so that the sides are of even thickness. Roll out the third piece of dough and place it over the second, after you have egg-washed the second piece. The egg wash or egg whites keep the layers of dough together, much like a paste. Be sure to remove any excess flour before washing the dough.

4 You now have 3 layers of dough. (You will have only 2 if you used only 2 pieces of colored dough.) Be sure the top piece of dough is washed with egg before you start to roll the dough. Fold the dough over at one edge and roll it up so that a pinwheel is formed after three or more turns. As soon as the roll of dough is about 1¼ inches thick, cut it away from the layered dough with a knife. Round the spiral of dough to an even roll about 1 inch thick. Place this roll on a sheet pan lined with waxed or parchment paper.

Roll the flat, layered dough up again and form another pinwheel. Continue this until the layered dough has all been made up into spiral rolls. Place the rolls of spiraled dough in the refrigerator to chill.

5 If you plan to use the dough for cookies soon after the spiraled rolls are shaped, put them into the freezer for about half an hour. They will quickly become firm. On the other hand, these rolls of cookies may be kept in the freezer for long periods of time and can be taken out, sliced, and baked as you need them.

6 Cut the frozen or chilled rolls into slices or cookies ¼ inch thick. Try to make all the cookies of equal thickness. This will enable you to bake them with an even crust color.

7 Place the cookies on a dry pan. It is best to bake them on parchment paper. Let the cookies return to room temperature so that they are completely defrosted. Cookies that are baked while still frozen may be slightly raw or gummy in the center. This is especially so if the cookies are sliced thick.

Bake the cookies at 380° until they are golden brown on the bottom. You do not want these cookies browned on top. This will cover the colors and the cookies will lose their unique appearance. If the oven does not bake evenly, shift the pans in the oven. Re-

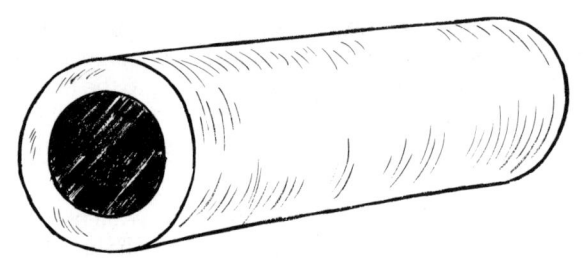

Fig. 22-2 A chilled roll of bull's-eye cookie dough. A round strip of one color is rolled in a sheet of cookie dough of another color.

member that the cookies continue to bake while they are still hot and on the baking pan. Allow the cookies to cool before removing them from the pan.

BULL'S-EYE COOKIES

Refer to Fig. 22-2.

1 Divide the dough into 2 equal parts, and color them as you wish. You may want the center to be chocolate and the outside to remain the natural yellow color of the dough. (Remember to melt the chocolate before mixing it into the dough.) Place the colored doughs in the refrigerator to chill. Use the freezer to hurry the chilling process.

2 Place the dough for the outside part on the floured cloth. Flatten the dough slightly with the palm of your hand. Roll the dough out about 2 inches wide and ¼ inch thick. (The length will depend upon the amount of dough you have.) Remove any excess flour from the top of the dough and brush the dough with egg wash or egg white wash.

3 Roll the second piece of dough into a roll about ¾ inch in diameter. Check to see that it is as long as the rolled-out dough. If it is shorter, roll it a bit longer. If it is longer, push the roll together with the palms of your hands. Lift the roll of dough gently and place it in the center of the first rolled-out piece of dough. Fold the edge of the flat layer of dough over the roll, and turn it over until the entire roll of dough is covered. If the dough does not stick to the roll, it means either that the egg wash has dried or that the flour has not been removed from the roll of dough. If this happens, unroll the outside dough and brush the center roll of dough with egg wash. Fold the bottom dough over the roll again and it will now stick.

4 Roll the dough to a thickness of 1¼ inches in diameter. Be sure it is of even thickness throughout. Make up other rolls of cookies in the same way. If you have a large piece of dough to begin with, divide it into an even number of equal parts and color half the pieces

UNIT 22: ICEBOX COOKIE VARIETIES 237

in one color and half in the other. Put the rolls of dough into the freezer, make them up, and bake them as you did the pinwheel cookies. *Do not overbake the cookies.*

SPIRAL COOKIES

Refer to Fig. 22-3.

1 Divide the icebox cookie dough you have just made into 3 equal parts, and color each part a different color. (Pastel shades of yellow, red, and chocolate make a pleasing combination.) Chill the dough.

2 Remove a small piece of dough from each unit and blend them together into a rectangular shape. Roll this piece of dough out on the floured cloth to a thickness of about ⅛ inch. Brush the top of the dough with egg wash or slightly beaten egg whites.

3 Roll out a strip of each color into a roll about ½ inch thick. Place the rolls alongside each other as though you were going to make a three-braid roll. Braid the 3 strips of colored dough together loosely. Now roll the braid into a roll about 1 inch in diameter.

4 Brush the top of the roll to remove excess flour. Lift the roll gently and place it on the rolled-out and egg-washed rectangular dough. Brush the top of the roll with egg wash; then lift the bottom edge of the rolled-out dough and place it over the roll. Roll the entire dough so that the inside roll is covered completely. Roll the dough to a diameter of 1¼ inches. Place the dough on a pan and store it in the freezer to chill it thoroughly.

5 Slice the roll into ¼-inch slices. If the color smears slightly after you have sliced some of the cookies, wipe the knife blade and continue. If the dough should become soft before you are finished slicing all the cookies, return the dough to the freezer to firm it again. Cut as many cookies as you plan to use. The rest of the dough may be kept in the refrigerator or the freezer.

6 Bake the spiral cookies as you did the pinwheel or bull's-eye cookies. *Do not overbake.*

Fig. 22-3 A roll of spiral cookie dough. Two or three different-colored strips of dough are braided together and then rolled up in a sheet of rolled-out dough.

CHECKERBOARD ICEBOX COOKIES

Refer to Fig. 22-4.

NOTE Read the instructions carefully and look at the sketches as you work. *Neatness and care* will give you a very attractive cookie for your efforts.

1. Divide the dough into 2 equal parts and color both halves as you wish. (The most popular combination is yellow and chocolate.)

2. Remove a small piece of dough from each part and place them to one side. These will later be used as the outside wrap for the cookies. Thus, one wrap will be yellow and the other chocolate.

3. Chill the pieces of dough before using them. Divide each piece of chilled or frozen dough again into 2 sections so that you may now have 2 pieces of chocolate dough and 2 pieces of yellow dough.

4. Dust a cloth lightly with flour, spreading it over the cloth. Place any one of the colored pieces of dough on the cloth and roll it out into a rectangular shape about ¼ inch thick. Be sure it is of even thickness all over. Remove excess flour from the surface of the dough. Lift the rolled dough gently and place it on a small pan that will fit into the freezer.

5. Now take a piece of dough from the contrasting (opposite) color dough. Roll this dough in the same way as you did the first piece. Brush the rolled-out dough on the pan with egg wash. Roll up the dough on the cloth around the rolling pin (Fig. 22-4*a*) and place it directly over the egg-washed dough of contrasting color. Then unroll it and press it down very gently so that it sticks to the egg wash. (Fig. 22-4*b*.) Take another piece of dough of the same color as the first, or bottom, piece of dough, roll it, and place it on top of the second piece. Follow this by rolling a fourth layer of dough the same color as the second layer and placing it on top of the third layer. You now have two alternate layers of yellow and chocolate— or any other two colors you may have used to color the dough. Place the four-layered dough into the freezer to chill or harden.

NOTE If you have difficulty lifting the rolled-out layers of colored dough to place on top of each other, roll the dough up gently on a rolling pin and place it over the first layer. Unroll the dough carefully so that it covers the other layer. Do not stretch the dough while you are rolling it up and unrolling it. Be sure to straighten the sides of the layered dough with your hands or the flat side of the knife.

6. When you are ready to make up the cookies and before you remove the layered dough from the freezer, roll out the small pieces of dough you had set aside. This dough should be rolled quite thin on the floured cloth and should be about 4 inches wide and as long as the size of the dough will permit you to roll it.

UNIT 22: ICEBOX COOKIE VARIETIES

Fig. 22-4 **Icebox cookies.**

    a To make checkerboard cookies, the dough is colored in 2 parts and then divided into 4 pieces. Each piece of dough is rolled out to ¼-inch thickness.

    b Brush each layer with water or egg whites. Stack the layers, alternating the two colors.

    c There should be four layers—two yellow and two chocolate. These layers are cut into strips about ¼ inch thick.

    d Roll out a piece of leftover dough into a thin sheet. The cut strips are placed over each other on the sheet, alternating chocolate and yellow so that a checkerboard effect is formed. Wrap the sheet around the square as a cover.

    e Chilled checkerboard-square cookie dough that is ready to be sliced into cookies.

PART SEVEN: VARIETY COOKIES

7. Remove the layered dough from the freezer and cut slices about ¼ inch thick. (Fig. 22-4c.) Wash the rolled-out dough with egg wash. Place the first strip you cut in the center of the rolled-out dough. Egg-wash this strip. Now cut the second strip. Lift it gently and turn it over so that the colors contrast with each other. In other words, by turning the cut strip you have placed it on the first cut strip so that the yellow is now over the chocolate and the chocolate is over the yellow. Wash the second strip and cut the third. Place this as you did the first in order to have alternate, or opposite, colors again on top of each other. Place the fourth cut strip over the third and you will have four layers of dough with alternating color strips. It will have the appearance of a checkerboard. (See Fig. 22-4d.)

8. Brush the top and sides of the four-layer square with egg wash. Lift the edge of the rolled-out dough and press it against the side of the square. Fold the dough over so that all four sides of the square are covered with the outside dough. Cut away excess dough with a knife. Square the sides with the flat side of a knife if necessary. (Fig. 22-4e.) Lift the square gently and place it back on the pan. If you have more dough that has to be made up, complete the other squares, using the other piece of dough for the outside.

9. The rolled-up checkerboard squares can be kept in the freezer until you are ready to cut and bake them. When ready to slice them, remove the dough from the freezer and use a sharp French knife to slice the cookies. Cut them about ¼ inch thick and slice them evenly. Place them on a pan about ¼ inch apart. Allow the cookies to defrost; then bake them at 380°. Check the bottoms of the cookies to see that they are light brown. Do not overbake so that a brown crust color dulls the appearance of the checkerboard colors.

VOCABULARY

accompany	contrast	fresh	lunch	stale
animal	creative	glazed (review)	nutmeats	unique
assortment	diamond	hazelnut	pastel	universal
center	elaborate	hearts	pecan	variation
checker	excessive	hundred	press	wafer
continue	firmly	imagine	similar	walnut

Refer to *Glossary* for the explanation of words you do not know. The dictionary will be helpful for terms not included in the *Glossary* because they are commonly used words.

PART EIGHT ■■■■■■■■

decorating cakes & pastries

INTRODUCTION:
PRACTICING AND PREPARING

AIM To learn how to decorate petits fours, French pastry, birthday cakes, and other special-occasion cakes.

THINGS YOU SHOULD KNOW There is really much pride and pleasure to be found in decorating your own cakes and pastries. The neatly decorated birthday cake, the little petits fours that you can finish with almost any design you wish, the larger French pastries, and the special-occasion or holiday cakes you decorate will give you a great deal of satisfaction. And your skill will be admired by others.

The attractiveness of cake or pastry lies in the neatness of its decoration. This depends on the way you use color combinations, how you apply the frosting, and the practical judgment you use in making the decorations. This is a wonderful chance for you to create many of your own artistic designs. You may become quite expert if you are artistically inclined. It does take time, patience, and a good measure of practice to develop these artistic abilities, but you will note that each cake you decorate will not only become easier to do but will look more and more attractive. *You must follow instructions, look at the sketches for guidance, and practice.*

PRACTICING DECORATING

Referring to the figures for Unit 24, do the following:

1 Learn how to cut parchment or freezer paper into triangles; then practice making them into paper cones. Roll them so that the point of the cone is closed until you fill the cone and then cut the point off. Make a number of cones for practice and place them one inside the other so that they will be ready whenever you need them.

2 Prepare some buttercream frosting and use it for practice decorating. Fill a paper cone with frosting and decorate the back of a baking pan or layer pan, pretending it is the top of a layer cake. (Refer to Figs. 24-2 and 24-3.) At first, you can expect the cone to come open while you fill it. The buttercream may back out of the top of the cone when you first try to squeeze it. Your designs may look like the first attempts you made to write or draw. These are all signs of the beginner. With practice, you will improve.

3 Scrape the frosting from the practice pan and return it to the bowl. Use it again and again for practice. Place it in the refrigerator for use again whenever you have time. Refer to the instructions you followed when you decorated the first layer cakes you made. (Figs. 16-2 and 16-3.) Practice using the pastry bag and tubes with the same frosting and pans.

INTRODUCTION

PREPARING THE VARIOUS CAKES FOR DECORATING

1. All cakes, layer cakes, loaf cakes, or flat sheet cakes to be cut into smaller sections should be cool or chilled before they are decorated.

2. A chilled cake will cut more easily and without crumbling. This is especially important with foam or sponge-type cakes. Chill these cakes for use after all the frostings and garnishes have been prepared.

3. To make petits fours or French pastries, it is best to use a close-grained cake, such as a pound cake. These cakes can be frozen or chilled before or after they are decorated. They cut neatly without crumbling, and the simple or fondant frosting sticks to the sides of the cake rather than peeling off of it as the frosting is poured.

4. Cakes that are frosted with a simple or flat type of frosting should be placed on an icing grate or a roasting rack over a pan. This will permit the frosting to be poured over the cake and the icing that runs off will be collected in the pan below the rack. The icing collected in the pan may be rewarmed and poured again so that there is little or no waste.

5. Icings should be smooth and without lumps. Leftover icings that have been refrigerated or stored in a cool place may be warmed in a double boiler and stirred to make them smooth. This is true for buttercream and fudge-type frostings, as well as the simple or flat frostings.

6. Check your needs before you begin. Such tools as spatulas, spoons, icing bowls, saucepans, icing grates, decorating bags and tubes, and other similar equipment should be ready for use. A prepared frosting may cool and become too firm while you look for a spatula or tube.

7. It is important to repeat that icings and frostings should be colored carefully. Pastel or light shades are best for most cakes. Deep or dark colors are used for special-occasion cakes and special color designs. Always be sure the colors are blended in well to avoid the streaks which cause an uneven color on the cakes.

UNIT 23

DECORATING PETITS FOURS AND FRENCH PASTRIES

DECORATING PETITS FOURS

Petits fours are small pieces of cake that are cut into various small shapes. These are best cut from sheets of pound cake that have been baked in flat sheet pans. The cake is usually about 1 inch thick.

1 Place the small units of cake on the icing grate. Be sure they are set firmly so that they do not turn over when the frosting is poured over them.

NOTE You may insert a fork into the bottom of the unit and dip it directly into the warmed frosting. Allow the icing to drip; then set the unit on the grate to dry and to complete the dripping of the icing. You may use sugar tongs or spoons to remove the unit from the fork.

2 Be sure that the frosting is warm and pours easily. Add the color at this time and stir it in well. Now lift the saucepan and pour some of

UNIT 23: DECORATING PETITS FOURS AND FRENCH PASTRIES

the frosting over each of the units. Be sure you pour over the center of each unit so that the icing runs down the sides and the entire unit is covered. With a spoon, add a little icing to any bare spots.

3 Scrape the frosting that drips on the pan together with a spatula or large spoon and return it to the saucepan. Warm it again and pour it over other unfrosted units. Allow the units to dry before removing them from the rack or grate.

4 Remove the units (petits fours) from the grate and place them on a pan lined with waxed paper.

NOTE The frosting may be colored with several shades or with chocolate, for greater variety. Some people prefer to color all the cakes with one pastel shade and then decorate them with different designs. Prepare the icings and cones for decorating after you have selected the design for each variety. Practice one design on a pan before you decorate the petits fours. Be neat and clean about your work. See Fig. 23-1 (page 246) for decoration of petits fours.

DECORATING FRENCH PASTRIES

French pastries are larger units of different designs. They are usually cut from two sheets of cake that have been sandwiched together with jam, jelly, or some other filling, and then chilled. When the sheets are chilled enough, they are cut into various shapes (squares, rectangles, diamond shapes, or round shapes).

1 The cut-out units may be iced with a simple or flat type of frosting in the same way that you covered the petits fours.

2 If the sides of the cake are to be decorated with buttercream or a fudge-type icing, lift the piece of cake and hold it in one hand between your thumb and forefinger. Now dip the spatula or table knife into the icing and spread the icing around the sides of the French pastry unit.

3 At this point, you must have ready the garnish you will use, so that it will be easy for you to dip the pastry into the garnish (chopped nuts, sprinkles, toasted cake crumbs, coconut, chocolate pieces, or other garnishes). Dip the unit into the garnish in the bowl so that the garnish is not spilled all over the table. Be sure the sides of the unit are completely covered but *do not get any of the garnish on the top,* for you will decorate this after the sides of all the units have been covered with frosting and dipped.

PART EIGHT: DECORATING CAKES & PASTRIES

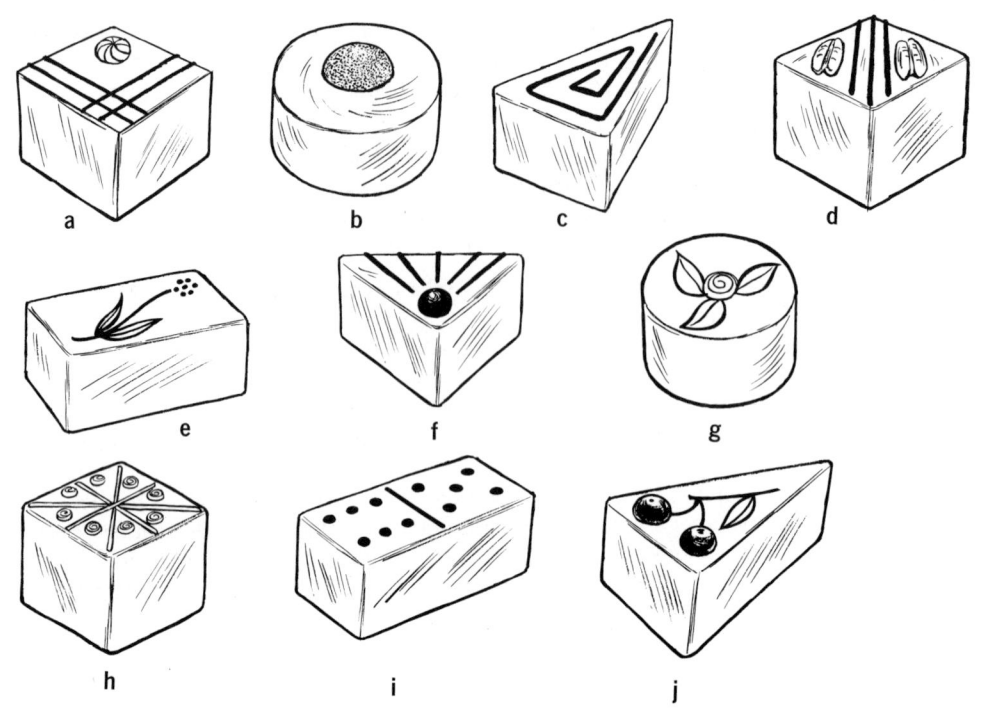

Fig. 23-1 **Decorated petits fours.**

- **a** Square-shaped petit four or pastry, glazed with simple icing and striped with contrasting frosting. The center may have a buttercream rosette or cherry.
- **b** A round-shaped petit four covered with fondant or simple frosting. In the center is a glazed cherry that has been rolled in granulated sugar.
- **c** A triangle-shaped petit four covered with simple icing and striped with a contrasting icing color.
- **d** A cube-shaped petit four glazed with fondant or simple icing and striped with contrasting colors. Pecan halves or other nuts are used for a garnish.
- **e** A rectangular-shaped petit four decorated with a green spray of small leaves with contrasting dots in a flower effect.
- **f** A triangle-shaped petit four coated with soft fudge or simple frosting. A glazed cherry or other fruit is at the peak with stripes of contrasting icing.
- **g** A round-shaped petit four has a rosette of colored buttercream with leaves extending from each side.
- **h** A cube-shaped petit four striped with a contrasting icing. Small rosettes of buttercream in various colors are spaced between the stripes.
- **i** A rectangular-shaped petit four finished like a domino.
- **j** This pyramid-shaped petit four is decorated by a green twig with a cherry placed at the end of each branch.

UNIT 23: DECORATING PETITS FOURS AND FRENCH PASTRIES   *247*

NOTE   At this point, you may place the units on a pan, wrap them well in parchment or waxed paper, and freeze them for later use. These are called "stock pieces," to be used whenever you need them.

4 The tops of the French pastries are usually decorated with a pastry bag and tube. Generally, a buttercream or fudge frosting is used to make the various designs. A single color or a combination of colors may be used on a single unit. You have had some practice in decorating layer cakes and cupcakes. Use this experience to help you decorate the French pastries.

5 The tops of the French pastry units may also be garnished. You may use any of the garnishes you have on the sides or you may add a glacé cherry, a whole nut, a dab of sprinkles, or any other topping to give added contrast and make the pastry attractive.

NOTE: STORING FRENCH PASTRIES AND PETITS FOURS

French pastries should be kept in the refrigerator until you are ready to serve them. Cover them with a light wrap. If they are to remain in the refrigerator for any length of time, they may be placed in a box and the box covered with paper. This will prevent staling and the absorption of odors from other foods.

Petits fours should be placed in boxes and wrapped well before they are refrigerated. The moisture of the refrigerator, if permitted to come into direct contact with a simple or flat type of frosting, will cause the frosting to become soft and sticky. If enough moisture is absorbed by the frosting, it will almost completely dissolve and the decoration will be totally lost. The petits fours, when properly wrapped, may be stored in the freezer for later use. (Allow them to defrost at room temperature before serving them.)

NOTE   It is desirable to place the petits fours or French pastries into paper cups. The petits fours can be put into the small, multicolored paper cups. This will make them even more attractive and much easier to handle for service. The French pastry units can be placed into the same paper liners that you used when you made cupcakes.

UNIT 24

DECORATING
BIRTHDAY CAKES
AND SPECIAL-OCCASION CAKES

It is important that you practice—at least once—decorating the back of an empty layer cake pan with a full cake design that you have drawn on paper. This experience will make you feel more secure when you decorate a real cake. It is also advisable to select a simple decoration (such as an inscription with a plain stem and bud design) for your first cake. The border design should be equally simple and easy to make. (Refer to Figs. 24-2 through 24-8 for illustrations of designs and inscriptions to help you.) Below are some basic rules you must follow when decorating cakes. Try to understand them and then apply them to the decorating you do.

1 Be sure the layers you are going to use for the cake are even. You may have to cut off some of the high round top to level the layers. Refer to the rules on preparing layers for frosting in Unit 16.

2 Learn your colors and how to blend them so that they do not clash. Remember to always add the color a drop or two at a time. You can always add more color to darken a frosting, but adding too much color at once will make it impossible for you to do anything to lighten it unless you can add more frosting.

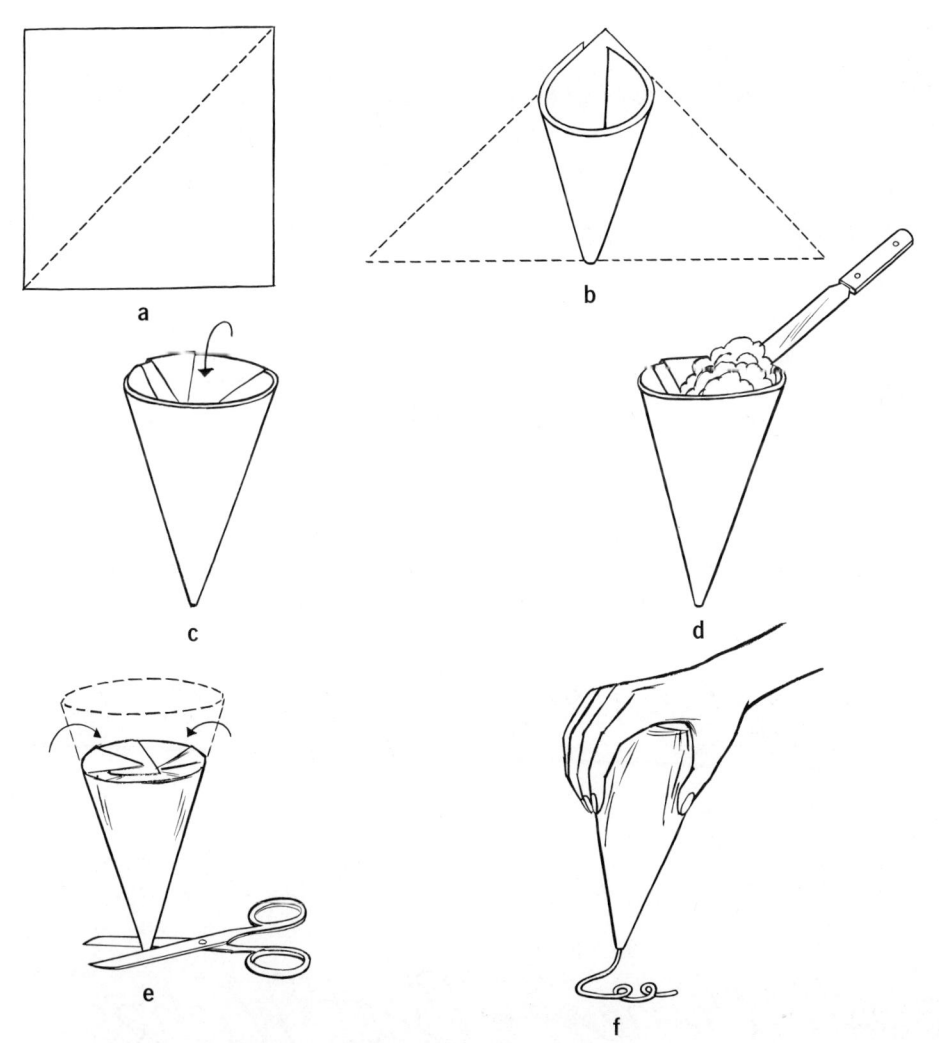

Fig. 24-1 Making a decorating cone for inscriptions.

- **a** To make a parchment paper cone for inscriptions, cut a square of parchment paper to form a triangle.
- **b** Shape the paper triangle to form a cone.
- **c** Fold an edge of the parchment paper into the cone to keep the paper cone from opening.
- **d** Fill the cone with icing or frosting.
- **e** Fold over the top part of the cone to seal it and then cut a small hole at the bottom with scissors.
- **f** Hold the cone in the palm of the hand and squeeze it from the top down to force the icing out.

PART EIGHT: DECORATING CAKES & PASTRIES

Happy Birthday   *Happy Birthday*

Congratulations   *Congratulations*

To Mother   *to Mother*

Halloween   *Halloween*

Happy Easter   *Happy Easter*

Sweet Sixteen   *Sweet Sixteen*

Best Wishes   *Best Wishes*

Thanksgiving   *Thanksgiving*

Merry Christmas   *Merry Christmas*

Fig. 24-2 **Inscriptions for decorating cakes.**

3 *Be sure you have in front of you the name or inscription to be placed on the cake. Spell carefully and correctly.*

4 Prepare the paper cones (Fig. 24-1*a, b, c*) and be sure they are rolled properly so that the point of the cone is completely closed until you cut it. Fill the cones, or pastry bag and tube, with the icing you will use for the inscription. (Fig. 24-1*d*.) (The inscription includes the name as well as the message such as "Happy Birthday.") Practice making the inscription on the back of a pan before writing it on the cake. (See Fig. 24-2 for inscriptions.)

5 Frost the cake so that the top is completely smooth. Buttercream icing, or even whipped cream, may be used to frost the top and sides of the cake. In order to smooth the frosting, dip the spatula in warm water; draw it gently over the top of the cake in wide, full strokes from one side of the cake to the other. Do not make small, jerky pats with the knife or spatula. This will make uneven lines or ridges on the cake. Practice will make this quite simple for you.

6 The sides of the cake may be garnished with chocolate sprinkles, chopped nuts, toasted cake crumbs, or other toppings. A dry type of garnish carefully placed on the sides of the cake will add color contrast and flavor, and make handling the cake easier.

7 The inscription should be *in proportion* to the size of the cake, which means that the writing should not be too small or too large. The letters you make should all be of equal size, except for the capital letters, so that the inscription is neat and can be read easily. Be careful that you space the letters evenly. Look at the sketch of the inscription you have made for guidance.

8 Cut the point of the cone that contains the icing you will use for the inscription. (Fig. 24-1*e*.) The hole should be small so that the icing will come out in a fine line. Be sure the top of the cone is closed well so that the icing does not come out of the top when you squeeze the cone. You should apply an even pressure, placed on top of the cone, to force the icing out of the hole at the bottom of the cone. (Fig. 24-1*f*.) If the line of icing cracks or breaks as you are squeezing, it means that you are not applying even pressure all the time.

    If the icing curls as it comes out of the cone, cut the hole at the bottom a little larger. If the curling continues, it may mean that there is a lump in the icing. If this is so, you will have to transfer the icing to another cone. Do this by making the hole larger and squeezing the icing into another cone. Try to remove the lump as you cut out the hole.

    If the icing curls as you make the letters, it means that you are applying too much pressure and the icing is coming out faster than you are writing or printing. Try to keep a steady pressure so that the icing comes out in an even line. As you use the icing, turn the top of the paper cone down to keep the pressure on the icing even.

9 Hold the cone squarely over the cake after you have decided where you are going to place the inscription. (For most cakes, the inscription is placed in the center of the cake.) *Refer to the cake design you prepared, and print or write slowly.* (See Fig. 24-2.)

10 When you are making stems, leaves, and flower supports, use green-colored frosting. For stems, fill the pastry bag or paper cone, cutting a small hole in the cone as you did for the inscription. (Fig. 24-1*e*.) Squeeze a little of the icing out to remove any air pockets. Air pockets will cause the icing to crack when the icing is pushed out. Look at the sketch or design you made for the cake, and then place the stem or garland design around the cake. The design should be about ¾ to 1 inch in from the edge of the cake. See Fig. 24-3 for different garland designs. Since this cone is filled with green frosting, place it to one side to use later when you are making leaves or supports for the buds and flowers.

11 Prepare a cone, or pastry bag and tube, with pink (or other) frosting to be used for buds or blossoms (see Fig. 24-4*a*). If you are using a paper cone, cut the cone at an angle, starting at the very point and cutting about ½ inch from the center to the outside of the cone. Refer to Figs. 24-4*b* and *c* for guidance. The icing will come out of the hole in a flat or ribbon-like strip when the cone is squeezed. Now refer to Fig. 24-5 and follow the steps shown there for making the buds or flat blossoms. *Practice these steps* until you have mastered the shaping of the various petals into buds or blossoms.

12 Space the buds and blossoms so that the cake decoration looks attractive and natural. Avoid crowding and overdecorating.

13 To make leaves (Fig. 24-6 and 24-7), use scissors to cut a cone filled with green icing. Start at the center point and cut about ¼ inch to the side. Do this on both sides of the cone. When the cone is squeezed, the icing will come out in a leaf effect. Squeeze these small leaves next to the blossoms or at spray twigs where there are no flowers. Try to have the leaf slightly cover the base of the rosebud. The leaves may be made larger by squeezing harder and moving the tube so that the leaf becomes longer and then tapers off to a point. Practice will improve your skill.

14 Lastly, the border or edge design placed on the cake is usually made with a pastel shade of icing lighter than that used for the inscription. It may also be the same shade as the inscription, but the color should not be darker than the inscription for, if it is, it will detract from the inscription. Remember that the inscription is the most important part of the cake. It carries the message which explains the purpose of the cake. Nothing should overshadow the inscription. All decorations should highlight the inscription. Make the border design as even as you can so that the edge or border acts as a frame for the cake. (Figures 24-8 and 24-9 show two finished decoration designs.)

UNIT 24: DECORATING BIRTHDAY CAKES & SPECIAL-OCCASION CAKES 253

a

b

c

d

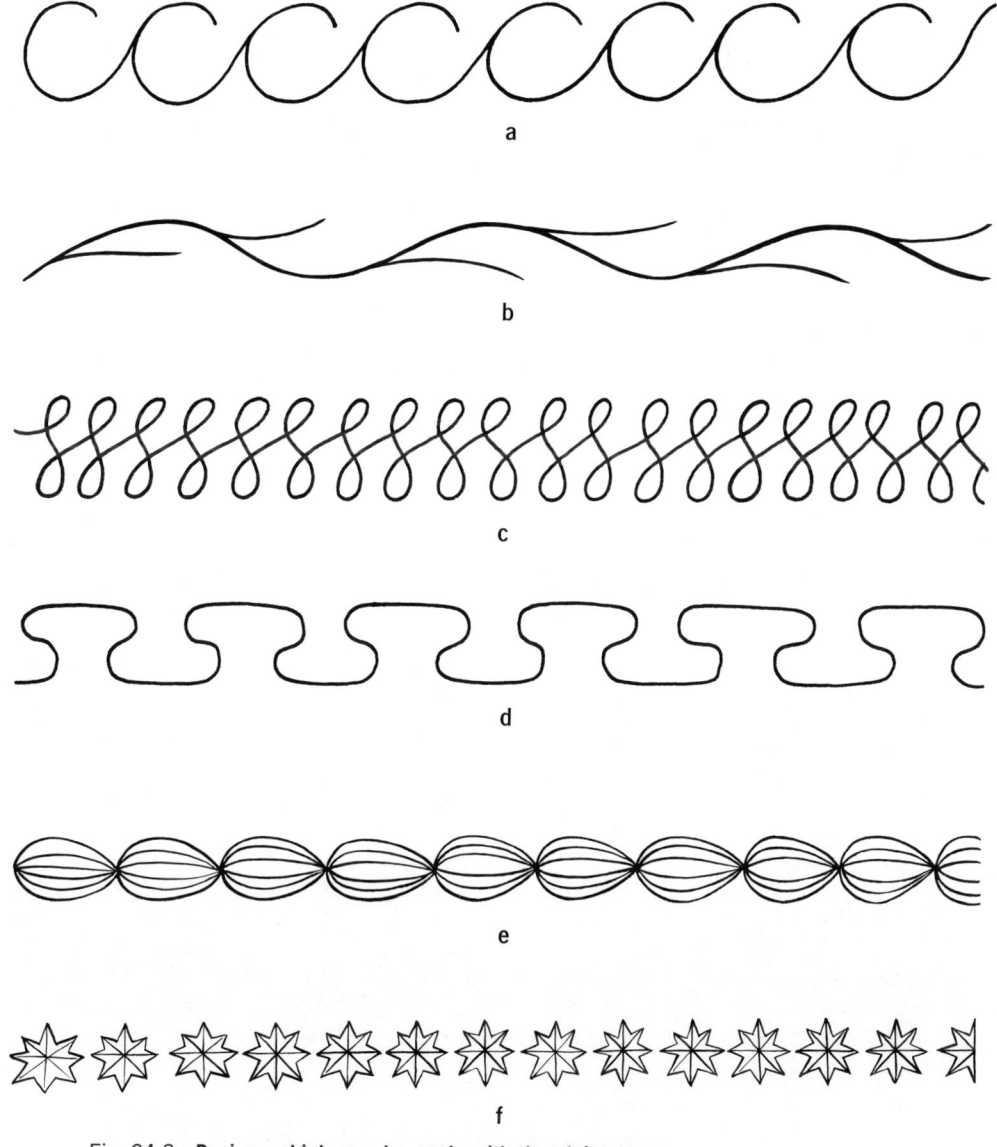

e

f

Fig. 24-3 **Designs which may be made with the plain cone.**

    a A C-shaped design for the border or edge of the cake.

    b A spray or twig design for inside borders and flowers.

    c A spiral loop for fine border designs.

    d Design of a running U with a flat base.

    e Pear-shaped border design made with a close star or French tube.

    f A star design made with a French tube or close star tube.

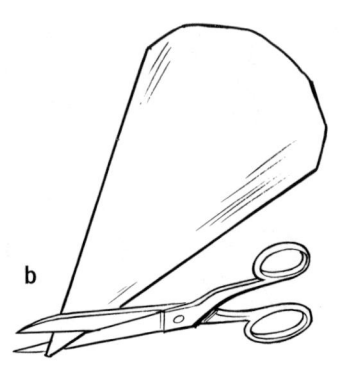

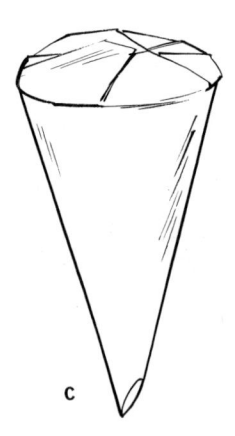

Fig. 24-4 **Cone for rosebuds.**

    a To make a rosebud tube from a paper cone, make and fill the cone as usual.

    b Cut one side of the point only.

    c The finished rosebud tube.

UNIT 24: DECORATING BIRTHDAY CAKES & SPECIAL-OCCASION CAKES   255

a

b

c

Fig. 24-5 **Blossom designs.**
    a The sweet pea design (three-petal flower).
    b The apple blossom (five-petal flower).
    c The orange blossom (six-petal flower).

256   PART EIGHT: DECORATING CAKES & PASTRIES

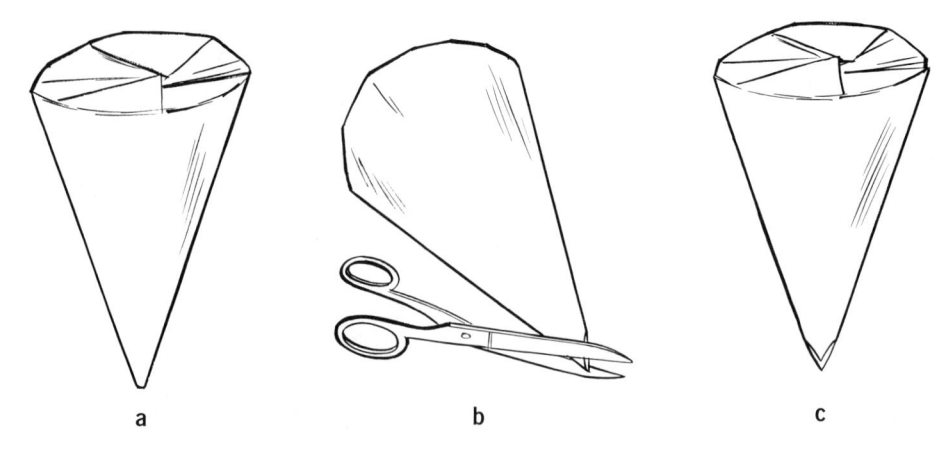

a   b   c

Fig. 24-6 **Leaf tube.**

    a To make a leaf tube out of paper for decorating, first fill the paper cone with icing.

    b Cut both sides of the cone's point equally. Keep the cuts short for small, dainty leaves.

    c A cone cut as a leaf tube.

Fig. 24-7 **Leaf designs.**

UNIT 24: DECORATING BIRTHDAY CAKES & SPECIAL-OCCASION CAKES   257

Fig. 24-8 **Cake design.**
A simple birthday cake design—a fine spray with small rosebuds and leaves.

258   PART EIGHT: DECORATING CAKES & PASTRIES

Fig. 24-9 **Cake design.**

This birthday cake design has a large spray design on one side of the cake with larger blossoms and leaves.

UNIT 24: DECORATING BIRTHDAY CAKES & SPECIAL-OCCASION CAKES

VOCABULARY

absorption	drawing	leaves	practice	*Review*
artistically	garland	mayonnaise	proportion	flavor
cones	gravy	message	uniformity	grain
crumbling	inclined	petals		sketch
detract	inscription	petits fours		texture

Refer to *Glossary* for an explanation of words you do not know. The dictionary will be helpful in the case of a term not included in the *Glossary* because the term is a commonly used word.

INDEX

Absorb, or *absorption* (*see* Glossary)
Acids, cream of tartar, 159, 187
  fruit juices, 22, 113, 187
  vinegar, 187
Angel cake, 155, 158–160
  baking, 155, 160
  cooling, 155
  decorating, finishing of, 160
  pan preparation for, 155, 159
Apples, 104–107, 196–199
  apple dumplings, 196–199
  fresh and canned, 104–107
  in pies, 104–107
    apple pie filling, 105–106
    syrup for apple pies, 104–105

Bag out (*see* Glossary)
Bake (*see* Glossary)
Baking powder, 7, 92–93, 140, 145
  action of, 7, 92–93, 140, 145
    in biscuits, 7
    in cakes, 140, 145
    in doughnuts, 92–93
Baking soda, 14, 19–20, 144–145
  action with molasses, 19–20
  in cakes, 144–145
  in muffins, 14, 19–20
Bananas, 22–26
  banana bread, 22–26
  contents of, 22
  oxidation of, 22
  ripeness of, 22
Beat, or *whip* (*see* Glossary)
Birthday cakes, 248–259
  basic rules for, 248–252
  decoration designs for, 252–253, 257–258
  floral designs for, 252, 254–256
  how to decorate, 251–252
    inscriptions, 250–251

Birthday cakes, how to decorate, planning, 249–252
  practice exercises, 242, 251
Biscuits, 2, 4–11
  baking, 6, 8
  eggs in, 12
  making, 4–11
  prepared mixes for, 11
  self-rising flour for, 11
  uses of, 2
  varieties of, 3–11
    cheese biscuits, 9
    cinnamon-raisin biscuits, 9–11
    combination biscuits, 7–8
    flaky-type biscuits, 6
    raisin biscuits, 9
    smooth-top biscuits, 3–5
Blend (*see* Glossary)
Blending method of cake mixing, 147–151
  high-ratio cakes, 147–151
    chocolate cake, 149–150
    white cake, 150–151
    yellow layer cake, 148–149
  ingredients used for, 147
  machine mixing, 148
  special shortening for, 148
Blueberries (huckleberries), 17, 110–111
  in muffins, 17
  in pie filling, 110–111
  types of, 110–111
Bow-tie doughnuts, 90–91, 93–95
  cake type, 93–95
  yeast-raised type, 90–91
Bread, quick-type, 18, 21–26
  varieties of, 21–26
    banana bread, 22–26
    banana-nut bread, 26
    prune bread, 26
    raisin-banana bread, 26
    Southern corn bread, 18

INDEX

Bull's-eye cookies, 236–237
Buns (sweet rolls), 64–77
  filled varieties, 64–77
    cinnamon buns, 64–67
    crescent buns, 67–70
    crumb buns, 73–76
    round filled buns, 76–78
    snail-shaped buns, 70–73
  refrigeration of, 64
  sweet yeast dough for, 64
    enrichment of, 64, 70
    fermentation of, 64
Butter, in puff pastry, 187–188
  (*See also* Basic Ingredients)
Buttercream frosting, 166–167
Butterflake rolls, 47–50
Butterfly cupcakes, 174, 176–177

Cakes, 141–151, 168–177, 248–259
  baking, 141–143, 145, 149
  birthday, 248–259
  cupcake varieties, 143–149
    devil's food, 143–145
    gold, 145–146
    yellow, 140–143, 148–149
  finishing and decorating, 168–177
  freezing, 149
  high-ratio (special blend) varieties, 147–151
    chocolate, 149–150
    white, 150–151
    yellow, 148–149
  layer cakes (creamed), 139–145, 148–149
    chocolate, 143–145
    yellow, 140–143, 148–149
  pound cake, 160–161
  prepared mixes for, 138
Cake-type doughnuts, 92–97
  bow-tie doughnuts, 95
  comparison with yeast-raised doughnuts, 92–93
  leavening of, 92–93
  ring doughnuts, 94
  specialty cake drops, 94
  twist doughnuts (crullers), 95

Can sizes (*see* Measurements)
Caramelize (*see* Glossary)
Checkerboard cookies, 238–240
Cherries, 109–110
  canned varieties, 109–110
    can sizes (pack), 109
  frozen, 110
Cherry pie filling, 109–110
Chocolate, 143–144, 146, 161, 165–166, 220
  in cakes, 143–144, 146, 161
  in cookies, 220
  fudge frosting, 165–166
  pie filling, 130–131
  (*See also* Basic Ingredients)
Chocolate chip cookies, 230–231
Cinnamon, 64–65, 85, 88, 91, 94
  buns, 64–67
  sugar, 64–65
    for doughnuts, 85, 88, 91, 94
  uses of, 64–65
Cloverleaf rolls, 44–47
Cocoa, 144–145, 233
  in cakes, 144–145
  in cookies, 233
  (*see* Basic Ingredients)
Coconut, 123, 158
  custard pie, 123
  types of, 123
  uses of, 123, 158
Colors (food), 163–164, 216, 252
  blending, 216, 252
  in frosting, 163–164
Combination doughnuts, 95–97
  characteristics of, 95
  leavening of, 95
  recipe for, 96
  varieties of, 95–97
Cookies, 214–231
  basic types of, 214
  dough-type cookies, 214–216, 217–222
    icebox, 232–240
    shortbread, 214–215, 220–222
    sugar, 217–220
  rules for making, 214–216
    dough-type, 217–222

INDEX

Cookies, general rules, 215–216
    spooned or bagged-out, 215–216, 223–231
        chocolate chip, 230–231
        French, 227–230
        jumble, 224–227
    uses of, 214
Corn muffins, 18–19
    Southern corn bread, 18–19
Cornstarch, 104–111, 121
Cream (*see* Glossary)
Cream, 131–132, 202, 212
    whipped cream, 131–132, 212
        in cream puffs, 212
        in eclairs, 212
        in napoleons, 202
        in pies, 132
    (*See also* Basic Ingredients)
Cream of tartar, 159, 187
    in angel cake, 159
    in puff pastry dough, 187
Cream puffs and eclairs, 205–212
    decorating and finishing of, 210–212
    description of, 205
    making and baking, 207–209
    recipe for, 206
    special fillings for, 205
        basic custard, 209
    special uses for, 205
Creaming method of mixing, 138–140
    curdling, 140
    for cake mixing, 138–140
        ingredients used, 139–140
        machine mixing, 139
        temperature of ingredients, 140
    effect on batter, 139
Crescent buns, 67–70
Crullers, 92–95
Crumb buns, 73–76
Crumb-topped pies, 117
Crumb topping, 73–74
Crust, 100–103, 118–121
    for fruit-filled pies, 100–103
        ingredients used, 101
        mixing, 102–103
        pie crust faults, 100–101
        recipe for, 102
    for soft-filled pies, 102, 118–121

Crystallization (*see* Glossary)
Cupcakes, 140–146, 148–151, 168–177
    blended batter type, 148–151
        chocolate, 149–150
        white, 150–151
        yellow, 148–149
    creamed batter type, 140–146
        devil's food, 143–145
        gold cake, 145–146
        yellow cake, 140–143
    finishing and decorating, 168–177
    making and baking, 145–146
    pan preparation for, 145
    variety fillings for, 145
Custards, 118–123, 201, 209–210
    basic custard, 209–210
    Bavarian custard, 201, 209–210
    French custard, 201, 209–210
    in napoleons, 201–202
    pie varieties, 118–123
        coconut-custard, 118, 123
        custard, 118, 123
        filling for, 121–122
Cut in (*see* Glossary)

Decoration (*see* Glossary)
Decorating cakes, 242–259
    basic rules for, 248–252
    birthday cakes, 248–259
    cupcakes, 168–177
    floral designs, 252, 254–256
    French pastry, 245–247
    garnishes, 245
    layer cakes, 168–169, 178–182
    petits fours, 244–245, 246
    practice for, 242, 251
    preparing cakes for, 179–180, 243
Develop dough (*see* Glossary)
Devil's food cake, 143–145
    characteristics of, 145
    cupcakes, 143–145
    layer cakes, 143–145
Dissolve (*see* Glossary)
Doughnuts, 80–97
    frying fat for, 81
        fats or oils used, 81

INDEX

Doughnuts, frying fat for, preparation of, 80, 84
  testing temperature of, 83
  varieties of, 80–97
    cake-type doughnuts, 92–97
    combination-type doughnuts, 95–97
    comparison with yeast-raised doughnuts, 92–93
    leavening of, 92–93
    varieties of, 93–96
      ring doughnuts, 94
      special cake drops, 95
      twisted crullers, 95
    yeast-raised doughnuts, 80–91
      bow-ties, 91
      doughnut centers, 87
      glazed doughnuts, 85–88
      jelly doughnuts, 81–85
      twisted doughnuts, 88–91
Doughs, 4–11, 34–63, 64–78, 80–91, 93, 214–217, 222
  combination, 7–8
    biscuits, 4–11
    doughnuts, 81, 93
  cookie, 214–216, 217–222
  yeast-raised, 37–40
    fermentation of, 34–35, 40
    freezing of, 35
    refrigeration of, 35
    sponge dough, 36
    sweet yeast dough, 37–40
      buns, 64–78
      doughnuts, 80–91
      soft rolls, 41–69
Drop cakes, 174
Dry yeast, 7
Dumplings, apple, 196–199
Dust (*see* Glossary)

Eclairs, 205–212
  (*See also* Cream puffs)
Egg wash, 5, 56
Eggs, 28, 121, 139–140, 150, 153–154, 158–159, 207
  adding to batters, 139–140
  composition of, 140, 150

Eggs, leavening effect of, 28, 153–154, 207
  thickening effect of 121
  types of, 153–154
    fresh eggs, 153–154
    frozen eggs, 153–154
  uses of, 153–154
  whites of, 150, 158–159
  yolks, 153
  (*See also* Basic Ingredients)
Equipment (*see* Basic Equipment)

Fermentation, factors affecting, 34–35
  slowing down fermentation, 34–35
  speeding up fermentation, 34–35
  of rich doughs, 64
  (*See also* Glossary)
Fillings, 64–65, 76, 78, 104–112, 158, 193, 215
  in buns, 76, 78
  cinnamon sugar, 64–65
  custard, 209–210
  in pies, 104–112
    fruit fillings, 104–112, 193
  jams, 76, 78, 158, 215
  jellies, 76, 78, 158, 215
  nutmeats, 145, 215
Flaky (*see* Glossary)
Flat icing or frosting, 162–164
Flavorings, 151, 163
  blend of, 151
  in cakes, 151
  (*See also* Basic Ingredients)
Flour, 14, 34–35, 101, 125, 187
  composition of, 14
  gluten in, 14
  types of, 14, 34–35, 101, 187
    all-purpose, 14, 101, 187
    bread (high gluten), 14, 34–35
    cake, 14
    pastry, 14, 101
    rye, 14
    self-rising, 14
    tapioca, 125
    whole wheat, 20
  uses of, 14, 20, 27, 34–35, 101, 140, 187, 214–215

INDEX

Flour, uses of, in cakes, 140
    in cookies, 214–215
    in doughs, 34–35, 101, 187
    in muffins, 14, 20
    in popovers, 27
    (*See also* Basic ingredients)
Flowers, 252–256
    blossoms, 252, 255
    buds, 252, 254
    garlands, 252–253
    leaves, 252, 256
    stems, 252–253
Fold (*see* Glossary)
Frankfurter rolls, 53–54
Freezing, 35, 149, 191, 247
    cakes, 149, 247
    doughs, 35
    puff pastry, 191
French cookies, 227–230
French pastry, 245, 247
    cakes for, 243
    decorating, 245, 247
    refrigeration and freezing, 247
    special notes about, 243
Frostings, 162–167
    icings, coloring of, 162–163
        as fillings, 163
    varieties of, 162–163, 164–167
        combination icing, 163, 164–167
        creamed icings, 163
        flat or simple icing, 162–164
        fudge icing, 163
    (*See also* Glossary, *Ice*)
Frozen foods, 35, 104–105, 110, 111, 149
    cakes, 149
    fruits, 104–105, 110–111
        apples, 105
        blueberries, 111
        cherries, 110
Fruits, 104–112, 192–198
    types of, 104–112
        canned, 104, 108
        fresh, 104–105
        frozen, 104–105
    uses of, 104–112, 192–198
        in pies, 104–112
        in puff pastry, 192–198

Fry (*see* Glossary)
Fudge-type frostings, 164–167

Gas, 34–35
    carbon dioxide, 34
    fermentation, 34–35
Gelatin (*see* Basic Ingredients)
Gelatinize (*see* Glossary)
Glazed doughnuts, 65, 85–88, 92–94
    cake type, 92–94
    icing for, 65, 87
    yeast-raised, 85–88
Gluten, 14, 28, 34
    effect on fermentation, 34
    in flour, 14
        development of, 34
    in muffins, 14
    in popovers, 28
    yeast and, 34
    (*See also* Glossary)
Gold cupcakes, 145–146
Gradually (*see* Glossary)
Grain (*see* Glossary)
Grease (*see* Glossary)

Hamburger rolls, 51–52
High-ratio cakes, 147–151
    cupcakes, 148–150
    layer cakes, 148–150
Humidity (*see* Glossary)

Ice (*see* Glossary)
Icebox cookies, 232–240
    varieties of, 234–240
        bull's-eye, 236–237
        checkerboard, 238–240
        pinwheel, 234–236
        spiral, 237
Icings, 65, 162–167
    types of, 162–163
        combination, 163
        creamed, 163, 164–167
        simple, 65, 162–164

INDEX

Ingredients, temperature of, 34–35
    effect on cake mixing, 140
    effect on fermentation, 34–35
    (*See also* Basic Ingredients)

Jelly doughnuts, 81–85
    finishing, 84–85
    frying, 83–84
    making, 81–83
Jelly roll, 156–158
Jumble cookies, 224–227

Knead (*see* Glossary)

Layer cakes, 138–182
    finishing and decorating, 168–169, 178–182
    methods of mixing, 139–161
    pan preparation for, 140–141
    types of, 139–156
        blended types, 147–151
            chocolate, 149–150
            white, 150–151
            yellow, 148–149
        creamed types, 139–145
            devil's food, 143–145
            yellow, 140–143
Leavening, chemical, 7, 14 19–20, 92–93, 140–145
    baking powder, 7, 92–93, 140, 145
    baking soda, 14, 19–20, 144–145
    natural, 153
        eggs, 139–140, 153, 207
        mixing, 140, 160
    organic, 34
    yeast, 34
    (*See also* Basic Ingredients; Glossary)
Lemon, 125–130
    composition of, 128
    filling for pie, 125
        fresh lemon filling, 128–129
        prepared puddings, 125
    meringue pie, 125–130
Liquids, 34, 104–110
    fruit juices, 104–110

Liquids, water, 34
    (*See also* Basic Ingredients)
Loaf cakes, 141, 143–145, 156, 160–161
    chocolate, 143–145
    pound, 160–161
    sponge, 156
    yellow, 141

Machines, 139–140, 148–149
    for cake mixing, 139, 148
    freezer, 149
    refrigerator, 140
    (*See also* Basic Equipment)
Margarine, 188–189
    in puff pastry, 188–189
    (*See also* Basic Ingredients)
Measure (*see* Glossary)
Meringue, 129–131
    composition of, 129
    pie faults, 130
    recipe for, 129
        application of, 129–130
    topping for pies, 131–132
        on chocolate pie, 131–132
        on lemon pie, 129–130
Milk (*see* Basic Ingredients)
Mix (*see* Glossary)
Mixes, prepared, 11–12, 92, 125, 128–131, 209
    biscuits, 11–12
    cakes, 11–12, 138
    cupcakes, 138
    custards, 125, 128, 131
    doughnuts, 92
    pie fillings, 128–131
    puddings, 125, 128, 131, 209
Moist (*see* Glossary)
Moisture, 35
    effect on fermentation, 35
Molasses, 19–20, 125
    acid in, 19–20
    color of, 19
    effect on batter, 19
    in leavening effect, 19–20
    in pumpkin pie, 125
Mold, or *Mould* (*see* Glossary)

Muffins, 13-19
  baking, 17
  leavening of, 14
  mixing procedures for, 13-14
  pan preparation for, 14
  prepared mixes for, 14
  self-rising flour in, 14
  variety of, 8, 17-19
    blueberry, 17
    corn, 18-19
    date-nut, 17
    orange, 18
    plain, 15-17
    raisin, 17
    Southern corn bread, 18-19
    whole wheat, 19-20

Napoleons, 199-202
  decorating and finishing, 201-202
  description of, 199
  making and baking, 199-202
  variety of fillings for, 201

Parker House rolls, 41-44
Pastry flour, 101
Patty shells, 202, 204
  special uses for, 202
Petits fours, 243-245, 246
  cake for, 243
  decorating, 244-245, 246
  refrigerating and freezing, 247
  special notes, 243
Pie, fruit-filled, 100-117
  crumb-topped, 117
  crust for, 100-103
  fillings for, 104-112
    apple, 104-107
    blueberry, 110-111
    cherry, 109-110
    pineapple, 108-109
  making and baking, 113-117
    common faults of, 101-102, 106, 112-113, 116
    leftover dough, 116, 133

Pie, making and baking, oven temperature (baking), 112, 116-117
  washing tops, 116
  prebaked and precooked pies, 118, 125-132
    chocolate cream, 130-132
    lemon meringue, 128-130
    shells for, 126-128
    variations (toppings), 129, 131-132
  soft-filled pies, 118-132
    baked variety, 118-125
      crust for, 118-121
      custard, 121-122
      pumpkin, 124-125
      shells for, 119-121
  turnovers (pie crust), 132-135
Pineapple, 108
  can sizes (*see* Measurements)
  filling for pies, 108
  types of, 108
Pinwheel icebox cookies, 234-236
Popovers, 27-32
  description of, 27
    baking, 28-31
    leavening, 27-28
  faults and causes of, 31-32
  pan preparation for, 29
  as quick bread, 27
  recipe for, 29
  varieties of, 31
    cheese, 31
    whole wheat, 31
Pound cake, old-fashioned, 160-161
Prepared mixes (*see* Mixes)
Proteins, 14, 34, 159
  in eggs, 159
  in flour, 14
  in gluten, 34
Puff pastry, 186-204
  description of 186-188
  dough for, 188-191
    composition of, 188-189
    recipe for, 188-191
  leavening of, 188
  special uses for, 186-187
  variety products, 194-204

Puff pastry, variety products, apple dumplings, 196–199
   fruit baskets, 194–196
   napoleons, 199–202
   patty shells, 202–204
   turnovers, 192–193
Pumpkin pie, 124–125
  recipe for, 124
  special points, 125
  substitutes for, 125
   squash, 125
   sweet potatoes, 125
   yams, 125

Quick breads, 21–26
  loaf-type varieties, 21–26
   banana bread, 22–26
   banana-nut bread, 26
   prune bread, 26
   raisin-banana bread, 26
   Southern corn bread, 18
  pan preparation for, 23–24
  popovers, 27–32

Raisins, 9, 66–67
  in biscuits, 9
  in buns, 66–67
Refrigeration, 35, 132, 158, 180, 191
  of cakes, 158, 180
  of doughs, 35
  of pies, 132
  of puff pastry, 191
  (*See also* Basic Equipment)
Ring-shaped doughnuts, 85–88, 94
  cake doughnuts, 94
  glazed doughnuts, 85–88
Rise (*see* Glossary)
Roll (*see* Glossary)
Rolls, 41–63
  muffin type, 44–50
   butterflake, 47–50
   cloverleaf, 44–47
   pan type, 41–44, 51–52, 53–54
    frankfurter, 53–54
    hamburger, 51–52
    Parker House, 41–44

Rolls, serving and storing, 50, 51–53
  twisted, 55–63
   braided figure-8, 59–61
   double-knot, 58–59
   single-knot, 56–58
   three-braid, 62–63
Round filled buns, 76–78

Salt, 35, 101
  effect on fermentation, 35
  in pie crust, 101
  (*See also* Basic Ingredients)
Scaling (*see* Glossary)
Scrape (*see* Glossary)
Shortbread cookies, 214–216, 220–222
Shortenings and fats, all-purpose, 101
  butter, 101
  emulsified, high-ratio, special, 147–148
  lard, 101
  margarine, 188–189
  mixing methods, 139–140, 147–148
   blending (special), 147–148
   creaming (all-purpose), 139–140
  oil (vegetable), 65, 67
   for frying, 81
  (*See also* Basic Ingredients)
Sift (*see* Glossary)
Simple frosting, 162–164
Snail-shaped buns, 70–73
Soft rolls, basic dough for, 38
  (*See also* Rolls)
Southern corn bread, 18–19
Spices (*see* Basic Ingredients)
Spiral cookies, 237
Sponge cake, 155–156
  layers, 156
  loaves, 156
Starch, corn, 104–111, 121
  as thickening agent in pie, 104
  (*See also* Basic Ingredients)
Steam, 28, 188
  as leavening agent, 28, 188
Stipple (*see* Glossary)
Stippling puff pastry, 188
Stir (*see* Glossary)

INDEX

Sugar cookies, 217–220
Sugars, varieties (*see* Basic Ingredients)
Sweet yeast dough, 37–40
  conditioning of, 40
  enrichment, 64
  recipe for, 38
  refrigeration of, 35
  [*See also* Buns (sweet rolls); Soft rolls]
Syrup wash, 65
Syrups (*see* Basic Ingredients)

Temperature, 34–35, 140
  effect on cake mixing, 140
  effect on fermentation, 34–35
Texture (*see* Glossary)
Thickening agents, 100–117, 118–131
  cornstarch, 104
  flour, 104, 124
  natural, 121
  in pie fillings, 100–117, 118–131
  tapioca flour, 121
Tools and utensils (*see* Basic Equipment)
Toppings, 64–65, 73–74, 76, 78, 104–112, 129–132, 158, 170–181, 215
  on cakes, 170–172, 177, 181
  cinnamon sugar, 64–65
  crumb topping, 73–74
  fruit varieties, 104–112
  jams and jellies, 76, 78, 158, 215
  meringue, 129–131
  whipped cream, 131–132
Tough (*see* Glossary)
Turnovers, 132–135, 192–193
  pie crust variety, 132–135
  puff pastry variety, 192–193
Twist shape, cake-type doughnuts, 88–91
  yeast-raised doughnuts, 92–95
Twisted rolls, 55–63
  braided figure, 59–61

Twisted rolls, double-knot roll, 58–59
  single-knot roll, 56–58
  three-braid roll, 62–63

Volume (*see* Glossary)

Wash (*see* Glossary)
Wash, egg wash, 5, 56
  syrup wash, 65
Water, in pie crust, 101
  (*See also* Basic Ingredients)
Wet peak (*see* Glossary)
Whip (*see* Glossary, *Beat*)
Whipping cream for pies, 131–132
Whipping method, cakes made with, 153–161
  angel cake, 155
  jelly roll, 156–158
  sponge cake, 155–156
  pan preparation for, 154
  special facts about, 154–155
White cake, 150–151
Whole wheat flour, blending of, 20
  in muffins, 20

Yeast, 7, 34–40, 64
  in combination biscuits, 7
  composition of, 34
  dry, 35–36
  effect of temperature on, 34–35
  fermentation process, 34–36
  gluten and, 34
  preparation of, 34
  salt and, 34
  sponge dough, 36
  storage of, 34–35
  sweet yeast dough, 37–40, 64
Yellow layer cakes, 140–143, 148–149
  cupcakes, 140–143
  layer cakes, 140–143, 148–149
  loaf cakes, 140–143